MICHELANGELO ANTONIONI

INTERVIEWS

CONVERSATIONS WITH FILMMAKERS SERIES
PETER BRUNETTE, GENERAL EDITOR

Credit: Associated Press

MICHELANGELO ANTONIONI

INTERVIEWS

EDITED BY BERT CARDULLO

UNIVERSITY PRESS OF MISSISSIPPI/JACKSON

www.upress.state.ms.us

The University Press of Mississippi is a member of the Association of American University Presses.

Copyright © 2008 by University Press of Mississippi

Manufactured in the United States of America

First printing 2008

Library of Congress Cataloging-in-Publication Data

Michelangelo Antonioni : Interviews / edited by Bert Cardullo.
     p. cm. — (Conversations with filmmakers series)
   Includes index.
   ISBN 978-1-934110-65-2 (cloth: alk. paper) — ISBN 978-1-934110-66-9
(pbk.: alk. paper) 1. Antonioni, Michelangelo—Interviews. 2. Motion picture
producers and directors—Italy—Interviews. I. Cardullo, Bert.
   PN1998.3.A58A3 2008
   791.43023′ 3092—dc22

                                                          2007044551

British Library Cataloging-in-Publication Data available

CONTENTS

Introduction *vii*

Chronology *xxiii*

Filmography *xxix*

A Conversation with Michelangelo Antonioni 3
ANDRÉ LABARTHE

An Interview with Antonioni 11
MICHÈLE MANCEAUX

A Talk with Michelangelo Antonioni on His Work 21
FILM CULTURE

An Interview with Michelangelo Antonioni 46
PIERRE BILLARD

Zabriskie Point 70
MARSHA KINDER

Michelangelo Antonioni 79
CHARLES THOMAS SAMUELS

Antonioni Discusses *The Passenger* 104
BETTY JEFFRIES DEMBY AND LARRY STURHAHN

Antonioni Speaks . . . and Listens 115
RENEE EPSTEIN

Antonioni after China: Art versus Science 121
GIDEON BACHMANN

An Interview with Michelangelo Antonioni 131
AMERICAN CINEMATOGRAPHER

Film Is Life: An Interview with Michelangelo Antonioni 138
BERT CARDULLO

Antonioni in 1980: An Interview 155
SEYMOUR CHATMAN

Life Is Inconclusive: A Conversation with
Michelangelo Antonioni 162
FRANK P. TOMASULO

A Love of Today: An Interview with Michelangelo
Antonioni 169
GIDEON BACHMANN

Index 175

INTRODUCTION

IN AN INTERVIEW with Michelangelo Antonioni in 1978, I asked, "In a world without film, what would you have made?" Like his work, the answer was concise. "Film," he said. And in a world *with* film, it could be said, Antonioni also created film, in the sense that he made a new art form or made the existing art form new. In *La notte* (1961) even more strikingly than in *L'avventura*, with which he scored his first international triumph in 1960, he was forging a new language apposite to a changed world.

For Western society, theistically based and teleologically organized, the concepts of drama that derived substantially from Aristotle had sufficed for centuries. The cinema was born to that inheritance and, out of it, still produced fine works in the 1960s (although with a perceptibly increasing tinge of nostalgia that has, by the twenty-first century, become overwhelmingly palpable). But Antonioni saw the dwindling force of this inheritance—"of an aging morality, of outworn myths, of ancient conventions," as he put it in a statement (reiterated in my interview with him) accompanying the initial screening of *L'avventura* at the Cannes Film Festival—and was finding new means to supplement it. He was achieving, in other words, what many contemporary artists in his and other fields were seeking but not often with success: renewal of his art rather than repetition.

It is a commonplace that the most difficult part of an artist's life in our time is not to achieve a few good works or some recognition, but to have a career, as Antonioni has done: to live a life *in* art, all through one's life, at the same time as one replenishes the life *of* that art. But since the beginning of the Romantic era and the rise of subjectivism, the use of synthesis—of selecting from both observation and direct experience, then imaginatively rearranging the results—has declined among serious artists, until by the 1960s art had taken on some aspects of talented diary-keeping. (The most obvious examples from the period are "confessional" poetry and "action" painting.) An artist's life and internal experience have thus become more and more circumscribedly his subject matter, and his willingness to stay within them has become almost a touchstone of his validity. This has led to the familiar phenomenon of the quick depletion of resources—all those interesting first and second works, and then the sad, straggling works that follow them—not to speak of the debilitation of art. The question is further complicated because the more sensitive a person is, the more affected he is in our time by Ibsen's Great Boyg—that shapeless, grim, and unconquerable monster from *Peer Gynt* who represents the riddle of existence—which increases the artist's sense of helplessness, of inability to deal with such experience as he does have.

One such response from the 1960s—the decade during which Antonioni made his great trilogy, which includes *L'eclisse* (1962) in addition to *L'avventura* and *La notte*—was that of Jackson Pollock, Hans Hofmann, and their kin, who were exponents of dissatisfaction rather than re-creation. Another was that of French anti-novelists like Alain Robbe-Grillet and Nathalie Sarraute, who, in their frustration with the limits of the conventional novel, asked readers to share their professional problems rather than be affected as readers. Bertolt Brecht, for his part, jostled the traditional drama healthily (ironically, more so subsequent to his death in 1956 than prior to it), but his theater was didactic and aimed towards a different godhead—a temporal one that now seems sterile to many. The so-called Theater of the Absurd faced reality rigorously and even poetically, but such a theater of images and few or no characters was limited to disembodied effects—and each of its playwrights (Ionesco, Beckett, Pinter) seemed to have one reiterated effect.

In films, too, the avant-garde—Man Ray, Jean Cocteau, and many others to follow—had tried to find new methods or forms; but they, too, concentrated so much on the attempt that they neglected to communicate much content. A more conventional artist like Ingmar

Bergman felt the spiritual discontent of the 1960s as keenly as anyone, but his films from this period, for all their superb qualities, exemplify Buck Mulligan's line to Stephen Dedalus in James Joyce's *Ulysses*: "You have the cursed jesuit strain in you, only it's injected the wrong way." The fountainhead of these Bergman films, that is, may be mysticism, but his asking whether the God-man relation was still viable seemed anachronistic—to put it mildly—by the second half of the twentieth century. Antonioni himself seemed, around the same time, to have answered that question in the negative; to have posited that human beings must learn self-reliance or crumble; to have begun hoping for the possibility of hope.

Nonetheless, Antonioni seemed to be forging a miracle, albeit of the secular kind: finding a way to speak to his contemporaries without crankily throwing away all that went before and without being bound by it. He was re-shaping the idea of the content of film drama by discarding ancient and less ancient concepts, by re-directing traditional audience expectations towards immersion in character rather than conflict of character, away from the social realism of his neorealist forbears and toward "introspective realism"—"to see," in his words from a 1962 *Film Culture* interview, "what remained inside the individual" after the nightmare of World War II (with its Holocaust and atomic weaponry) and all the political as well as economic upheavals that followed. Particularly in the trilogy but also in the film immediately following it (and his first one in color), *Il deserto rosso* (1964), Antonioni arrived—without inventing a totally new *language* of cinema—at a new and profoundly cinematic mode of expression or exposition, in which every aspect of style, of the purely visual realm of action and object, reflects the interior state of the characters.

The same cannot be said for such films of his from the previous decade as *Le amiche* (1955) and *Il grido* (1957), though it's true that as early as *Cronaca di un amore* (1950), Antonioni's "habit of shooting rather long scenes was born spontaneously," as he himself has reported:

> On the first day of filming *Cronaca di un amore*, having the camera fixed to its stand immediately caused me real discomfort. I felt paralyzed, as if I were being prevented from following closely the one thing in the film that interested me: I mean the characters. The next day I called for a dolly, and I

began to follow my characters till I felt the need to move on to another exercise. For me, this was the best way to be real, to be true. Real: inside the scene, exactly as in life. I have never succeeded in composing a scene without having the camera with me, nor have I ever been able to make my characters talk in accordance with a pre-established script. . . . Already, even then, I needed to see the characters. (Antonioni quoted in the entry on him in John Wakeman, ed., *World Film Directors, 1945–1985* [1988].)

Antonioni was thus re-shaping not only the idea of the content of film drama, he was also re-shaping time itself in his films: taking it out of its customary synoptic form and wringing intensity out of its distention; daring to ask his audience to "live through" experiences with less distillation than they were accustomed to; deriving his drama from the very texture of such experiences and their juxtaposition, rather than from formal clash, climax, and resolution. Fundamentally, he was giving us characters whose drama consists in facing life minute after minute rather than in moving through organized, cause-and-effect plots with articulated obstacles—characters who have no well-marked cosmos to use as a tennis player uses a court, and who live and die without the implication of a divine eye that sees their virtues (whether people do or not) and will reward them.

Over such characters, Antonioni ever hovered with his camera: peering, following, and then lingering to savor a place after the people have left it. Again, he was more interested in personality, mood, and the physical world than in drama, in setting as a way of expressing states of mind— so much so that in *Il deserto rosso*, he even had the natural surroundings painted to serve the film's underlying psychological scheme as well as to connote the seemingly metaphysical world of its characters. (As Antonioni told Charles Thomas Samuels in a 1969 interview included here, "The relationship between people and their surroundings is of prime importance.") He was interested, that is, more in the observation of characters than in the exigencies of storytelling. And it is this interest—if we apply conventional cinematic standards—that at times makes his pictures, with their elliptical approach to narrative, seem to have lost their way.

For Antonioni was trying to exploit the unique powers of film as distinct from the theater. Many superb film directors (like Vittorio De Sica) were oriented theatrically; Antonioni was not. He attempted to get from the cinema the same utility of the medium itself as a novelist whose point is not story but tone and character, and for whom the texture of the prose works as much as what he says in the prose. In this way, Antonioni's movies, like other great works of film art, can be seen as sharing in the flexibility and potential subtlety of imaginative prose, which stems from the very abstractness of words, their not being "real" objects—just as film, being made of reflections cast on a screen, is not "real" either.

Indeed, by purely *theatrical* standards, any of Antonioni's major feature films could easily be condensed by a skilled cutter—in *L'avventura*, for example, the search on the island, the visit to the deserted town, the kisses of Sandro and Claudia in the field. But when the film is all over, you see that such condensation would sharpen the pace at the expense of the purpose. Antonioni wants the discoveries of this pair—of every one of his characters, as I intimated earlier—to occur in something more like real time than theatrical time, because long, lingering shots, by their very leisurely immobility, suggest the overbearing pressure that time exerts upon human emotions. Obviously, this is not real time or we would all have to bring sandwiches and blankets with us to the movie theater; but a difference of ten seconds in a scene is a tremendous step towards veristic reproduction rather than theatrical abstraction.

John Grierson once said that when a director dies, he becomes a photographer; but Antonioni got emotional utility—in films about *people*, let us not forget—out of such quasi-veristic reproduction of surfaces and compositions. (Even his early documentaries, like *Gente del Po* [1947], were about people, as he himself observed to Michèle Manceaux in the 1961 interview that follows: "Up to [*Gente del Po*], documentary directors in my country had concentrated on places, objects, works of art. But my film was about sailors, fishermen, and daily life . . . about people.") He used photography for enrichment, in other words, not to elicit salon gasps. Thus the overwhelming sense of characterological estrangement and malaise conveyed by *L'avventura*, for one, is as much a product of the style of the movie as of its events or dialogue.

In the island settings that dominate the first third of the film, for instance, characters stand two or three in a shot, looking away from each other and isolated against the sea or the arid volcanic landscape; indeed, the studied compositions work to emphasize the space between characters as much as the characters themselves. And cutting and camera movement are unconventional, not simply for the sake of being so, but to lend force to the film's ideas. To wit: point-of-view shots are rare (part of Antonioni's battery of techniques precluding simple emotional involvement on our part), and the basic narrative resource of the shot-reverse-shot pattern is carefully modified, so as simultaneously to express or visualize the internal dislocation of this world and to position us in relation to it. *L'avventura's* breaking the "rules" of film grammar is not merely capricious, then, and the much admired "beauty" of the film's photography is not simply pictorialism. Our very awareness of such composition, texture, and montage helps to keep us at the contemplative distance that the picture requires.

The sequence that best represents Antonioni's style, however, can be found in *La notte*: the one in which Lidia, the wife of the novelist Giovanni, slips away from the publisher's party and wanders through the streets of Milan. Conditioned as we are, we *expect* something to happen; we that think she is off to meet a lover, or that she may get involved in an accident, even that she may intend to kill herself. But nothing happens, and everything happens. Lidia strolls past a bus conductor eating a sandwich and is fascinated both by his existence and his appetite in the same universe with her; she passes two men laughing uproariously at a joke and she smiles, too, although she has not heard it, anxious as she is to join them, to be one of the human race; she encounters a crying child and kneels briefly but unsuccessfully to comfort it; she tears a flake of rust off a corroding wall; she sees two young men punching each other ferociously, watches horrified, then screams for them to stop. Next, in the suburbs, Lidia watches some boys shooting off rockets. She finds she is in a neighborhood where she and Giovanni used to come years before, so she telephones him and he drives out to pick her up.

Now by film-school definition, this is not a cumulative dramatic sequence. It is a miniature recapitulation, deftly done, of the possibilities of life: there is a child but there is also an old woman; we see a man eating and a man punching; sunlight on a fountain gets juxtaposed, at one point, against the lewdness of a greasy stall-keeper. Antonioni holds it all together with something like the surface tension of liquids and, by not commenting, comments. His art is essentially as drastic a revolution as abstract expressionist painting or Samuel Beckett's litany-like deconstruction of dialogue, but Antonioni has not estranged us in order to speak to us about loneliness, and he has not sacrificed the link of recognition in order to create new images. Put another way, he has not had to use absurdity to convey the absurd—an absurd made manifest in our age by the crisis of faith, for which, in *La notte*, Lidia and Giovanni's vitiated marriage itself serves as one large metaphor.

When, in my early twenties, I followed Lidia's long, meandering stroll through the streets, that arc of despair which led to the truth—the assurance, that is, in knowing that one can live without assurances—I knew that it traced what I had been prepared to feel next, what I was going to be like, what I was about to do; that from then on it would be impossible not to see existence with the same narrowed, dry-eyed, precipice-crawling intentness as Michelangelo Antonioni. Now we have all had the experience of watching a film that seems to be changing our perception as it unfolds, affecting the way we see and not simply offering us exotic or heightened images of what we have already perceived without the camera's intervention. And when subsequently we leave the movie theater, we discover that the world, which we thought we knew, has changed to meet the new ways in which it's being regarded. This reciprocity—a new reality being summoned by a new perceptiveness and in turn compelling that perceptiveness into being—seems to me to be at the heart of the filmmaker's art and of the filmgoer's experience on the level of creative spectatorship. On any other level a film, like every object of popular culture, is there to console, divert, flatter, bludgeon, or confirm—in any case to see to it that we remain unchanged.

In the preface (not included in this collection) to the 1963 volume of screenplays for four of his films, Antonioni himself wrote that "the problem for a director is to catch reality an instant before it manifests itself and to propound that movement, that appearance, that action as a new perception." In its rescuing of the director from the status of a recording agent who decides which aspects of established reality are to be photographed (or, rather, who enhances or "dramatizes" those aspects of reality that lie open to the ordinary eye), this seems to me to be as useful a description of the art of filmmaking as we are likely to find. Or at least of one aspect of filmmaking; there is another, which is the *inventing* of reality, the making of something that hasn't existed before.

I'd like to think, however, that Antonioni would agree that the two functions are ultimately the same, that the act of discovery of what reality is going to be next, the apprehension of its impending face, is a mysterious cause of the new, a procedure that brings it into being and that thus invents reality anew. If this weren't true, then the director would merely be prescient and his art only one of prediction. The artist is indeed a kind of prophet, but prophecy isn't simply prediction; it is a force, a pressure on things to be other than they would be if left to themselves. And this power, while it may partake of or draw upon fantasy, isn't in its most serious uses a faculty of fantasy at all; there is nothing "unreal" or escapist in what it brings to birth.

To say all these things, though, is not to say why Antonioni's best works, those of the 1960s, are so much greater than, say, Federico Fellini's *La dolce vita* (1960)—another picture, like Antonioni's trilogy, on the theme of well-heeled decadence and the moral crisis of the *haute bourgeoisie*, but one marred by its obviousness and the mechanical application of its ideas. The critical failure, however, has always been in not seeing that Antonioni's films transcend their ostensible subject and milieu, as *La dolce vita* does not, that *L'avventura*, *La notte*, and *L'eclisse* are creations of universal validity and not simply portraits of a particular class or of a particular species of decadence. I say this despite Antonioni's own statement to me, as well as to a number of other interviewers over the years, that "the experience which has been most important in making me the director I have become is that of my own middle-class background. It is that world which has contributed most to my predilection for certain themes, certain conflicts, certain emotional or psychological problems." (Read closely, however, this statement cannot be equated with the declaration that Antonioni's films directly concern, and only concern, the middle class.) His films are not really about decadence at all. Like Henry James's novels, these pictures employ privileged characters, men and women with the total physical and economic freedom to choose their lives, precisely in order to exhibit the difficulties of such choice, the anguish of such freedom, for *anyone* who has it—even if only in part.

Thematically, Antonioni was treating of human connections no longer sustained by traditional values, or by any convictions at all (a humanity with too much freedom of choice, as it were), and therefore forced to abide with the most fragile and precarious of justifications. One might say that his films were the first truly existential ones. When I first saw them I was filled with a sense of discovery of a world—a visual one this time, not a theoretical, abstract one as in Kierkegaard or Sartre—which no longer replied to the questions I had about it and gave me no feeling of nurture, acceptance, or invitation. And that is the way Antonioni's characters move through their environments, in a new and strange alienation, an individual isolation in the midst of constant social interaction: a condition very different from, and far more subtle than, what is suggested by the clichés of modern sophisticated awareness, all our talk (even more feverish in the twenty-first century) about the failure of communication, technological dehumanization, the death of God, the fragmentation or atomization of society, and the like.

This new alienation—this despair or desolation in spite of the superficial appearance of affluence and pleasure, this emotional barrenness that Antonioni called (in a public appearance at the 1962 Cannes Festival) "the eclipse of all feelings"—is what we might call his subject or theme, but that isn't the same thing as his art and it is a great mistake to think it is. The basis for my argument that Antonioni's films are not "about" a decadent class—let alone the death throes of capitalism—is that the visual world he composes, the one he discovers beneath appearances and calls into being, is the one we all inhabit, whether or not we have been summoned into any of its particular scenes. This is one reason why *L'avventura*, *La notte*, and *L'eclisse* are related in an indestructible unity: in the first, we move through physical landscapes, bare islands, the sea, or through nature and whitewashed ancient towns that seem to be part of nature; in the latter two films, we move through the city (Rome, rather than Milan, in *L'eclisse*), with its geometry of streets and its assembly of artifacts, the coldest products of modern materialistic "wit" and inventiveness, the new nature. Between them these hemispheres make up the world for all of us. But it is Antonioni's characters that have been given the task of being its explorers—and its exhibited sacrifices.

Coherence, unity, connection between interior self and exterior reality are no longer sustained by this world of commerce and utility, so its inhabitants have to establish for themselves the very ground of their behavior. What is mistaken for boredom in Antonioni's characters, then, is actually a condition of radical disjunction between personality and circumstance. For a vital connection has been broken: the physical world has been dispossessed of the inherited meanings and principles according to which we had previously motivated our lives and structured its psychic as well as moral events. In such a world the idea of a "story," in the sense of a progressive tale leading from a fixed starting point to a dénouement that "settles" something or solves some problem, no longer has any use and is in fact inimical to the way this world is actually experienced.

This is the reason for the broken narratives, the conversations in a void, the events leading nowhere—the search for the lost girl in *L'avventura*, Jeanne Moreau's wandering without destination through the city in *La notte*, the final, fifty-eight-shot montage in *L'eclisse* from which not only the couple Vittoria and Piero but all human contact is banished. For a story implies a degree of confidence in the world, or at least a trustfulness that the environment, no matter how painful or brutal it might be, is knowable, makes sense, hangs together. But of course there is a "story" in Antonioni's films, though not of the traditional kind. Will I be understood if I say that this story is in one sense the tale of the end of the stories with which the screen, along with the novel (which art form film most nearly resembles), has heretofore beguiled us? I mean that our former modes of fiction—the love story, the romantic quest, the action epic—have lost their power of conviction because the world we experience has lost its own such power. The essence of Antonioni's art in these films therefore is to forge, in the face of our lost convictions and acceptances about the world—convictions and acceptances upon which we had based our narrative arts—a new, mercilessly stripped "telling" of our condition of bereftness and chill, one that refuses to find "endings" or resolutions or definitive images that reassure us.

This art might be described as accession through reduction, the coming into truer forms through the cutting away of created encumbrances: all the replicas we have made of ourselves; all the misleading, because logical or only psychological, narratives we have told and been told; the whole apparatus of reflected wisdom, inherited sensations, received ideas, reiterated clichés. For, as the leading woman, Claudia, says in *L'avventura*: "Things are not like that . . . everything has become so terribly simple." And Antonioni himself once said, in a 1967 interview with Pierre Billard reprinted in this volume, that the nonverbal logic of his otherwise narrative films depends upon neither a conceptual nor an emotional organization: "Some people believe I make films with my head; a few others think they come from the heart; for my part, I feel as though I make films instinctively, more with my belly than with my brain or my feelings."

Instinct or "gut response," abstraction, reduction, irony, parody: they are all forms of aggression against the traditional subject, against what art is supposed to treat. They are, much more than direct violence, our most effective means of liberating our experience, of releasing those unnamed emotions and perceptions that have been blockaded by everything we have been taught to see and hear and feel. This blockage is the reason why, despite the fact that Antonioni's films are far from experimental in the sense of the work of Hollis Frampton, Michael Snow, or Andy Warhol, his fictional narratives always feel flattened, or, to borrow a term from Roland Barthes, why they seem curiously *mat*, as if the spectator's ability to gain immediate access to this fiction were being impeded by something. Put another way (and to recast a line from Shaw's *Major Barbara*), we are learning something in the act of watching a film by Michelangelo Antonioni, and that always feels at first as if we are losing something.

And what we learn from Antonioni's world of alienation and disjunction is exemplified, as I have tried to make clear, not merely by what his characters do and say, but by the images they compose and that are composed as the context for their cinematic existence. I think now of the revelers eddying like dry leaves across the rich man's lawn in *L'avventura*; the rain on the car window making a screen between the woman and her potential lover in *La notte*; the camera tracking slowly around the woman's room in *Il deserto rosso*, painstakingly exhibiting every domestic object in its absolute separateness from, and indifference to, her feelings; the seven-minute take at the end of *The Passenger* (1975) that proceeds, in a 360-degree pan, out of the reporter Locke's hotel room, through a wrought-iron grill on to a dusty Spanish plaza, and then finally returns to the room where Locke now lies dead. All these images are of a world newly forced to yield up its true face, to *look like* what we have secretly felt it to be.

"The fundamental problem of the cinema is how to express thought," the great critic and theorist of the French New Wave, Alexandre Astruc, wrote sixty years ago. *L'avventura*, *La notte*, *L'eclisse*, and two or three other Antonioni films are works in which thought (impulsive or instinctual though it may be in Antonioni's case)—indissolubly fused with image, lying behind it, selecting it and justifying it—produces an art worthy of ranking with any other. Indeed, I don't think it too much to say that the movies, having come into their maturity at this time—around the middle of the twentieth century—have been giving us, ever since, more (or more useful) freedom than any other form. In Antonioni's own day, that freedom ranged from the narrowest and most preliminary liberation as bestowed by British movies such as *Room at the Top* (1959), *Saturday Night and Sunday Morning* (1960), and *A Taste of Honey* (1961), with their mostly traditional procedures but temperamental and thematic rebelliousness, to the far more solid and revolutionary, because more purely cinematic, achievements of *L'avventura*, *La notte*, *L'eclisse*, and *Il deserto rosso*.

In between were the films of the Frenchmen Jean-Luc Godard and François Truffaut, with their neo-existential adventures proceeding by non-motivated or arbitrary acts, the camera jiggling or running along at eye-level and sometimes freezing fast in not entirely successful visual implementation. There was Alain Resnais, who seemed to be doing with time what Antonioni was doing with space, if such a distinction is admissible in a medium that is preeminently the fuser of the temporal and the spatial. (The reality of his *Last Year at Marienbad* [1961] is that of time, of memory and anticipation, in which past, present, and future are mixed, the images from each realm advancing and retreating, fading, reemerging, repeating, coalescing, and finally coming to exist simultaneously—the way the mind actually but unavowedly contains them.)

There was also Éric Rohmer, whose physically handsome films were otherwise controlled by a hard intelligence that worked almost metaphysically to limit the things that "happen" and so to make the cinematic landscapes and interiors dispose themselves as mute backgrounds for meanings (and not, as in "action" movies, the meanings themselves). And then there was the Swede Bergman, with his new, not wholly convincing legends and his preachy discontent, but also his powerful and clean, unlavish images—or isolations—of (im)mortality in a context of abrasive psychology, harsh topography, and inclement weather. Let us not forget Fellini, either, whose *La dolce vita* may have been vastly overrated, but some of whose earlier films—particularly *I vitelloni* (1953) and *La strada* (1954)—were full of lucid, plangent vision less dependent on narrative devices than juxtaposed observations, and whose later *8½* (1963) combined the plangent and the observational with something close to the hallucinogenic.

In the entire range of Antonioni's own calculated "boredom" and refusal of clear resolution—as of Godard's anti-novelistic, anti-illusionary, anti-culinary devices; Resnais's solicitation of time as something unprogressive and non-consecutive; and—lest I forget—Robert Bresson's extreme leanness of image, austerity of incident, rigorousness of perception, and procedure by indirection—we see being fought this tendency of narrative to turn into an extended anecdote that serves either to legitimate or mythologize actuality, and thus to turn it into nothing more than an illustration of what we have already undergone, surmised, or wished for. That Antonioni, like other filmmakers (you can add to the list above Carl Theodor Dreyer, Yasujiro Ozu, and the later Roberto Rossellini in a film like *The Rise to Power of Louis XIV* [1966]) who try to present not new stories but new relationships between consciousness and reality, was expected to do otherwise was the basis not only of complaint against ostensible failures of his like *L'avventura* and *L'eclisse*. It was also the basis of extreme outcry (particularly in American film circles) against the apparently more "mod," more mainstream *Blow-Up* (1966)—even among many of Antonioni's erstwhile supporters.

But in *Blow-Up* Antonioni was not attempting a portrait of London, swinging or otherwise, so that the accusation at the time, "That's not what it's like," was especially obtuse. If anything, Antonioni's stranger's eye on London provided him with the perspective of strategic *naïveté*, the freedom from any complacent conviction of knowledge, the anti-sophistication that he needed to be able to set about his real business. (And Antonioni, like any artist, was in need of such unsophistication on the level of the human and the social, for one creates in order to find out, not to exemplify what one already knows.) This was precisely to deal with the relationship between what we think the world is like—our ideas derived mainly from what others have thought it is like and, especially today, from *publicized* ideas about it—and what the imagination together with all other perceptive powers is compelled to decide.

Blow-Up is really "about" something society, as society, cannot know in regard to itself: the fact of life caught between complacent knowledge and radical doubt, passion and enervation, reality and illusion. Its subject isn't London or sexual mores and ennui among the chic, but the way in which the imagination attends to such things. The film's central sequence—the fashion photographer Thomas's "discovery" of a murder concealed in the fine grain of one of his photographs—conveys the theme concisely. It is only by blowing up tiny sections of the picture that this new reality, of death, is revealed; that is, only by adopting an alternative perspective can we get a different sense out of what we perceive. All of Antonioni's movies are similarly new forms of perception about, and artifacts of, our continuing dilemmas and contradictions and perplexities, not representations of them. That is why I still remember my first experience of such a picture, have gone back to it here, and will continue to re-visit it, like my experiences of other Antonioni films—in movie theaters as well as in the movie theater, or mind screen, of my imagination.

Obviously, Antonioni knows that only by adopting an alternative perspective, particularly in film, can we get a different sense out of what we perceive. That he appears to do so in life as well—thus lending credence to his argument to Pierre Billard that his "films have always had an element of autobiography, in that I shoot any particular scene according to the mood I'm in that day, according to the little daily experiences I've had and the settings I've inhabited"—became clear to me when, subsequent to my interview with him in New York, I visited Antonioni in Rome late in July of 1978.

The living room of his apartment reflected intellectual restlessness—the will to multiple perspectives, as it were—rather than a desire for comfort. Except for a plush couch, the room was sparsely furnished, yet everywhere there were books, records, and a wild array of bric-a-brac. One table held a collection of antique weaponry—arrowheads, knife blades, and the like. Crowding the windowsills was a profusion of *objects trouvés*, including some television circuitry. Even the low glass coffee table was covered with an assortment of boxes, fragments of statuary, enormous ashtrays, and other items, some unidentifiable. Overwhelming the whole were striking, sometimes garish paintings, particularly a Lichtenstein and an enormous Francis Bacon of a semi-human figure installed in an easy chair but, for all that, apparently losing its innards.

We talked, off the record, for three more hours, despite the intense summer heat and Antonioni's preoccupation with preparations for the upcoming *Il mistero di Oberwald* (1980). His voice was as soft and toneless as I had remembered (he does not like the sound of his voice and prefers to limit its circulation—so much so that he refused to let the tapes of my earlier interview with him out of his hands, having them transcribed in full at his own expense); his eyes were as lugubrious as they had seemed in New York; and, though the face and body were far younger than his nearly sixty-six years at the time, Antonioni's apparent virility was belied by an extremely austere manner and by a series of nervous tics that became more intense as he found himself struggling for words—even in Italian. Despite showing some capacity for wit and relaxation during my afternoon with him, he seemed genuinely burdened, as he had in New York, by his earnest attempt to answer my questions.

Words, it was clear, were not his medium. And not just because they are not images, but because they don't move—the *eye* moves as it reads them. The camera-eye moves, too, hence films move, are a tracing of movement, and in Antonioni the movement is everything: action, summation, meaning; idea, emotion, impulse; shifting perspective, manifold vision, moving picture.

As is customary with all books in the Conversations with Filmmakers series, the interviews in this volume are reproduced in their entirety, with very little editing. Consequently the reader will at times encounter repetitions of both questions and answers, but it is my feeling that the same questions being asked and the consistency (or inconsistency) of responses will prove of significance to readers in their unexpurgated form.

BC

CHRONOLOGY

1912   Born in the northern Italian city of Ferrara on September 29 to Elizabetta Roncagli Antonioni and Ismaele Antonioni, a successful small industrialist.

1922–30 Develops an interest in puppetry, designing the figures and building model settings for them. Also develops an interest in architecture and, during his teenaged years, begins painting.

1931–35 Studies business, economics, mathematics, and commerce at the University of Bologna's Technical Institute, receiving the Dottore degree.

1935–39 Returns to Ferrara, working for a short time as a bank teller. With friends, establishes a drama company, putting on plays by Pirandello, Ibsen, and one by Antonioni himself titled *The Wind*; he directs some of these productions. He writes stories as well, and also wins a number of regional tennis tournaments. Begins writing film criticism for the local newspaper, *Il Corriere Padano*. Makes his first attempt at filmmaking, a 16mm documentary shot in a lunatic asylum; but it remains uncompleted after the inmates go into paroxysms of terror when the lights are switched on.

1939–40 Leaves Rome to assist with Mussolini's World's Fair, the Esposizione Universale Roma (E.U.R.), which was to be held in 1942 but never took place. Leaves this job after a few months and becomes a writer and editor for *Cinema*, the official film magazine of the Fascist party. Travels as a journalist to the Italian colonies in Africa.

1940–41   Studies at the Centro Sperimentale di Cinematografia in Rome.

1942   Co-scenarist of *Un pilota ritorna* (*A Pilot Returns*), directed by Roberto Rossellini. Co-scenarist and assistant director of *I due Foscari* (*The Two Foscaris*), directed by Enrico Fulchignoni; assistant director of *Les visiteurs du soir*, directed by Marcel Carné. Drafted into the Italian army. Marries the Venetian Letizia Balboni, a Centro student of editing who acted in the short film he made at the school in order to get his diploma.

1943   Returns to Ferrara to direct his first film, the documentary *Gente del Po* (*People of the Po Valley*), released in 1947. After the Nazis assume control of Italy, Antonioni refuses offers to go north and do film work with Mussolini's new Fascist regime, the Republic of Salò. Becomes involved in the anti-Fascist Action Party's underground network. Survives this difficult period by translating various works into Italian, among them Gide's *La porte étroite*, Morand's *Monsieur Zéro*, and Chateaubriand's *Atala*, as well as by selling the trophies and medals he had won at tennis tournaments.

1944   After the Allies liberate Rome, Antonioni writes film criticism for the new *Cinema* magazine, as well as for *Film d'oggi, Lo schermo*, and *L'Italia libera*. Director of photography for some of the covers of the magazine *Bis*. Works with Luchino Visconti on two scripts that are never filmed: *Furore* and *The Trial of Maria Tarnowska*.

1947   Co-scenarist of *Caccia tragica* (*Tragic Pursuit*), directed by Giuseppe De Santis.

1948   Directs the documentary shorts *Roma-Montevideo, Oltre l'oblio* (*Over Oblivion*), and *N.U.* (*Nettezza Urbana; Sanitation Department*). *N.U.* wins the Silver Ribbon for best documentary, an annual award made by the Italian Guild of Film Journalists.

1949   Directs the documentary shorts *Ragazze in bianco* (*Girls in White*), *Bomarzo, L'amorosa menzogna* (*Lies of Love*), *Superstizione* (*Superstitions*), and *Sette canne, un vestito* (*Seven Reeds, One Suit*). *L'amorosa menzogna* wins the Silver Ribbon for best documentary.

1950   Directs the documentary shorts *La villa dei mostri* (*The Villa of Monsters*) and *La funivia del Faloria* (*The Funicular of Mount Faloria*). Directs his first fiction feature film, *Cronaca di un amore* (*Story of a Love Affair*), which wins a Silver Ribbon in 1951.

1952   Co-scenarist of *Lo sceicco bianco* (*The White Sheik*), directed by Federico Fellini. Directs *I vinti* (*The Vanquished*), a feature film in three episodes.

1953   Directs the feature film *La signora senza camelie* (*The Lady without Camelias*). Directs *Tentato suicidio* (*Attempted Suicide*), an episode of *L'amore in città* (*Love in the City*), a six-episode anthology film whose directors also include Federico Fellini, Alberto Lattuada, Carl Lizzani, Francesco Maselli, and Cesare Zavattini.

1954   Letizia Balboni leaves Antonioni, and their marriage is later annulled.

1955   Producer of the documentary short *Uomini in più* (*More People*), directed by Nicolò Ferrari. Directs the feature film *Le amiche* (*The Girlfriends*), which wins the Silver Lion at the 1955 Venice Film Festival and a Silver Ribbon for best direction.

1956   Completes two scripts, *Ida e i porci* (*Ida and the Pigs*) and *Le allegre ragazze del 24* (*The Happy Girls from 24*), but neither is filmed.

1957   Directs the feature film *Il grido* (*The Outcry*), which wins the Critics' Grand Prize at the Locarno Film Festival. Directs the play *Scandali segretti* (*Secret Scandals*), co-written with Elio Bartolini, at the Teatro Eliseo in Rome. Meets Monica Vitti, who dubbed the Italian voice for English-speaking Dorian Gray in *Il grido* and who also is a theater actress, and they begin living together.

1958   Second-unit director of *La tempèsta* (*The Tempest*), directed by Alberto Lattuada. Director of the reshoot of *Nel segno di Roma* (*In the Sign of Rome*), after the death of its director-screenwriter, Guido Brignone. Technical supervisor on *Questo nostro mondo* (*This, Our World*), directed by Ugo Lazzari, Eros Macchi, and Angelo Negri. With Tonino Guerra, prepares *Makaroni*, a screenplay based on Ugo Pirro's novel

Le soldatesse (*The Camp Followers*), but their hopes for production
fall through at the last minute.

1959–60   Directs the feature film *L'avventura* (*The Adventure*), which is
awarded a Special Jury Prize at the 1960 Cannes Festival and
wins the British Film Institute's award for Best Foreign Film
of 1960.

1960–61   Directs the feature film *La notte* (*The Night*), which wins
the 1961 Silver Ribbon for best director and the Golden Bear
(or Grand Prize) at the 1961 Berlin Festival.

1962   Directs the feature film *L'eclisse* (*The Eclipse*), which is awarded
a Special Jury Prize at the 1962 Cannes Festival. This work is
considered by Antonioni as part of a trilogy that also includes
L'avventura and *La notte*. A British Film Institute poll of seventy
international critics names *L'avventura* the second-best film
ever made.

1963   Publication in English, in New York and London, of *The
Screenplays of Michelangelo Antonioni* (includes *Il grido,
L'avventura, La notte*, and *L'eclisse*).

1964   Directs his first feature film in color, *Il deserto rosso* (*Red Desert*).
It wins the Golden Lion (or Grand Prize) and the International
Critics' Prize at the 1964 Venice Festival.

1965   Directs *Prefazione: il provino* (*The Screen Test*), the introductory
episode of the three-episode anthology film *I tre volti* (*Three
Faces*). The other two episodes were directed by Franco
Indovina (Antonioni's assistant on three films) and Mauro
Bolognini, respectively.

1966   Directs the feature film *Blow-Up*, which wins the Best Director
Award from the National Society of Film Critics in New York,
the Palme d'Or at the 1967 Cannes Film Festival, the BFI's
1967 award for Best British Film, and a Silver Ribbon for Best
Director of a Foreign Film.

1969   Publication in English, in New York, of the screenplay of
L'avventura.

1970   Directs the feature film *Zabriskie Point*.

1971   Publication in English, in London, of the screenplay of
Blow-Up.

1972   Directs the feature-length documentary *Chung Kuo (China)*,
in 16mm.

1974–75   Directs the feature *Professione: Reporter* (*The Passenger*), his
first film written entirely by someone else (Mark Peploe).
Its script is published in English, in London, and the film wins
a Silver Ribbon for Best Director. Plans to make *Tecnicamente
dolce* (*Technically Sweet*), which would have involved working
on location in the Amazon jungle, fall through.

1976–78   Conceives a number of film projects, all of which are
ultimately abandoned at one stage or another: *The Crew*,
co-written with Mark Peploe, which would have been shot
in Australia; *The Color of Jealousy*; a science-fiction film titled
L'aquilone (*The Kite*), with a script by Tonino Guerra, which
was to have been filmed in the southern Asiatic part of the
Soviet Union; and *Patire o morire* (*Suffer or Die*), with a script
by Guerra and Anthony Burgess, which was first to star
Richard Gere and then Giancarlo Giannini.

1979–80   Directs the feature film *Il mistero di Oberwald* (*The Mystery of
Oberwald*), based on the play *L'aigle à deux têtes* (*The Two-
Headed Eagle*), by Jean Cocteau. It is shown on (Italian)
television first, then transferred from videotape to film to
be shown in some theaters and at several festivals.

1982   Directs the feature film *Identificazione di una donna*
(*Identification of a Woman*), which wins a Special Prize at the
Cannes Festival. At the same festival, Antonioni receives a
special award for the entire body of his work.

1983   Directs *Renault 9*, a publicity spot, as well as *Ritorno a Lisca
Bianca* (*Return to Lisca Bianca*), a short documentary for the
television program *Falsi ritorni* (*Fake Returns*). Exhibitions in
Venice and Rome of a collection of his artwork titled *The
Enchanted Mountain*: it consists of small watercolors, shown
beside photographic enlargements made by the director.

1984   Plays himself in *Chambre 666* (*Room 666*), a documentary
film by Wim Wenders. Directs *Fotoromanza*, a music video
made for the song of the same title by Gianna Nannini.

1985   Suffers a stroke that leaves him partially paralyzed and unable
to speak.

1986   Publication of *That Bowling Alley on the Tiber: Tales of a
Director*, a short-story collection. Second marriage, to Enrica
Antonioni.

1989   Directs the documentary *Kumbha Mela*.

1990   Directs *Roma '90*, a documentary for the television program *12 autori per 12 città* (*Twelve Authors for Twelve Cities*).

1992   Directs *Noto-Mandorli-Vulcano-Stromboli-Carnevale* (*Volcanoes and Carnival*), a documentary on Sicily.

1993   Receives Lifetime Achievement Award from the European Film Academy.

1995   Appears as himself in the documentary *Making a Film for Me Is Living*, directed by his wife, Enrica. Co-directs, with Wim Wenders, the feature *Al di là delle nuvole* (*Beyond the Clouds*), based on material from *That Bowling Alley on the Tiber*. It wins the International Critics' Prize at the Venice Film Festival. Receives the Award for Lifetime Achievement in Film from the American Academy of Motion Picture Arts and Sciences.

1997   Receives the Golden Lion at the Venice Film Festival for Outstanding Career.

1998   Co-produces, with Robert Altman, the fiction short *Liv*, directed by Edoardo Ponti.

1999   Begins to direct the fiction feature *Tanto per stare insieme* (*Just to Be Together*), based on Antonioni's 1973 short story "Two Telegrams," and starring Robin Wright Penn, Sam Shepard, Winona Ryder, Andy Garcia, and Johnny Depp, but the film is abandoned in production.

2000   Begins to direct the fiction feature *Destinazione Verna*, co-written with Tonino Guerra, and starring Anthony Hopkins and Sophia Loren, but the film is abandoned in production.

2001   Special citation from the National Society of Film Critics in the United States.

2004   Directs the episode "The Dangerous Thread of Things," based on material from *That Bowling Alley on the Tiber*, for the three-episode omnibus film *Eros*; its other episodes are directed by Steven Soderbergh and Wang Kar-Wai. Directs the documentary short *Lo Sguardo di Michelangelo Antonioni* (*Michelangelo Eye to Eye*), in which he appears as himself.

2007   Dies on July 30 at his home in Rome.

FILMOGRAPHY

1943–1947
GENTE DEL PO [PEOPLE OF THE PO RIVER]
Producer: Artisti Associati, I.C.E.T.-Carpi (Milan)
Director: **Michelangelo Antonioni**
Screenplay: **Michelangelo Antonioni**
Cinematography: Piero Portalupi
Editing: C. A. Chiesa
Music: Mario Labroca
B & W, in Italian
10 minutes, documentary

1948
N. U. (NETTEZZA URBANA [DEPARTMENT OF SANITATION])
Producer: I.C.E.T. (Lux Film)
Director: **Michelangelo Antonioni**
Screenplay: **Michelangelo Antonioni**
Cinematography: Giovanni Ventimiglia
Editing: **Michelangelo Antonioni**
Music: Giovanni Fusco, with a prelude by Johann Sebastian Bach
B & W, in Italian
9 minutes, documentary

1948–1949
L'AMOROSA MENZOGNA [LIES OF LOVE]
Producer: Edizioni Fortuna Film Roma (Filmus)

Director: **Michelangelo Antonioni**
Screenplay: **Michelangelo Antonioni**
Cinematography: Renato del Frate
Editing: **Michelangelo Antonioni**
Music: Giovanni Fusco
Cast: Anna Vita, Sergio Raimondi, Annie O'Hara, Sandro Roberti
B & W, in Italian
10 minutes, documentary

1949
SUPERSTIZIONE [SUPERSTITION]
Producer: I.C.E.T.-Carpi (Giorgio Venturini)
Director: **Michelangelo Antonioni**
Screenplay: **Michelangelo Antonioni**
Cinematography: Giovanni Ventimiglia
Editing: **Michelangelo Antonioni**
Music: Giovanni Fusco
Narrator: Gerardo Guerrieri
B & W, in Italian
9 minutes, documentary

1950
LA VILLA DEI MOSTRI [THE VILLA OF MONSTERS]
Producer: Filmus
Director: **Michelangelo Antonioni**
Screenplay: **Michelangelo Antonioni**
Cinematography: Giovanni de Paoli
Editing: **Michelangelo Antonioni**
Music: Giovanni Fusco
B & W, in Italian
10 minutes, documentary

1950
LA FUNIVIA DEL FALORIA [THE CABLE CARS OF FALORIA]
Producer: Theo Usuelli
Director: **Michelangelo Antonioni**
Screenplay: **Michelangelo Antonioni**

Cinematography: Goffredo Bellisario and Ghedina
Editing: **Michelangelo Antonioni**
Music: Theo Usuelli
B & W, in Italian
10 minutes, documentary

1950
CRONACA DI UN AMORE [STORY OF A LOVE AFFAIR]
Producer: Franco Villani and Stefano Caretta, for Villani Films
Director: **Michelangelo Antonioni**
Screenplay: **Michelangelo Antonioni**, Danièle d'Anza, Silvio
Giovaninetti, Francesco Maselli, Piero Tellini
Cinematography: Enzo Serafin
Editing: **Michelangelo Antonioni**
Music: Giovanni Fusco, with solo saxophone by Marcel Mule
Art Direction: Piero Filippone
Cast: Lucia Bosè (Paola Molon Fontana), Massimo Girotti (Guido),
Ferdinando Sarmi (Enrico Fontana), Gino Rossi (Carloni, the
detective), Marika Rowsky (Joy, the model), Rosi Mirafiore
(barmaid), Rubi D'Alma
B & W, in Italian
96 minutes

1952
I VINTI [THE VANQUISHED; a.k.a. THE BEATEN ONES or YOUTH AND
PERVERSION]
Producer: Film Constellazione, S.G.C.
Director: **Michelangelo Antonioni**
Screenplay: **Michelangelo Antonioni**, Suso Cecchi D'Amico, Diego
Fabbri, Turi Vasile, Giorgio Bassini; Roger Nimier (French episode)
Cinematography: Enzo Serafin
Editing: Eraldo Da Roma
Music: Giovanni Fusco
Set Design: Gianni Polidori and Roland Berthon
Sound: Alberto Bartolomei
Cast: Italian episode: Franco Interlenghi (Claudio), Anna-Maria Ferrero
(Marina), Evi Maltagliati (Claudio's mother), Eduardo Cianelli

(Claudio's father), Umberto Spadaro, Gastone Renzelli; French episode:
Jean-Pierre Mocky (Pierre), Etchika Choureau (Simone), Henri Poirier,
André Jacques, Annie Noel, Guy de Meulan, Jacques Sempey; English
episode: Peter Reynolds (Aubrey), Fay Compton (Mrs. Pinkerton),
Patrick Barr (Ken Whatton), Eileen Moore, Raymond Lovell, Derek
Tansley, Jean Stuart, Tony Kilshaw, Fred Victor, Charles Irwin
B & W, in Italian
110 minutes

1952–1953
LA SIGNORA SENZA CAMELIE [THE LADY WITHOUT CAMELIAS]
Producer: Domenico Forges Davanzati, for E.N.I.C.
Director: **Michelangelo Antonioni**
Screenplay: **Michelangelo Antonioni**, Suso Cecchi D'Amico, Francesco
Maselli, P. M. Pasinetti, adapted from the novel *La Dame aux camélias*
(1848) by Alexandre Dumas fils
Cinematography: Enzo Serafin
Editing: **Michelangelo Antonioni**
Music: Giovanni Fusco, as played by the Marcel Mule Saxophone Quintet
Set Design: Gianni Polidori
Cast: Lucia Bosè (Clara Manni), Andrea Cecchi (Gianni Franchi), Gino
Cervi (Ercole), Ivan Desny (Nardo Rusconi), Alain Cuny (Lodi), Monica
Clay (Simonetta), Anna Carena (Clara's mother), Enrico Glori (director),
Laura Tiberti, Oscar Andriani, Elio Steiner, Nino Del Fabbro, Gisella
Sofio, Louisa Rivelli
B & W, in Italian
105 minutes

1953
TENTATO SUICIDIO [ATTEMPTED SUICIDE, an episode of the
anthology film AMORE IN CITTA (LOVE IN THE CITY)]
Producer: Faro Film
Director: **Michelangelo Antonioni**
Screenplay: **Michelangelo Antonioni**, Cesare Zavattini, Aldo Buzzi,
Luigi Chiarini, Luigi Malerba, Tullio Pinelli, Vittorio Veltroni
Cinematography: Gianni di Venanzo
Editing: Eraldo Da Roma

Music: Mario Nascimbene
Set Design: Gianni Polidori
Cast: The principals are all played by non-actors, who tell their own personal stories.
B & W, in Italian
20 minutes

1955
LE AMICHE [THE GIRLFRIENDS]
Producer: Giovanni Addessi, for Trionfalcine-Titanus
Director: **Michelangelo Antonioni**
Screenplay: **Michelangelo Antonioni**, Suso Cecchi D'Amico, and Alba de Céspedes, from Cesare Pavese's story "Tra Donne Sole," published in his volume *La bella estate* (1949)
Cinematography: Gianni di Venanzo
Editing: Eraldo Da Roma
Music: Giovanni Fusco, with guitar played by Libero Tosoni and piano by Armando Trovajoli
Set Design: Gianni Polidori
Cast: Eleanora Rossi Drago (Clelia), Valentina Cortese (Nene), Yvonne Furneaux (Momina De Stefani), Gabriele Ferzetti (Lorenzo), Franco Fabrizi (the architect Cesare Pedoni), Ettore Mani (the architect's assistant, Carlo), Madeleine Fischer (Rosetta Savone), Annamaria Pancani (Mariella), Maria Gambarelli (Clelia's employer), Luciano Volpato
B & W, in Italian
104 minutes

1956
IL GRIDO [THE CRY; a.k.a. THE OUTCRY]
Producer: Franco Cancellieri, for S.P.A. Cinematografica, in collaboration with Robert Alexander Productions (New York)
Director: **Michelangelo Antonioni**
Screenplay: **Michelangelo Antonioni**, Elio Bartolini, Ennio de Concini
Cinematography: Gianni di Venanzo
Editing: Eraldo Da Roma
Music: Giovanni Fusco, with piano played by Lya de Barberis

Set Design: Franco Fontana
Costumes: Pia Marchesi
Cast: Steve Cochran (Aldo), Alida Valli (Irma), Betsy Blair (Elvia), Dorian
Gray (Virginia), Gabriella Pallotta (Edera), Lynn Shaw (Andreina), Mirna
Girardi (Rosina), Gaetano Matteucci, Guerrino Campanili, Pina Boldrini
B & W, in Italian
116 minutes

1960
L'AVVENTURA [THE ADVENTURE]
Producer: A Cino del Duca Co-Production (Amato Pennasilico):
Produzioni Cinematografiche Europee (Rome) and Société
Cinématographique Lyre (Paris)
Director: **Michelangelo Antonioni**
Screenplay: **Michelangelo Antonioni**, Elio Bartolini, Tonino Guerra
Cinematography: Aldo Scavarda
Editing: Eraldo Da Roma
Music: Giovanni Fusco
Set Design: Piero Poletto
Costumes: Adriana Berselli
Cast: Gabriele Ferzetti (Sandro), Monica Vitti (Claudia), Lea Massari
(Anna), Dominique Blanchar (Giulia), Renzo Ricci (Anna's father), James
Addams (Corrado), Dorothy De Poliolo (Gloria Perkins), Lelio Luttazzi
(Raimondo), Giovanni Petrucci (young painter), Ruspoli (Patrizia), Joe
the fisherman from Panarea (old man on the island), Prof. Cucco
(Ettore), Enrico Bologna, Franco Cimino, Giovanni Danesi, Rita Molè,
Renato Pinciroli, Angela Tommasi Di Lampedusa, Vincenzo Tranchina
B & W, in Italian
145 minutes

1961
LA NOTTE [THE NIGHT]
Producer: Emanuele Cassuto, for Nepi-Film, Silva-Film (Rome), and
Sofitedip (Paris)
Director: **Michelangelo Antonioni**
Screenplay: **Michelangelo Antonioni**, Ennio Flaiano, Tonino Guerra
Cinematography: Gianni di Venanzo

Editing: Eraldo Da Roma
Music: Giorgio Gaslini, as played by the Quartetto Giorgio Gaslini
Set Design: Piero Zuffi
Costumes: Biki
Cast: Marcello Mastroianni (Giovanni Pontano), Jeanne Moreau (Lidia), Monica Vitti (Valentina Gherardini), Bernhard Wicki (Tommaso), Maria Pia Luzi (patient), Rosy Mazzacurati (Resy), Guido A. Marsan (Fanti), Gitt Magrini (Signora Gherardini), Vincenzo Corbella (Gherardini), Giorgio Negro (Roberto), Roberta Speroni (Berenice), Ugo Fortunati (Cesarino), Vittorio Bertolini, Valentino Bompiani, Salvatore Quasimodo, Giansiro Ferrata, Roberto Danesi, Ottiero Ottieri
B & W, in Italian
122 minutes

1962
L'ECLISSE [ECLIPSE]
Producer: Robert and Raymond Hakim, for Interopa Film, Cineriz (Rome), and Paris Film Production
Director: **Michelangelo Antonioni**
Screenplay: **Michelangelo Antonioni**, Tonino Guerra, Elio Bartolini, Ottiero Ottieri
Cinematography: Gianni di Venanzo
Editing: Eraldo Da Roma
Music: Giovanni Fusco, with the "Eclipse Twist" sung by Mina
Set Design: Piero Poletto
Cast: Monica Vitti (Vittoria), Alain Delon (Piero), Lilla Brignone (Vittoria's mother), Francisco Rabal (Riccardo), Louis Seignier (Ercoli), Rossana Rory (Anita), Mirella Ricciardi (Marta), Cyrus Elias (drunk)
B & W, in Italian
124 minutes

1964
IL DESERTO ROSSO [THE RED DESERT]
Producer: Antonio Cervi, for Film Duemila, Cinematografica Federiz (Rome), and Francoriz (Paris)
Director: **Michelangelo Antonioni**

Screenplay: **Michelangelo Antonioni**, Tonino Guerra
Cinematography: Carlo Di Palma (in Technicolor)
Editing: Eraldo Da Roma
Music: Giovanni Fusco, with singing by Cecilia Fusco; electronic music
by Vittorio Gelmetti
Set Design: Piero Poletto
Costumes: Gitt Magrini
Cast: Monica Vitti (Giuliana), Richard Harris (Corrado Zeller), Carlo
Chionetti (Ugo), Xenia Valderi (Linda), Rita Renoir (Emilia), Aldo Grotti
(Max), Giuliano Missirini (radio-telescope operator), Lili Rheims (his
wife), Valerio Bartoleschi (son of Giuliana), Emanuela Paola Carboni
(girl in the fable), Bruno Borghi, Beppe Conti, Giulio Cotignoli,
Giovanni Lolli, Hiram Mino Madonia, Arturo Parmiani, Carla Ravasi,
Ivo Cherpiani, Bruno Scipioni
Color, in Italian
120 minutes

1965
PREFAZIONE: IL PROVINO [PREFACE: THE SCREEN TEST, the preface to
I TRE VOLTI (THREE FACES OF A WOMAN), directed by Mario Bava
and Salvatore Billitter]
Producer: Dino de Laurentiis, Cinematografica
Director: **Michelangelo Antonioni**
Screenplay: Piero Tosi
Cinematography: Carlo Di Palma (in Technicolor)
Editing: **Michelangelo Antonioni**
Music: Piero Piccioni
Set Design: Piero Tosi
Costumes: Piero Tosi
Cast: Princess Soraya, Ivano Davoli, Giorgio Sartarelli, Piero Tosi, Dino
de Laurentiis, Alfredo de Laurentiis, Ralph Serpe
Color, in Italian
25 minutes

1966
BLOW-UP
Producer: Bridge Films (Carlo Ponti), for Metro-Goldwyn-Mayer

Director: **Michelangelo Antonioni**
Screenplay: **Michelangelo Antonioni**, Tonino Guerra, from a story by
Julio Cortásar, "Les babas del Diablo," published in his volume *Las
Armas Secretas* (1964); English dialogue written in collaboration with
Edward Bond
Cinematography: Carlo Di Palma (in Metrocolor)
Photographic Murals: John Cowan
Editing: Frank Clarke
Music: Herbie Hancock ("Stroll On," as performed by the Yardbirds);
John Sebastian ("Make Up Your Mind," as sung by The Lovin' Spoonful)
Set Design: Assheton Gorton
Costumes: Jocelyn Rickards
Cast: Vanessa Redgrave (Jane), David Hemmings (Thomas), Sarah Miles
(Patricia), Peter Bowles (Ron), Verushka, Jill Kennington, Peggy Moffitt,
Rosaleen Murray, Ann Norman, Melanie Hampshire (models), Jane
Birkin, Gillian Hills (teenagers), Harry Hutchinson (antique dealer),
John Castle (painter), Susan Broderick (antique shop owner), Mary Khal
(fashion editor), Ronan O'Casey (Jane's lover), Tsai Chin (receptionist)
Color, in English
III minutes

1970
ZABRISKIE POINT
Producer: Carlo Ponti, for Metro-Goldwyn-Mayer
Director: **Michelangelo Antonioni**
Screenplay: **Michelangelo Antonioni**, Tonino Guerra, Fred Gardner,
Sam Shepard, Claire Peploe
Cinematography: Alfio Contini (in Panavision and Metrocolor)
Editing: **Michelangelo Antonioni**, Franco Arcalli
Music: Pink Floyd; Kaleidoscope; The Rolling Stones ("You've Got the
Silver"); The Youngbloods ("Sugarable"); The Grateful Dead ("Dark Star");
John Fahey ("Dance of Death"); Roscoe Holcomb ("I Wish I Was a
Single Girl Again"); Patti Page ("The Tennessee Waltz")
Production Design: Dean Tavoularis
Special Effects: Early McCoy
Cast: Mark Frechette (Mark), Daria Halprin (Daria), Rod Taylor (Lee Allen),
Paul Fix (café owner), G. D. Spradlin (Lee Allen's associate), Bill Garaway

(Marty), Kathleen Cleaver (Kathleen), and the Open Theater of Joseph Chaikin
Color, in English
110 minutes

1972
CHUNG KUO [CHINA]
Producer: Radiotelevisione Italiana (RAI)
Director: **Michelangelo Antonioni**, with the collaboration of Andrea Barbato
Cinematography: Luciano Tovoli
Editing: Franco Arcalli
Sound: Giorgio Pallotta
Musical Consultant: Luciano Berio
Color, in Chinese
220 minutes, documentary

1975
THE PASSENGER
Producer: Carlo Ponti, for Metro-Goldwyn-Mayer. A Co-production with Compagnia Cinematografica Champion, Rome; Les films Concordia, Paris; and C.I.P.I. Cinematográfica, Madrid
Director: **Michelangelo Antonioni**
Screenplay: Mark Peploe, Peter Wollen, **Michelangelo Antonioni**
Cinematography: Luciano Tovoli (in Metrocolor)
Editing: Franco Arcalli, **Michelangelo Antonioni**
Art Direction: Piero Poletto
Costumes: Louise Stjensward
Make-Up: Franca Freda
Hairdresser: Adalgisa Favella
Cast: Jack Nicholson (Locke), Maria Schneider (girl), Jenny Runacre (Rachel), Ian Hendry (Knight), Stephen Berkoff (Stephen), Ambroise Bia (Achebe), José Maria Cafarel (hotel keeper), James Campbell (witch doctor), Manfred Spies (German stranger), Jean Baptiste Tiemiele (murderer), Angel Del Pozo (police inspector), Chuck Mulvehill (Robertson)
Color, in English
122 minutes

1980
IL MISTERO DI OBERWALD [THE MYSTERY OF OBERWALD]
Producer: Radiotelevisione Italiana (RAI)
Director: **Michelangelo Antonioni**
Screenplay: **Michelangelo Antonioni**, Tonino Guerra, from the play
The Eagle Has Two Heads (1946), by Jean Cocteau
Cinematography: Luciano Tovoli
Editing: **Michelangelo Antonioni**, Francesco Grandoni
Music: Johannes Brahms, Arnold Schoenberg, Richard Strauss
Art Direction: Mischa Scandella
Costumes: Vittoria Guaita
Sound: Gian-Franco Desideri, Claudio Grandini
Video Color Consultant: Franco De Leonardis
Color Mattes: Francesco Grandoni
Cast: Monica Vitti (The Queen), Paolo Bonacelli (Count Foehn), Franco
Branciaroli (Sebastian), Luigi Diberti (Felix, Duke of Willenstein),
Elisabetta Pozzi (Edith de Berg), Amad Saha Alan (Tony, the
manservant)
Color, in Italian
129 minutes

1982
IDENTIFICAZIONE DI UNA DONNA [IDENTIFICATION OF A WOMAN]
Producer: Giorgio Nocella and Antonio Macri, for Iter Film (Rome) and
Gaumont (Paris)
Director: **Michelangelo Antonioni**
Screenplay: **Michelangelo Antonioni**, Gérard Brach, Tonino Guerra,
from a story by **Michelangelo Antonioni**
Cinematography: Carlo Di Palma
Editing: **Michelangelo Antonioni**
Music: John Foxx
Art Direction: Andrea Crisanti
Costumes: Paola Comencini
Sound: Mario Bramonti
Cast: Tomás Milián (Niccolò), Christine Boisson (Ida), Daniela Silverio
(Mavi), Marcel Bozzuffi (Mario), Lara Wendel (girl at the pool), Veronica
Lazar (Carla Farra), Enrica Fico (Nadia), Sandra Monteleoni (Mavi's
sister), Giampaolo Saccarola (stranger), Itaco Nardulli (Lucio), Carlos

Valles (close-up man), Sergio Tardioli (butcher), Paola Dominguin (girl in window), Arianna de Rosa (Mavi's friend), Pierfrancesco Aiello (young man at party), Maria Stefania d'Amario (landlady's friend), Giada Gerini (landlady), Alessandro Ruspoli (Mavi's father), Luisa della Noce (Mavi's mother)
Color, in Italian
128 minutes

1995
AL DI LÀ DELLE NUVOLE [BEYOND THE CLOUDS]
Producer: Philippe Carcassonne, Vittorio Cecchi Gori, Brigitte Faure, Ulrich Felsberg, Danièle Gegauff Rosencranz, Felice Laudadio, Pierre Roitfeld, and Stéphane Tchal-Gadjieff
Director: **Michelangelo Antonioni**, Wim Wenders
Screenplay: **Michelangelo Antonioni**, from *That Bowling Alley on the Tiber* (1983), Wim Wenders
Cinematography: Alfio Contini (Antonioni segment: four short tales of love); Robby Müller (Wenders segment: a story linking the four short tales)
Editing: Claudio Di Mauro, Peter Przygodda, Lucian Segura
Music: Johann Sebastian Bach, from Suite in E minor, BMV996; Bono and Adam Clayton (as U2); Van Morrison, Laurent Petitgand, Lucio Dalla, Brian Eno, Beatrice Banfi
Art Direction: Thierry Flamand
Sound: Thierry Levon, Jean-Pierre Ruh
Set Design: Denis Barbier, Marie-Noëlle Giraud
Costumes: Esther Walz
Cast: Fanny Ardant (Patricia), Chiara Caselli (mistress), Irène Jacob (a girl), John Malkovich (the director), Sophie Marceau (a girl), Vincent Perez (Niccolò), Jean Reno (Carlo), Kim Rossi-Stuart (Silvano), Inés Sastre (Carmen), Peter Weller (husband), Marcello Mastroianni (the man of all vices), Jeanne Moreau (friend), Enrica Antonioni (boutique manager), Carine Angeli, Alessandra Bonarota, Laurence Calabrese, Tracey Caligiuri, Hervé Décalion, John-Emmanuel Gartmann, Sherman Green, Veronica Lazar, Suzy Lorraine, Cesare Luciani, Muriel Mottais, Bertrand Peillard, Sara Ricci, Sophie Semin, Sabry Tchal

Gadjieff, Giulia Urso, Frère Jean-Philippe Revel, Frère Daniel
Bourgeois
Color, in French, English, and Italian
115 minutes

2004
IL FILO PERICOLOSO DELLE COSE [THE DANGEROUS THREAD OF
THINGS, an episode of the anthology film EROS]
Producer: Domenico Procacci, Stéphane Tchal-Gadjieff, Raphel
Berdugo, and Jacques Bar, for Fandango, Roissy Films, Solaris
Productions, Cité Films (Paris), Deluxe, and Jet Tone Films
Director: **Michelangelo Antonioni**
Screenplay: **Michelangelo Antonioni**, from *That Bowling Alley on the
Tiber*, Tonino Guerra
Cinematography: Marco Pontecorvo
Editing: Claudio Di Mauro
Music: Enrica Antonioni, Vinicio Milani
Cast: Luise Ranieri (the girl, Linda), Christopher Buchholz (the
husband), Regina Nemni (Chloë, the wife)
Color, in Italian
32 minutes

MICHELANGELO ANTONIONI

INTERVIEWS

A Conversation with Michelangelo Antonioni

ANDRÉ LABARTHE / 1960

Q: *You are the author of all the stories of your films. Is that because you
haven't found any other way of illustrating what you have in mind; or is it that,
for you, to create a film story and to direct it become one and the same thing?*
A: For the principle of the cinema, as for that of all the arts, there is one
choice. As Camus says, it is the revolt of the artist against actuality. If you
stick to that principle, how important are the means by which reality is
disclosed? Whether the author of a cinema finds it in a novel, in a news
item, or in his own fantasy, what counts is his way of isolating it, of styl-
izing it, of making it his own. If he achieves that, the source has no
importance. The plot of *Crime and Punishment* without the form which
Dostoyevsky gave it is a mediocre plot. It could become either a very
beautiful—or very ugly—film. That is why I have almost always written
my own films. Once I was struck by one of Pavese's novels. As I worked on
it, I knew that I loved it for reasons entirely different from those which
had originally made me think of it as a film. And the pages which had
interested me the most were those which lent themselves least to a cinematic translation. On the other hand, it is very difficult to find oneself an
original story line, since the original material is already selected in terms
of a very definite narrative style. Finally, I find it much simpler to invent
the story completely. A director is a man, therefore he has ideas; he is also
an artist, therefore he has imagination. Whether they are good or bad,

English translation from *New York Film Bulletin* 2nd series, 8 (34), 1960. Originally
published in *Cahiers du cinéma*, no. 112 (October 1960).

there are so many stories to tell, it seems to me. And that which I see, that which happens to me is constantly changing these stories.

Q: *The subjects of your films resemble one another curiously; they always revolve about the same problem: the couple, the woman, solitude. Why?*
A: The characteristic choices of a director answer to the same logic which determines his limits: if you accept the latter, it is much easier to evaluate the first. It is possible that the public (at least the part of the public which is interested in my work) is tired of seeing me constantly returning to the same subject. But, if it is true that, up to now, I have only produced variations on the same theme, it is also true that I have tried to develop this theme, to enrich it, to renew it in the light of my own experience. I have been making films for ten years. I began with *Story of a Love Affair*, here in Milan, where I am now making *La notte*. The places, the atmosphere, are the same. The characters belong, more or less, to the same social class. However, this film seems so different to me—if I didn't know that it is much more autobiographical than *Story of a Love Affair*, I would say that *La notte* is the film of another director. Probably, just like the surroundings, I have also changed countenance.

Take *The Cry*, for example. In that film, while you will find my favorite theme, I pose the problem of the emotions in a different aspect. If, before this, my characters usually accepted their failures and emotional crises, this time we meet a man who reacts, who tries to overcome his unhappiness. I have treated this character with much more mercy.

The landscape also has a different function. If in my other films I used it to add better definition to a situation or a spiritual state, in *The Cry* I wanted it to be the landscape of memory: the countryside of my childhood, seen through the eyes of someone returning home after an intense cultural and emotional experience. In *The Cry*, this return takes place in the most appropriate season: winter—when the wide, open horizon becomes a counterpoint to the psychology of the film's central character. *L'avventura*: this is the story of a cruise on a yacht. The disappearance of a girl during the period of several days is meant to symbolize the fragility of emotions in a real situation. In a certain sense, it is the answer to *Il grido* provided by the characters who peopled my preceding films. To make a play on words, you might say that *L'avventura* is *The Cry* of *The Girlfriends*. At any rate, it is not a question of truth seen from different perspectives, but of two different ways of seeing the same truth. The result is the same: solitude. With *La notte* I will arrive at one result of compromise: the compromise that is found today in morality and even in politics. The characters this time find themselves, but they have trouble in communicating because they have discovered that the truth is difficult, that it demands great courage and decision—impossible to achieve in their way of life.

Q: *What does your work bring you? What would you do if you could no longer make films?*
A: If you have an enemy, don't try to beat him up, or curse him, or humiliate him, or hope he will have a traffic accident. Simply hope that he will be left without work. It is the most horrible fate that can strike a man. Every vacation, even the most marvelous, makes no sense except as a way to counteract fatigue. I consider myself privileged in this: I do work that pleases me. I don't know many Italians who can say as much. This work is the most important thing in my life. It is superfluous to ask me what it gives me. It gives me everything. It gives me the chance to express myself, to communicate with others. Being inept at speaking, I would have the sensation of not existing at all—without the cinema.

The other things I would have been able to do are, in order: architecture and painting. As a kid I didn't design puppets as most children of my age did; I designed doorways, capitals, plans of absurd battlements; I constructed city districts in cardboard and painted them in violent colors. I have always loved colors. The few times that I dream, it is in color. The thing that strikes me first about a face is its coloring. I don't say this to make myself singular: it's simply a characteristic like any other. I am naturally very impatient to make a film in color.

Q: *What does the word "directing" mean to you?*
A: Authoritative critics have written essays and books on that subject. I am not a theoretician of the cinema. If you ask me what directing is, the first answer which comes to mind is: I don't know. The second is this: My opinions on that are all in my films. And then, among other things, I am against the separation of various phases of the work. This separation has only a practical value. It is valuable for all who participate in the work: all but the director, especially if he is also the author of the film story and

directing the picture. To speak of direction as one phase of the work is to carry on a theoretical discussion which seems to me antithetical to the concept of unity of creation to which each artist dedicates himself during his work. Doesn't one edit and do the montage during the shooting these days? And during the shooting, isn't everything automatically in question: from the story to the lines of dialogue which reveal their true meaning only when heard in the voices of the actors?

To be sure, there is always a moment when—from ideas, images, intuitions about movements, whether psychological or physical—you must arrive at a concrete realization. For the cinema, as in all the other arts, it is the most delicate moment; when the poet or the writer puts his first words on paper, the artist his brush to canvas, or the director arranges his characters in their setting, makes them speak and move, establishes by composition and framing a reciprocal harmony between people and things, between the rhythm of the dialogue and that of the entire sequence, makes the movement of the camera follow the psychological situation, etc. But the decisive moment above all is when he receives from all these and all that surrounds him all possible suggestions in such a way that his work acquires a more improvised direction, becomes more personal and even, in the broadest sense, more autobiographical.

Q: *What importance do you give to Italian neorealism? Do you consider yourself attached to it, for example, by the sketch in* Love in the City, *and in what way?*
A: To answer a question of this kind, I would have to write an entire essay on Italian neorealism. At present I am engaged in making a film. I find myself in a creative period and not a critical one. All I can say is that Italian neorealism has produced some very beautiful films; in that way it has been important. For me the sketch in *Love in the City* belonged completely to the neorealistic current. But how can one judge from the fragment of a film which the exigencies of length forced me to mutilate so much. I should have and I wished to have—related so many stories, I even shot certain others. There was one in particular that I had to cut out because of the unbearable ugliness of the principal character: a servant. Nevertheless it was a strong, dramatic story. And it is precisely then during the shooting of *Love in the City* that I learned how much can be discovered while making a film. These people who tried to commit

suicide were great characters. They were that during the making of
the film itself by virtue of the understanding they established among
themselves and because of what they told me. They were terribly proud
of their deed, but at the same time so happy (almost against their will)
that they were still alive, that they were truly touching. I should have put
all that on film there, right away: perhaps that would have been the true
neorealistic film that Zavattini talks of so much.

Q: *What is the most important moment for you in the creation of a film?*
A: I've already answered that in discussing directing. All the moments
in the creation of a film are of equal importance. It's not true that any
sharp distinction between them can exist. They are all in synthesis. Thus,
during the elaboration of the story, it can happen that you decide on a
tracking shot, or while planning scenes you may change a character or situation, and even during recording change one or more cues. From the
moment when the first idea of the film came to mind—still formless—
up to the projection of the rushes, for me the making of a film represents
a single, unified work. I mean that I cannot interest myself in anything
but that film, day and night. That shouldn't be considered a romantic
attitude—on the contrary, I become, rather, more lucid, more attentive;
I almost have the feeling of becoming more intelligent and ready to
understand. But, if you want a single answer to your question: the
moment of shooting, beyond any doubt. Since it is then that all
thoughts, all other moments an author experiences, come together.

Q: *In each of your films, framing plays an important role. Do you think of
the composition of an image, or are you more concerned about following your
characters? Or both?*
A: Both, naturally. I always try to manage so that each element of the
image serves the narrative, serves to specify a particular psychological
moment. An image is only essential if each square centimeter of that
image is essential.

Q: *What do you call "improvising," then, when at the moment of shooting
you have written a detailed script?*
A: You cannot help but recognize that direction today is less detailed
than formerly, less detailed even than several years ago. Technical

indications have virtually disappeared, also the "column on the right"—
the dialogue. In my directing I have almost eliminated the numbers
that used to indicate shots. Only the script girl uses them to facilitate
her job. This, because it seems to me more logical to decide the angles
and aspects even at the moment of shooting the scenes. That is already
one way of improvising. But there are more. I seldom care to reread a
sequence on the eve of shooting it. Now and then I arrive at the location
where we are working and I don't even know what we must shoot. This
is the system I prefer, arriving at the moment of shooting, absolutely
without preparation, virginal. I often ask that they leave me alone for
fifteen minutes or a half hour, on the location, and I let my thoughts
wander freely. I confine myself to looking around me. I use the things
around me too: they always suggest ideas to me. I have great sympathy
for objects, perhaps more than for people, but the latter interest me
more. In every way I find it useful to gaze at the surroundings and sense
the atmosphere for a while, in anticipation of the characters. It can
happen that the images I have before me at that moment coincide with
those I have in my imagination, but that doesn't happen often. More
often, the image in mind has something insincere, artificial. This, then,
is a way of improvising. But that's still not all. It may also happen that
in rehearsing a scene I change my mind abruptly. Or I change it
progressively as the electricians set up their lights and I see the actors
move and talk under them. I believe it is only then that you really
evaluate a scene and correct it. Speaking of improvisation also, I refer
you to another thing which I have already spoken of in my answer to
your fourth question.

Q: *When you are preparing and making a film, do you think of the public
and does this thought influence you?*
A: I believe I've answered that above. I repeat it: I certainly think
about the public in the sense that I need someone to show what I have
done, with whom I can communicate. However, I don't consider that
the public influences me. If I made films for the public, shouldn't
I make them for money or for glory? One makes films by thinking only
about films and above all *not* about that sort of thing. I try to make
films that have the greatest possibility of pleasing myself, and I am
certain that, the more beautiful they are, the more they please me.

Q: *Chiefly in your last films, the sound seems to have been the object of*
particular care. Have you any ideas about the relationship between sound and
image which are uniquely yours?
A: I give enormous importance to the soundtrack and I always try to
give it the greatest attention. And when I say "soundtrack," I allude to
natural sounds, to noises, rather than to music. Music rarely reinforces
the image, more often it serves merely to put the spectator to sleep and
to keep him from appreciating clearly what he is seeing. All things
considered, I am rather opposed to "musical commentary," at least in
its original form. I feel something old-fashioned, rancid in it. The ideal
would be to compose with noises an impressive soundtrack and to
appoint an orchestra conductor to direct it. But then the only orchestra
conductor capable of doing it—wouldn't he be the director of the film?

Q: *Which is in your career the film that seems to you, today, to be most*
important and why?
A: I have always thought that a certain amount of frivolity was necessary
to answer such questions. These are questions which only aim to satisfy
the curiosity of readers. It is obvious to say that all my films have as much
importance in my career as in my life. Finally, I don't seem to understand
how I should answer: from a critical viewpoint, certainly not, that is not
my business. I would not be objective, and I would try in vain to identify
the reasons for a preference among my films. From the human viewpoint,
let us say, then. In this case, I would say the most important of my films is
L'avventura, because it is the one which cost me the most, which taught
me the most, which more than any other film forced me to be present to
myself. In respect to that I ought to explain how it often happens that
I am absent from myself, but we get into the realm of gossip there—and
I don't enjoy that.

Q: *What are the ties in your work with that of Pavese?*
A: Here is another embarrassing question. Perhaps (excuse me for
saying this to you) it is badly worded. I could always reply that it is not
for me to say, or even that no particular empathy exists beyond that of
a reader for an author. I believe I have read Pavese pretty thoroughly,
but there are writers I love and esteem more than I do him. What I love
in *Among Women Only*, the story (by Pavese) from which I drew my film

The Girlfriends, are the feminine characters and what goes on in their inner selves. Besides, one of these characters resembles extraordinarily another character whom I knew only too well in reality, and I wanted to speak of it, to demonstrate it. It will be said that this answer eludes the question: if it is accepted literally, the sense of it will escape you. But, frankly, I have little to add. Critics have mentioned a certain analogy between Pavese and me, recognizing in our mutual pessimism a very small common denominator. Personally, it seems to me the intellectual experiences of Pavese coincide tragically with his personal experiences. Can as much be said for me? Am I not here engaged in making a film, I would even say obstinately? And, everything added up, this obstinacy, isn't it a proof of optimism?

An Interview with Antonioni

MICHÈLE MANCEAUX/1960

ANTONIONI LOOKS PALE and tense. He has been filming now for thirty-two nights, right through from five every evening until seven in the morning, and his own fatigue is matched by that of his cast and technical crew. The location is a golf club near Milan, transformed for screen purposes into a private villa. The action of *La Notte*, which concerns a couple (Jeanne Moreau and Marcello Mastroianni) on the verge of a break-up, brings the director back to one of his favourite themes: the failure of communication which has bankrupted their relationship.

Antonioni is not especially anxious to retain his reputation as a "difficult" director; and in *La Notte*, to satisfy his producer, he has contrived a happy ending of a sort. But Antonioni has a genius for despair, and this attempt at reconciliation should constitute one of the most poignant embraces the screen has shown us. It is a key scene in the film; and at dusk and dawn each day, in the few moments of half-light, Antonioni is filming it in short snatches.

It's now seven in the evening. The actors, made up and ready, have been there since five, and they're waiting while preparations are made for an immense tracking shot across the park. At last everything is in place. Jeanne Moreau crosses the park, tracked by the camera. There's barely time to begin the shot two or three times, and already the light is fading.

From *Sight and Sound*, vol. 30, no. 1 (Winter 1960–61), pp. 5–8. Reprinted by permission of the British Film Institute.

Back to the house. Since Antonioni is shooting inside a room, each shot requires a shift in the placing of the furniture and lights. Between each take one sees, in this vast house, people wandering about rather like fish in an aquarium. It's a long night; and towards five in the morning, curled up in armchairs, one stumbles upon a weary stills cameraman, a sleeping hairdresser.

The scene Antonioni is shooting involves three people: Jeanne Moreau, Marcello Mastroianni, and Monica Vitti. There's something aquarium-like about this as well. They criss-cross about the room, to and fro, unspeaking and communicating only through looks and gestures. Antonioni controls his *mise-en-scène* like a ballet. The players, cut off from one another by window panes, placed on different levels, carrying on back-to-back conversations, are manoeuvred with an attention which goes beyond the merely aesthetic. Antonioni looks after every detail: he straightens a lock of hair, rips the corner off a whiskey bottle label to make it look less new, throws a towel down on a chair, takes his time about picking a tie for his leading man. To the actors, however, he does no more than indicate positions and gestures, never intonations.

It's a damp evening, and moths are fluttering into the clusters of lights. Calmly, one after another, Antonioni brushes them away.

"There, Jeanne, you say, 'The weight of all these years on one's shoulders'. Then you sink down." Jeanne Moreau, who is playing in both French and Italian, smokes one cigarette after another. Throughout the night, the atmosphere stays very quiet.

Four-thirty in the morning, and suddenly it gets cold. They all look tired, ill, as they pull on boots and jerseys and go out again to the park. The grass is shiny with dew. Jeanne Moreau, bare-shouldered in a black crêpe dress, is sitting beside Mastroianni. He kisses her, pulls her down on to the sand.

Antonioni asks everyone to move away. Then, and exceptionally, he gives Jeanne Moreau an indication of the psychology of the scene . . . "He kisses her. She kisses him, but it's out of pity; for him, for herself, for their love. She thinks he's understood her and feels the same way. But, once again, they're at odds with each other. He wants to sleep with her, like men who think this is the way to set everything right. When she understands this, she resists; she doesn't want that."

"Camera."

Antonioni kneels close to them on the ground. "I don't love you anymore," says Jeanne, "and you no longer love me." "Be quiet," answers Mastroianni, as the light comes up.

"*Basta cosi*," says Antonioni. "Cut."

MICHÈLE MANCEAUX: *You were already 37 when you made* Cronaca di un Amore *in 1950. Could you tell me what you had done before that and how you came to the cinema?*

MICHELANGELO ANTONIONI: I was born at Ferrara, which is a lovely, quiet old town in the middle of the sort of flat landscape you see in *Il Grido*. I took my degree at the University of Bologna. During this time I interested myself in the theatre; we had set up a student company and put on plays. I produced Pirandello, Ibsen, and even a play I'd written myself—terrible! In fact, I had been attracted to the theatre since I was a child. One year, in the country, some of my friends and I built a little theatre and put on some absurd show. I suppose I was about twelve. My job was to make thunder noises by rolling rocks down a gulley behind the stage. They fell with a noise that echoed in the channel, at the bottom of which ran a stream. I loved this deep and mysterious noise. I made thunder noises all through the show . . .

The first time I ever went behind a camera (it was a 16 mm Bell and Howell) was in a lunatic asylum. I was determined to shoot a real-life documentary, that's to say with actual patients, and was so insistent that at last the hospital director let me try it. We put the camera in place, set up the lights, and disposed the patients about the room as we wanted them for the first shot. I ought to say that they were touchingly obedient and very careful to do nothing wrong. Finally, I ordered the lights to be switched on. It was rather a moving moment for me. Suddenly the room was blazing with light: for a second the patients stayed motionless, almost petrified, and I've never seen on any actor's face quite such expressions of overwhelming terror . . . But that lasted only a moment, and the rest of it was almost indescribable. They tried desperately to shield themselves against the light, as though it were some kind of prehistoric monster attacking them. Their expressions were disintegrated, devastated. Now, of course, we were the petrified ones. The cameraman hadn't the strength even to shut off the motor and I wasn't up to giving any kind of order. It was the hospital director, at last, who shouted out,

"Stop! Cut the lights!" And in the half-darkness we saw bodies grovelling and shivering as though in agony.

MM: *Wasn't this experience enough to put you off film-making?*
MA: Not a bit. But it's a scene I've never forgotten. It was then, though without being aware of it, that we began to talk of neorealism. After the war, when these films became fashionable, I often thought of this documentary—which was never made—as a sort of classic text . . . I felt this even more when I made my first film, *Gente del Po*, in 1943.

. . . I had come to Rome in 1940, on a job connected with the big International Exhibition which was planned for 1942, and which, of course, never took place. This job didn't last long, and during this period I was often really hungry. I remember that I stole a piece of meat once, and I'm not ashamed to admit it . . . Later, I became editor of the magazine *Cinema* and also worked as assistant to Rossellini on his film *Un Pilota Ritorna*. In 1942 I went to France, as assistant to Carné on *Les Visiteurs du Soir*. I was called up and had to go back to Italy as soon as the film was finished, and I suppose my career might have taken quite a different course if I'd been able to stay in France.

After that I did some work as assistant both to Visconti and De Santis and wrote some scripts, including Fellini's *Lo Sceicco Bianco*. And in 1947 I finally managed to get together the footage I'd shot for *Gente del Po*, which hadn't been possible before because of the post-war division of Italy. When I got the negative, I was bitterly distressed to find that half was missing: a 2,000-ft. documentary was reduced to only 1,000 feet. But let me be a little presumptuous for a moment: this short really did go some way towards anticipating the neorealist films. Up to then, documentary directors in my country had concentrated on places, objects, works of art. But my film was about sailors and fishermen and daily life . . . about people.

In 1948 I made my second documentary, *N.U.*, which was about street-cleaners. Then I made some others, and was awarded some prizes. And finally, in 1950, I found someone in Turin who was prepared to finance a feature for me. I suggested the subject of *Cronaca di un Amore*, and although he didn't much like the sound of it he invited me to come and see him. I suppose the hours I spent talking to him in his hotel room were some of the most difficult in my life, especially since I'm not by nature a talker. I talked altogether for four or five hours, without much real idea of how he was reacting or what effect I was making. At last he told me that he still didn't think much of the subject, but he could see what I felt about it and that was good enough.

MM: *Do you feel that there's a line of progression in your own work, from* Cronaca di un Amore *to* L'Avventura *and* La Notte? *What are you moving towards?*

MA: That's a very difficult question, and I'm tempted to answer: I just make films, and that's that. I don't feel, in any case, that the things a director has to say about his own work really go very far towards illuminating it . . . and in my own case, I know enough about myself to know that anything I said would just define a particular moment or state of mind, or throw a certain light on the imaginative process. Here, you should be able to say, I remember such and such motives . . . nothing more. An artist's line of development, I think, is something that comes about unconsciously.

My feeling, too, is that films aren't "understood" simply by spying out their content. You have to ask much more of a film—or something different. But I suppose there is always a kind of lowest common denominator in my films, or at least in the best of them. It's an analysis of the sentiments, as they are today. I think *La Notte* will probably end this analysis and I may follow it with something quite different.

MM: *Which of your own films satisfies you most?*

MA: Apart from *La Notte*, and of course I can't judge that yet, I would say that *L'Avventura* is the best . . . Superficially, this film may look like a rather complicated and perhaps mysterious love story. During a holiday trip, a girl disappears; and the fact of this disappearance creates a gap which is immediately filled by other factors. For the missing girl's fiancé and her friend, the search becomes a kind of sentimental journey, at the end of which they've reached a new and unforeseen situation. On one level, it could be a kind of thriller, with enough sophistication and enough weight to the characters to give it the pseudo-dignity of the psychological thriller.

Well, there are elements of that in the story construction. But *L'Avventura* has other ambitions . . . Not towards a message but, more humbly, a demonstration. I wanted to show that sentiments which convention and rhetoric have encouraged us to regard as having a kind of definite weight and absolute duration, can in fact be fragile, vulnerable, subject to change. Man deceives himself when he hasn't courage enough to allow for new dimensions in emotional matters—his loves, regrets, states of mind—just as he allows for them in the field of science and technology.

Well, what's to be done? *L'Avventura* naturally does not pretend to have the answer to the disturbing questions it raises. It's enough for me to have posed them in cinematic terms.

MM: *Why do you use only natural settings?*
MA: Because I find them the most stimulating. It's rather like telling a painter, "Here's this wall, so long and so high, which you have to cover with frescoes." Limitations of this sort help the imagination much more than they constrict it. There's another reason as well. I am interested in the relationship between the internal space and the external space of a setting. In reality one cannot exist without the other, and in fact the second often conditions the first. It's a natural circumstance which one can't ignore. It's true that on the set you can construct interior and exterior as you please. But for me something is missing, an occasional quality of reality, perhaps even a particular light. In a sense, I can say that to direct in a natural setting is to continue writing the film.

MM: *Sometimes you transform your natural decor, work over it and select from it so that it looks like something it isn't . . .*
MA: Yes, that's true. But this has to do with a temptation I'm always giving way to, whether it's in someone's office or a private house or even my own home. I'll be talking to someone and suddenly, during the conversation, I'll begin to feel uncomfortable. Somehow we seem badly placed in the scene. We may be sitting next to each other, for instance, and I feel we should be facing one another, or perhaps I'd rather have a window than a wall behind him . . . When I'm shooting a film I do no more than this: I manoeuvre objects and people as they seem to go best.

MM: *How important are the actors to you? Are they simply objects to be manipulated as the situation demands?*

MA: A very important element in the action, but one which I need to have entirely in my own hands. During rehearsals I never get very close to the actors. Instinctively, I would want to treat them badly, to consider them as individuals only to the extent to which they're useful to the film. For this reason, I explain as little as possible what I think about the characters they're playing or the scene they're just about to shoot. In effect, I try to direct them not so much through their intelligence as through their nerves and instincts. I want them rather to lose control of themselves—though without being aware of it—and to get down, as it were, to the raw material. The important thing then is to select and assemble the right expressions. That's the difficult part about this system . . . if you can really call it a system.

MM: *You know Robert Bresson's films? He's another director who doesn't want his players to "act."*
MA: I know Bresson's films and think very highly of them. But my own feeling is not that actors ought not to act, only that they ought to act with the least possible lucidity. What I want to avoid is actors becoming their own directors.

MM: *You often work with non-professionals. Do you choose them because they can represent the characters rather than because they are good actors?*
MA: Yes, quite often. Some of the small parts in *La Notte* are played by people who have never acted before, not even in school productions, and they are very good. On the other hand, there are times when one must have good professional actors to develop certain characters. As I said, it has to do with using them in a certain way.

MM: *Watching you at work, I was very struck by the way in which you supervise the smallest details. You leave nothing to chance, and yet your films are not entirely realistic. How do you reconcile this very precise method and the sort of atmosphere you get?*
MA: Why should I leave things to chance? Nothing in a work of art comes about by accident . . . Moreover, chance has never worked well for me. From the moment when it inspires us, in any case, the real becomes our number one enemy. And, too, isn't it really you French critics who've chosen this expression "interior realism" to describe my work?

MM: *How big a part does improvisation play in your films?*

MA: Generally I come to work without knowing exactly what I'm going to shoot. I ask the members of the company to leave me alone, and for about fifteen or thirty minutes I'm by myself. This is the time when I resolve my various problems, and I suppose you might say that I'm virtually inventing a little piece of film.

MM: *The women in your films are generally free and aware of what they are doing, often initiating action on their own account. This doesn't seem to reflect the usual Italian attitude towards women. Would you say that, if the women were more submissive, there wouldn't be this kind of breakdown in relationships?*

MA: No, I don't think that this is the reason why relations between men and women are liable to deteriorate so easily. It's more of a natural process, and it isn't particularly the fault of society. The world is changing very quickly, and why should we be surprised that human psychology and the mechanics of sentiment are changing as well?

MM: *Do you regard your own heroes as particularly weak men?*

MA: Perhaps. But the important thing is that they should be strong as characters.

MM: *But aren't they, for the most part, men who have renounced their work?*

MA: A man who renounces something is also a man who believes in something . . .

MM: *All the same, my impression is that you are more indulgent to women. You generally allow them more strength than your male characters. In* Le Amiche, *for instance, it's Clelia who takes the decision to leave the man.*

MA: But in *L'Avventura* the woman is no less weak than the man . . . In any case, I don't feel that this word "weak" is really the right one. We're living in an impasse. Is it weak to try to get out of it, even if, for the moment, you lose the battle?

MM: Le Amiche *was an adaptation from a novel by Pavese. What do you feel about adaptations generally and do you think that they are a proper thing for the cinema?*

MA: I don't think there is any problem here. When you read a novel or story and think about it in film terms, what matters is what there is in the story that strikes off completely new possibilities. You take the narrated incidents as a living reality, that is, and this constitutes your new point of departure. What is left of a story by Bandello in Shakespeare? Absolutely nothing. And, on my own account, I was never particularly troubled by considerations of remaining faithful to Pavese's novel.

MM: *Is there any writer whom you particularly admire?*
MA: Of course. I imagine everyone has a favourite writer. You always become aware of coincidences between your own experiences and personal reflections and what you read. There's a period in which Stendhal gets you, a period when Gide gets you, when Malraux gets you, when Musil gets you . . . Something certainly stays with us from this reading; it is part of the cultural baggage to which we cling, more or less unconsciously and at the most unlikely moments. I've enjoyed reading Conrad immensely, for instance, but I could never make a film from one of his novels.

MM: *But you might one day make a Conradian film?*
MA: Perhaps. But that would be something for the critics to judge, not for me.

MM: *How is it that you are almost the only Italian director whose work strikes one as entirely secular? There's almost always a whiff of religion in Italian films, but one never senses it in your work.*
MA: Do you think this is a failing or a virtue?

MM: *For me, a virtue.*
MA: My impression is that people abroad are very badly informed about Italian questions. You aren't probably aware that there has been a kind of Jansenist tradition in Italy. And if it is true that I'm a secular artist, it's also true that I'm part of a cultural tradition, both in literature and in the cinema. Svevo, for instance, was a secular writer; so was Pavese. The Italian silent and pre-war cinemas were secular. There has always been this minority in Italy. So I would say, simply, that if I am a secular artist I'm not some kind of freak or monster. If I seem isolated in our

cinema, it may be because in our surroundings opportunism is almost a habit of mind. I don't, of course, mean to deny that some artists, and the best of them, are entirely sincere. There's an authentic Catholic nostalgia in Fellini's work and even in Rossellini's; and in the films of De Sica and Zavattini there is always hope, or at least there is not that compulsion to look pitilessly right to the bottom, which is a characteristic secular trait.

MM: *It seems to me that there is one recurring theme in all your films: the impossibility of fidelity.*
MA: Fidelity is linked to the sentiments, and I've already said what I feel about those questions. It's a vicious circle. If the sentiments are fragile . . . But, please, I don't want to begin the interview all over again.

A Talk with Michelangelo Antonioni on His Work

FILM CULTURE/1962

THE FOLLOWING ARTICLE IS BASED on the transcript of an open discussion that took place at the Centro Sperimentale di Cinematografia in Rome on March 16, 1961, after a retrospective screening of Antonioni's films for students and faculty members, arranged by the Centro's director, Leonardo Fioravanti.

ANTONIONI: Someone once said that words, more than anything else, serve to hide our thoughts. Nevertheless, in answering your questions, I will try to be as direct and honest as possible, as I try to be when I'm working on a film. I didn't come prepared to make a speech, so I've been asking myself what I should say to you and what it is that you want to know about me. I am a film-maker who began making feature films about ten years ago, and who forced himself to follow a certain direction, to maintain a certain coherence. Now I'm not saying this to pat myself on the back, but I'm saying it because it was the only way I would have been interested in making films. Had I done them in any other way, I probably would have made worse films than the ones I did make.

Now, if you ask me what were the motives and the reasons that led me to make films in this particular manner, I think I can say today that I was motivated by two considerations. (And bear this clearly in mind, these statements are being made *ex post facto* and not *a priori*, that is, I had no

From *Film Culture*, no. 24 (Spring 1962), pp. 45–61.

conception of them until I actually became involved in making feature-length dramatic films.) The first had to do with those crucial events that were taking place around us immediately after the war, and even later, in 1950, when I first started working in films; the second was simply a technical matter more closely related to cinematography per se. With reference to the first consideration, I will most certainly say that as far as their particular period was concerned, all those so-called Italian neorealistic films, among which are some genuine masterpieces, were representative of the most authentic and the most valid cinematic expression possible, and they were also the most appropriate. After all, it was a period in which everything happening around us was quite abnormal; reality was a burning issue. The events and situations of the day were extraordinarily unusual, and perhaps the most interesting thing to examine at that time was the relationship between the individual and his environment, between the individual and society. Therefore, a film such as *The Bicycle Thief*, for example, where the main character was a laborer who lost his job because someone had stolen his bicycle, and whose every motivation stemmed from that specific fact, and that fact alone, which in itself was the most important aspect of the film and around which its entire story was centered—this, I say, was the type of film necessary and appropriate for its time. (I know I've said this all before, but I don't mind repeating it because it's something of which I'm profoundly convinced.) It really wasn't necessary to know the protagonist's inner thoughts, his personality, or the intimate relationship between him and his wife; all this could very well be ignored. The important thing was to establish his relationship with society. That was the primary concern of the neorealist films made at that time. However, when I started making films, things were somewhat different, and my approach therefore was also different. I had arrived a little late on the scene, at a time when that first flowering of films, though still valid, was already beginning to show signs of exhaustion. Consequently, I was forced to stop and consider what subject matter was worth examining at that particular moment, what was really happening, what was the true state of things, what ideas were really being thought. And it seemed to me that perhaps it was no longer so important, as I said before, to examine the relationship between the individual and his environment, as it was to examine the individual himself, to look inside the individual and see, after all he had been through (the war, the immediate post-war situation, all the events that were currently taking place and which were of sufficient gravity to leave their mark upon society and the individual)— out of all this, to see what remained inside the individual, to see, I won't say the *transformation* of our psychological and emotional attitudes, but at least, the symptoms of that restlessness and behavior which began to outline the changes and transitions that later came about in our psychology, our feelings, and perhaps even our morality.

And so I began with *Cronaca di un amore*, in which I analyzed the condition of spiritual aridity and a certain type of moral coldness in the lives of several individuals belonging to the upper middle-class strata of Milanese society. I chose this particular subject because it seemed to me there would be plenty of raw material worth examining in a situation that involved the morally empty existence of certain individuals who were only concerned with themselves, who had no interest whatsoever in anything or anyone outside of themselves, and who had no human quality strong enough to counterbalance this self-centeredness, no spark of conscience left which might still be ignited to revitalize themselves with a sense of the enduring validity of certain basic values. It was this, unfortunately, which led the French critics quite innocently to define my style of film-making as being a kind of internal neorealism. At any rate, this seemed to be the right road for me to follow at that time. Later, I will also tell you how and why I had adopted a certain technical approach that was directly in line with this choice.

The second consideration that led me along this particular road was an ever-increasing feeling of boredom with the current standardized methods of film-making and the conventional ways of telling a story. I was already instinctively aware of this feeling when I first started working on my early documentaries, especially *N.U.*, which I had filmed in a somewhat different manner than what was then considered the orthodox way of making a film. (You will recall, however, that in 1943 I had already started shooting my very first documentary, which wasn't completed until 1947. Ever since then, in addition to making films about landscapes and places of interest, which were the usual kind of films being done in Italy at that time, I began making films about people, and in a way that was much more intense, much more sympathetic, much more involved.) As far as the documentary form was concerned, and especially with *N.U.*,

I felt a need to avoid certain established and proven techniques. Even Paolucci, who was then one of the most noted documentarists, was making his documentaries in accordance with the set standards of the day, that is, in blocks of sequences. Each one of these blocks had its own beginning, its own end, and its own order; when joined together, these blocks constituted a certain parabola that gave the documentary a unity of its own. And they were impeccable documentaries, even from a formal point of view; but I felt somewhat annoyed with all this sense of order, this systematic arrangement of the material. I felt a need to break it up a little. So, having a certain amount of material in my hands, I set out to do a montage that would be absolutely free, poetically free. And I began searching for expressive ways and means, not so much through an orderly arrangement of shots that would give the scene a clear-cut beginning and end, but more through a juxtaposition of separate isolated shots and sequences that had no immediate connection with one another but which definitely gave more meaning to the idea I had wanted to express and which were the very substance of the documentary itself; in the case of *N.U.*, the life of street-cleaners in a particular city.

When I was ready to start work on *Cronaca di un amore*, I found myself with these observations already acquired and with this basic experience already assimilated. So, as I was saying before, when I used that particular technical approach which consisted of extremely long shots, of tracks and pans that followed the actors uninterruptedly (the longest shot in *Cronaca di un amore* was 132 meters and it was the one taken on the bridge), I did it perhaps instinctively, but reflecting upon it now I can understand what led me to move in that particular direction. In effect, I had the feeling that it wasn't quite right for me to abandon the actor at a time when, having just enacted an intensely dramatic scene, he was left alone by himself to face the after-effects of that particular scene and its traumatic moments. Undoubtedly, those moments of emotional violence had had a meaningful effect upon the actor and had probably served to advance him one step further psychologically. So I felt it was essential for me to follow the actors with the camera a few moments after they had completed their performance of the written scene. And though this may have seemed pointless, it actually turned out that these moments were exactly those which offered me the best opportunity to select and utilize on the moviola screen certain spontaneous movements in their gestures and facial expressions that perhaps could not have been gotten in any other way. (Many times, of course, I had the camera follow the actors even without their being aware of it, that is, at a time when they had thought the shot was finished.)

All this experimentation provided the basis for the results achieved in *La notte*. And I want to say this, that ever since then I believe I have managed to strip myself bare, to liberate myself from the many unnecessary formal techniques that were so common at the time. I am not using the word "formal" in the sense that I had wanted to achieve results that would be strictly figurative. That wasn't the case at all. In fact, this has never been of any interest to me. Instead I have always tried to fill the image with a greater suggestiveness—by composing the shot in a way that would assist me to say precisely what I intend, and at the same time to assist the actors to express exactly what they are required to express, and also to assist in establishing a working rapport between the actors and the background, that is, the activity going on behind them as they perform their particular scene.

So, film by film, I gradually began to divest myself of certain precious and professionalized techniques. However, I must say that I don't regret having had them, for without them perhaps I would not have been able to finally arrive at what I feel is a greater simplicity. Now I can actually permit myself to make some minor technical errors. And I do make them. In fact, sometimes I even do it on purpose, in order to obtain a greater degree of effectiveness. For example, certain unorthodox uses of "field" and "counter-field," certain errors regarding position or movement. Thus, I have rid myself of much unnecessary technical baggage, eliminating all the logical narrative transitions, all those connective links between sequences where one sequence served as a springboard for the one that followed. The reason I did this was because it seemed to me—and of this I am firmly convinced—that cinema today should be tied to the truth rather than to logic. And the truth of our daily lives is neither mechanical, conventional, nor artificial, as stories generally are, and if films are made that way, they will show it. The rhythm of life is not made up of one steady beat; it is, instead, a rhythm that is sometimes fast, sometimes slow; it remains motionless for a while, then at the next moment it starts spinning around. There are times when it appears almost static, there are other times when it moves with tremendous speed, and

I believe all this should go into the making of a film. I'm not saying one should slavishly follow the day-to-day routine of life, but I think that through these pauses, through this attempt to adhere to a definite reality—spiritual, internal, and even moral—there springs forth what today is more and more coming to be known as modern cinema, that is, a cinema which is not so much concerned with externals as it is with those forces that move us to act in a certain way and not in another. Because the important thing is this: that our acts, our gestures, our words are nothing more than the consequences of our own personal situation in relation to the world around us.

And for this reason it seems most important nowadays for us to make these so-called "literary" or "figurative" films. (Obviously, these terms are paradoxical, because I am absolutely sure that no such thing as a literary film or a figurative film exists. There exists only cinema, which incorporates the experience of all the other arts.) I think it is important at this time for cinema to turn towards this internal form of film-making, towards ways of expression that are absolutely free, as free as those of literature, as free as those of painting which has reached abstraction. Perhaps one day cinema will also achieve the heights of abstraction; perhaps cinema will even construct poetry, a cinematic poem in rhyme. Today this may seem absolutely unthinkable, and yet little by little, perhaps even the public will come to accept this kind of cinema. I say this because something of the sort is already taking shape, something which even the public is becoming aware of, and which I think is the reason why certain so-called difficult films today are even achieving commercial success; they no longer remain in the film libraries, they no longer remain in the can. Instead, these films are reaching the great masses of people; in fact, I would say the more widespread they become, the more they are being understood.

ENZO BATTAGLIA *(student of the Centro's directing class):* *With reference to that shot in* La notte *where Jeanne Moreau, at a certain point, moves along that white wall against which she appears almost crushed—was this a planned shot, one that was in the original script, or was it improvised there on the spot? In other words, what I'd like to know is to what extent you plan your shots in advance and to what extent you let yourself be influenced by the locale during the actual shooting.*

ANTONIONI: I believe that in every form of artistic endeavor, there is
first of all a process of selection. This selection, as Camus once said,
represents the artist's revolt against the forces of reality. So whenever
I'm ready to start shooting a scene, I arrive on location in a fixed state
of "virginity." I do this because I believe the best results are obtained by
the "collison" that takes place between the environment in which the
scene is to be shot and my own particular state of mind at that specific
moment. I don't like to study or even think about a scene the night
before, or even a few days before I actually start shooting it. And when
I arrive there, I like to be completely alone, by myself, so that I can get
to feel the environment without having anybody around me. The
most direct way to recreate a scene is to enter into a rapport with the
environment itself; it's the simplest way to let the environment suggest
something to us. Naturally, we are well acquainted with that area in
advance, from the moment we have selected it, and therefore know
that it offers the proper setting for the particular scene that's being shot.
So it's only a matter of organizing and arranging the sequence, adapting
it to the characteristic details of the surrounding environment. For this
reason, I always remain alone in the area for about half an hour before I
start shooting a scene, whether it's an indoor scene or an outdoor scene.
Then I call in the actors and begin testing out the scene, because this
too is a way of judging whether the scene works well or not. In fact, it's
possible that a well-planned scene that was written while sitting behind
the desk, just won't work anymore once it's laid out in a particular locale,
so it has to be changed or modified right there and then. Certain lines
in the script might take on a different meaning once they're spoken
against a wall or against a street background. And a line spoken by an
actor in profile doesn't have the same meaning as one given full-face.
Likewise, a phrase addressed to the camera placed above the actor doesn't
have the same meaning it would if the camera were placed below him.
But the director (and, I repeat, this is my own personal way of working)
becomes aware of all these things only when he's on the scene and starts
moving his actors around according to the first impressions that come
to him from being there. So, it is extremely rare that I have the shots
already fixed in my mind. Obviously, in the various stages of preparing
a film, a director creates images in his mind, but it is always dangerous
to fall in love with these formulated images, because you eventually

end up by running after images abstracted from the reality of the environment in which the scene is being shot and which are no longer the same as they first appeared while sitting behind the desk. It is really much better to adapt yourself to a new situation, and this is especially so since the nature of film scripts today, as you know, is that they are becoming less and less detailed and less and less technical. They are the director's notes, and serve as a model on which one works during the course of the shooting. So, as I was saying a short while ago, improvisation comes directly from the rapport that is established between the environment and ourselves, from the rapport between the director and the people around him, both the usual professional collaborators and the people who just happen to be gathered in that particular area when the scene is being shot. In other words, it is possible that the rapport itself could suggest the outcome of a scene; it could suggest the modification of a line; it could suggest so many things, inasmuch as it too is a method of improvisation. So, I repeat, for this reason I very seldom give much advance thought to the shot but prefer to think about it when I'm there on the scene and when I put my eye behind the camera.

GIULIO CESARE CASTELLO (*film critic and member of the Centro faculty*): *This pertains to a natural setting, but what about the studio where the set is constructed according to a pre-conceived design?*
ANTONIONI: What I said also applies to a studio set.

CASTELLO: *Certain reciprocal stimuli inherent in a scene that is shot in a natural environment do not exist in one that is shot in a studio, which, to some extent, always creates a kind of limitation, if for no other reason than there exists a scenography; the set, therefore, is constructed in a specific way and there are certain movements which you simply cannot make, unless you plan and construct the scenography in a different way.*
ANTONIONI: Aside from the fact that I've been working less and less in a studio (I've now made two films without once setting foot in a studio), I can say that even there the situation I described holds true. Of course, when preparing a set within a studio, I sketch out an idea for the designer or architect as to what I think the scene should be like, establishing thereby a certain rapport with the surroundings. But not until I actually find myself on the finished set, at that moment and that

moment only, do I have the exact feeling of what the scene should really look like. And to some extent even those surroundings, which I myself to a certain extent have set up, can offer me surprises and suggest some changes, some new ideas. And I never reject those suggestions. Even here, before I start shooting, I remain alone by myself for a period of twenty minutes, a half hour, and sometimes even longer.

ANTONIO PETRUCCI *(member of the Centro faculty):   If I'm not mistaken, you once wrote somewhere that just before you start shooting a scene, you put yourself in a state somewhat similar to that of a writer in front of a blank page. And yet, undoubtedly, you must have some clue in mind as to what you want to do, just as a writer does; he doesn't sit down in front of a blank page unless he first has a definite idea what he wants to write about.*

ANTONIONI: No, but to continue your metaphor, you might say it's more like a writer who has an idea in mind as to what the house in which his character lives should be like, but has not yet begun to describe it. The creation doesn't take place until he describes it. Just as a scene in a film isn't depicted until the actual shooting of that scene takes place. Now there are more than a thousand ways an actor can enter a room and slap someone across the face. But there is only one right way; the other fifty thousand are all wrong. It's a matter of finding the right way. So, when I enter upon a new environment, I feel as though I were in front of a blank page—I have no idea where to begin. And I'm pursued by doubts right up until that moment when I see the material on the moviola screen. Therefore, I would think that even the studio can offer some surprises. Because the moment you place the actors on the scene, then, from the rapport established between the actors and their surroundings—a rapport that is absolutely new and spontaneous—you get an idea as to what should follow, depending on how the situation affects you. If every detail in the sequence were foreseen, well, then there wouldn't be any need at all for the dolly. Today a film is made while in progress; it is written right there on the spot, with the camera.

CASTELLO: *This method makes it necessary for you to shoot much more than the usual amount of footage. For example, how many feet of film did you shoot for* L'avventura *and* La notte?

ANTONIONI: Not so much. At least, not an extreme amount. For *L'avventura*, I shot about 170,000 feet; for *La notte* about 140,000. So that's not much.

CASTELLO: *I would like to ask another question of a more general nature. There being no doubt that everything you did to date was done the way you wanted to do it, inasmuch as you never have had to compromise yourself with the producers, is there anything in your films that you yourself reject, anything with which you are dissatisfied, not in the sense that every artist is always more or less dissatisfied with almost everything he has done in the past, but rather something you feel you shouldn't have done or which you should have done differently?*

ANTONIONI: Although I'm not completely satisfied with everything I've done—which is something natural and logical—I believe there's no particular film that leaves me more dissatisfied than any other. However, there are certain parts in some films that displease me more than other parts. For example, in *I vinti*, and also some sections in *Signora senza camelie*, which is a film I consider to be a mistake, mainly because I started off on the wrong foot from the very beginning of the film by concentrating on a character who then turned out to be the wrong one. Others may find that this is not so, but for me, knowing what I had in mind, I felt very bitter over the fact that I had to make so many changes from the original idea. However, there are some sequences in the film which I would do exactly the same way today. In *I vinti*, I was particularly dissatisfied with the Italian episode. And even in the French episode, I would now change many things, since I have come to know France a little better since then. Perhaps I'd leave the English episode as it is. But it's very difficult to judge this way, because even in *L'avventura* it seems to me there are certain things that I don't like anymore; even in *La notte*. And then, with *La notte*, I'm still so close to it that I haven't come to like it yet, and I'm not sufficiently detached from the film to really judge it.

FIORAVANTI: *In* L'avventura, *what are the parts that least satisfy you?*

ANTONIONI: Well, for example, today I would do the entire party scene at the end in a different way. I don't mean it's not good as it is now: I mean I would just do it differently, perhaps worse, but in any case, differently. Then, certain scenes on the islands, for example, certain things with the father, certain things with the helicopter.

KRYSTYNA STYPULKOWSKA *(student in the Centro's acting classes):   First of all, I would like to speak about* L'avventura, *or more precisely, about the significance of its ending, its conception.*

I understand one should never put such questions to a director, and for this I apologize, but some of us have spent many hours, actually entire nights, in discussing this very problem because every one of us saw it in a different way. Some said it dealt with an almost Pascalian conception of life, which lays bare the solitude of man, his perpetual failure, his humiliation, his attempt to escape from a world in which there is no way out. Others found in this ending, however disconcerting, a conception of life that is perhaps more optimistic than any of your other films. What are your thoughts on the subject?

My second question, though banal, interests me enormously inasmuch as I'm a student of acting. I would like to know how you work with actors. To be more precise, do you change your methods according to the personality of the actors? For example, let's take three actresses who have worked with you and who are quite different from each other: Lucia Bosè, Jeanne Moreau, and Monica Vitti.

ANTONIONI: I think it would be appropriate at this time to read you a statement I made at a press conference given for the opening of L'avventura at Cannes. It pretty well reflects my thoughts regarding the motives and the considerations that moved me to make L'avventura and, in a general way, sort of answers the young lady's question, which I will reply to more directly later on.

"Today the world is endangered by an extremely serious split between a science that is totally and consciously projected into the future, and a rigid and stereotyped morality which all of us recognize as such and yet sustain out of cowardice or sheer laziness. Where is this split most evident? What are its most obvious, its most sensitive, let us even say its most painful, areas? Consider the Renaissance man, his sense of joy, his fullness, his multifarious activities. They were men of great magnitude, technically able and at the same time artistically creative, capable of feeling their own sense of dignity, their own sense of importance as human beings, the Ptolemaic fullness of man. Then man discovered that his world was Copernican, an extremely limited world in an unknown universe. And today a new man is being born, fraught with all the fears and terrors and stammerings that are associated with a period of gestation. And what is even more serious, this new man immediately finds himself burdened with a heavy baggage of emotional traits which cannot exactly be called old and outmoded but rather unsuited and inadequate. They condition us without offering us any help, they create problems without suggesting any possible solutions. And yet it seems that man will not rid himself of this baggage. He reacts, he loves, he hates, he suffers under the sway of moral forces and myths which today, when we are on the threshold of reaching the moon, should not be the same as those that prevailed at the time of Homer, but nevertheless are.

"Man is quick to rid himself of his technological and scientific mistakes and misconceptions. Indeed, science has never been more humble and less dogmatic than it is today. Whereas our moral attitudes are governed by an absolute sense of stultification. In recent years, we have examined these moral attitudes very carefully, we have dissected them and analyzed them to the point of exhaustion. We have been capable of all this but we have not been capable of finding new ones, we have not been capable of making any head-way whatsoever towards a solution of this problem, of this ever-increasing split between moral man and scientific man, a split which is becoming more and more serious and more and more accentuated. Naturally, I don't care to nor can I resolve it myself; I am not a moralist and my film is neither a denunciation nor a sermon. It is a story told in images whereby, I hope, it may be possible to perceive not the birth of a mistaken attitude but the manner in which attitudes and feelings are misunderstood today. Because, I repeat, the present moral standards we live by, these myths, these conventions are old and obsolete. And we all know they are, yet we honor them. Why? The conclusion reached by the protagonists in my film is not one of sentimentality. If anything, what they finally arrive at is a sense of pity for each other. You might say that this too is nothing new. But what else is left if we do not at least succeed in achieving this? Why do you think eroticism is so prevalent today in our literature, our theatrical shows, and elsewhere? It is a symptom of the emotional sickness of our time. But this preoccupation with the erotic would not become obsessive if Eros were healthy, that is, if it were kept within human proportions. But Eros is sick; man is uneasy, something is bothering him. And whenever something bothers him, man reacts, but he reacts badly, only on erotic impulse, and he is unhappy. The tragedy in *L'avventura* stems directly from an erotic impulse of this type—unhappy, miserable, futile. To be critically aware of the vulgarity and the futility of such an overwhelming erotic impulse, as is the case with the protagonist in *L'avventura*, is not enough or serves no purpose. And here we witness the crumbling of a myth, which proclaims it is enough for us to know, to be critically conscious of ourselves, to analyze ourselves in all our complexities and in every facet of our personality. The fact of the matter is that such an examination is not enough. It is only a preliminary step. Every day, every emotional encounter gives rise to a new adventure. For even though we know that the ancient codes of morality are decrepit and no longer tenable, we persist, with a sense of perversity that I would only ironically define as pathetic, in remaining loyal to them. Thus moral man who has no fear of the scientific unknown is today afraid of the moral unknown. Starting out from this point of fear and frustration, his adventure can only end in a stalemate."

That was the statement I read in France. I believe one can deduce from its premise the significance of the film's ending, which, depending on how you look at it, might be considered either optimistic or pessimistic. Georges Sadoul has made a little discovery which I later found to be in agreement with what I had intended when I shot the final scene. I don't know if you still remember it. On one side of the frame is Mount Etna in all its snowy whiteness, and on the other is a concrete wall. The wall corresponds to the man and Mount Etna corresponds somewhat to the situation of the woman. Thus the frame is divided exactly in half; one half containing the concrete wall which represents the pessimistic side, while the other half showing Mount Etna represents the optimistic. But I really don't know if the relationship between these two halves will endure or not, though it is quite evident the two protagonists will remain together and not separate. The girl will definitely not leave the man; she will stay with him and forgive him. For she realizes that she too, in a certain sense, is somewhat like him. Because—if for no other reason— from the moment she suspects Anna may have returned, she becomes so apprehensive, so afraid she may be back and still alive, that she begins to lose the feeling of friendship that she once had for Anna, just as he had lost his affection for Anna and perhaps is also beginning to lose it for her. But what else can she do but stay with him? As I was saying before, what would be left if there weren't this mutual sense of pity, which is also a source of strength? In *La notte* the protagonists go somewhat further. In *L'avventura* they communicate only through this mutual sense of pity; they do not speak to one another. In *La notte*, however, they do converse with each other, they communicate freely, they are fully aware of what is happening to their relationship. But the result is the same, it doesn't differ. The man becomes hypocritical, he refuses to go on with the conversation because he knows quite well that if he openly expresses his feelings at that moment, everything would be finished. But even this attitude indicates a desire on his part to maintain the relationship, so then the more optimistic side of the situation is brought out.

CASTELLO: *I find it a bit ridiculous, this wanting to establish whether an ending is optimistic or pessimistic. However, I have noticed there is a certain divergence of opinion. I find the ending of* L'avventura *far more optimistic than that of* La notte. *And yet there are some who find* La notte *more optimistic.*

ANTONIONI: Once, in a situation similar to this, Pirandello was asked some questions about his characters, his scenes, his comedies. And he replied: "How should I know? I'm the author." Now for the young lady's second question about acting. With actors, I use certain ideas and methods which are strictly personal, and I don't know if they are right or wrong. Looking back at what has been my experience with actors, I can say that I directed them in a certain way only because I didn't care to work in any other way since my way seemed to give me the best results. And then, I am not like those directors, such as De Sica and Visconti, who can "show" the actor exactly how the scene is to be enacted. This is something I wouldn't know how to do inasmuch as I myself do not know how to act. I believe, however, that I know what I want from my actors. As I see it, an actor need not necessarily understand everything he is doing. In this respect, I always have a great deal of trouble when I first begin working with my actors, especially with some foreign actors. There is a general belief that actors must understand everything they do when enacting a scene. If this were so, then the best actor would be the one who is the most intellectual, which is simply not the case; the facts show us that often the reverse is true. The more an actor forces himself to comprehend the meaning of a scene, the more he tries to achieve a deeper understanding of a given line, a sequence, or the film itself, the more obstacles he sets up between the really natural spontaneity of that scene and its ultimate realization. Aside from the fact that by doing such, he tends to become, in a certain sense, his own director; and this is more harmful than beneficial. Now, I find it's not necessary for a director to have his actors rack their brains; it's better, in every respect, for them to use their instinct. As a director, I shouldn't have to consult with them regarding my conception of the way I feel a scene should be done. Otherwise, by revealing to them what is after all my own personal plan of action, they automatically become a kind of Trojan horse in what is supposed to be my citadel, which is mine by virtue of the fact that I am the one who knows what I want from them and I am the one who knows whether their response to what I ask for is good or bad. Inasmuch as I consider an actor as being only one element in a given scene, I regard him as I regard a tree, a wall, or a cloud, that is, as just one element in the overall scene; the attitude or pose of the actor, as determined under my direction, cannot but help to affect the framing of that scene, and I, not the actor, am the one who can know whether that effect is appropriate or not. Furthermore, as I said previously, a line spoken by an actor where the camera is facing him from above has one meaning, while it has another meaning if the camera is facing him from below, etc., etc. Only the director can judge these things, not the actor. And the same applies to intonation, which is primarily a sound and only secondarily a line in a piece of dialogue. It is a sound that should be made to integrate with the other sounds accompanying a given image, and at that moment, when the actor speaks his line, all the sounds, including his delivery of that line, that combine to make up the total sound pattern appropriate to that image or sequence, are not there yet. The actor pays no attention to all these details, but the director does. And that's not all. Even improvisation is a factor in connection with this particular subject. For instance, when an actor makes a mistake in delivering a line, I let him make that mistake. That is, I let him go ahead with his mistake because I want to see how it sounds, how it works, before he goes ahead and corrects that mistake. I want to see whether I can somehow utilize that mistake. Because at that moment his mistakes are the most spontaneous things he can give me, and it is that spontaneity of his which I have need of, even though he gives it to me against his will. When going through a scene before shooting it, I often try out certain pieces of dialogue or certain actions which may not have anything to do with the actual scene itself, and I am forcefully embarrassed when the actors ask me for explanations. Because beyond a certain point, I don't want to tell them anything. When I was doing *Il grido*, that excellent actress Betsy Blair wanted to go over the script with me, and she would ask me for an explanation of every line. Those two hours I spent with her going over that script were the most hellish hours of my life, since I was forced to invent meanings that weren't there at all. However, they were the meanings she had wanted me to give her, so she was satisfied. And this should also be taken under consideration.

There is another reason why I feel it really isn't necessary to explain every scene to your actors, for if you did so that would mean you'd have to give the same explanation to each actor. And this would not do, at least not for me. In order to get the best results, I know that I have to say one thing to one actor and something else to another actor. Because I am supposed to understand his temperament, I am supposed to know how he reacts, that when affected a certain way, he reacts a certain way, and when affected another way, he reacts differently. So it's not possible to use the same approach with every actor. To the director, the scene itself remains always the same, but when I approach the actors, in order for me to obtain the desired results, my explanations to them have to vary in accordance with the nature and temperament of each actor.

STEFANO SATTA *(student of the Centro's acting classes):   Although* L'avventura *and* La notte *both end with a new awareness on the part of the protagonists (you mentioned a mutual feeling of pity) while* Il grido *ends with a suicide, it seems to me that* L'avventura *and* La notte *are more imbued with agony and despair than* Il grido. *Is this merely coincidental or is it actually because of the different social climate involved?*
ANTONIONI: This is a question the critics can answer more efficiently than I can. You are not really asking me a question, you are making an observation. In other words, what you're telling me is that *L'avventura* and *La notte* succeeded in achieving their aims while *Il grido* did not. When the critics said—with regards to *Il grido*—that I was cold, cynical,

and completely inhuman, they evidently weren't aware of what I was trying to say. Perhaps I was not precisely aware of it myself at the time, and it only became clear to me after having done the other two films. Perhaps *L'avventura* and *La notte* help somewhat to explain *Il grido*, which, if shown in Italy today, might receive a greater success than when it first came out. I would say that *Il grido* is a more pessimistic film, more full of despair, which may be due to the fact that I myself, at that particular moment in my life, was in a certain state of depression. So if the film didn't reflect this, I'd really be surprised.

SATTA: *I would like to express myself more precisely. In* Il grido *I found a greater feeling of human warmth than I did in* L'avventura *and* La notte.

FIORAVANTI: *I think he means that* Il grido *ends in a more dramatic and tragic manner, that is, with a suicide; but, in certain aspects, he finds this film is actually more optimistic than either* L'avventura *or* La notte, *which seem colder to him in spite of the fact that they contain certain glimmers of hope.*

ANTONIONI: But insofar as this human warmth is no longer of any value to the protagonist, insofar as it doesn't help to prevent him from destroying himself, the ending of this film is more pessimistic than the others. I don't know. In spite of everything, this quality of human warmth as expressed by the main character in *Il grido* doesn't serve him at all as any link to the rest of humanity. He is a person who is no longer attached to life.

SATTA: *I would like to ask you another question. Regarding the final scene in* La notte, *I feel that you have departed from your usual style; in the sense that whereas you have been accused at times of making your characters say so very little to each other, in the final scene of* La notte *almost the opposite is true. With that final conversation between the husband and wife it almost seems that you want to give an explanation for the benefit and comfort of the spectators.*

ANTONIONI: I don't know if it gives that impression or not. Actually, that conversation, which is really a soliloquy, a monologue by the wife, is a kind of summing-up of the film to clarify the real meaning of what took place. The woman is still willing to discuss, to analyze, to examine the reasons for the failure of their marriage. But she is prevented from doing so by her husband's refusal to admit its failure, his denial, his inability to remember or unwillingness to remember, his refusal to reason things out, his incapacity to find any basis for a new start through a lucid analysis of the situation as it is. Instead, he tries to take refuge in an irrational and desperate attempt to make physical contact. It is because of this stalemate that we do not know what possible solution they could come to.

CHRISTA WINDISCH-GRATZ *(student of the Centro's acting classes): Between* L'avventura, La notte *and* Il grido, *I particularly liked* Il grido. *I liked the ending of* Il grido *because it clarifies something, it arrives at a definite conclusion, one that is perhaps too cruel, that needn't be so, but nevertheless that's the way it is. Whereas* L'avventura *and* La notte *leave me cold because they don't come to any definite conclusion.*

ANTONIONI: Lucretius, who was certainly one of the greatest poets who ever lived, once said, "Nothing appears as it should in a world where nothing is certain. The only thing certain is the existence of a secret violence that makes everything uncertain." Think about this for a moment. What Lucretius said of his time is still a disturbing reality, for it seems to me this uncertainty is very much part of our own time. But this is unquestionably a philosophical matter. Now you really don't expect me to resolve such problems or to propose any solutions? Inasmuch as I am the product of a middle-class society, and am preoccupied with making middle-class dramas, I am not equipped to do so. The middle class doesn't give me the means with which to resolve any middle-class problems. That's why I confine myself to pointing out existing problems without proposing any solutions. I think it is equally important to point them out as it is to propose solutions.

BANG-HANSEN *(student of the Centro's directing class):   I would like to know to what extent you believe lucidity could be a form of salvation or a way out.*

ANTONIONI: Now, look, lucidity is not a solution. In fact, I would say it puts you at a greater disadvantage, because where you have lucidity there is no longer any reason for the existence of a scale of values, and therefore one finds one's self even more at a loss. Certainly, I am for lucidity in all things, because this is my position as a secular man. But in a certain sense I still envy those who can draw upon their faith and somehow manage to resolve all their problems. But this is not so with everyone. You ask me questions of such magnitude that I feel I'm much too small to answer them.

PAOLO TODISCO *(student of the Centro's acting classes): To go back to your experiences with actors, you said that you try to create a characterization, giving the actor a minimum amount of directions, and then wait to see how he himself develops a certain theme.*
ANTONIONI: No, that's not quite right. I never let the actor do anything on his own. I give him precise instructions as to what he is supposed to do.

TODISCO: *Okay, then here is my question: In your films, you have worked with the following three actors: Lucia Bosè, Steve Cochran, and Monica Vitti. Three kinds of experiences, three different types of actors: Lucia Bosè, who had done very little before she started working with you; Steve Cochran, whose experience is that of a school much different than ours; and Monica Vitti, who comes to films from the stage. Which of the three gave you the most difficulty?*
ANTONIONI: Steve Cochran. Because he is the least intelligent of the three.

CASTELLO: *Just a moment. Only a short while ago you said you didn't want intelligent actors; you wanted it this way yourself, so why do you regret it now?*
ANTONIONI: Let me explain. He was less intelligent in the sense that when I specifically asked him to do something, he simply refused to do it. If I gave him certain directions and told him to follow those directions to the letter, he would abruptly tell me, "No." "Why not?" I would ask him. And he would reply, "Because I'm not a puppet." Now that was too much to tolerate . . . After all, there's a limit to everything. As a result, I had to direct him by using tricks, without ever telling him what it was I wanted.

GUIDO CINCOTTI *(Centro's film archivist): But it was resolved one way or the other. Either Cochran finally resigned himself to following your directions or else this underhand method you used went well. Because the end results were excellent.*

ANTONIONI: No, because he just went ahead and did everything he wanted—only he never became aware of the tricks I had to use in order to get what I wanted from him. With regards to Lucia Bosè, I had to direct her almost with a sense of violence. Before every scene, I had to put her in a state of mind appropriate to that particular scene. If it was a sad scene, I had to make her cry; if it was a happy scene, I had to make her laugh. As for Monica Vitti, I can say she's an extremely serious actress. She comes from the Academy, and therefore possesses an extraordinary sense of craft. Even so, there were many times when we were not in agreement on certain solutions, and I was forced to beg her not to interfere in my domain.

TODISCO: *It is said that a stage actor generally creates some difficulties for the director of a film. Now have you had such difficulties with, for example, Monica Vitti, who was originally a stage actress?*
ANTONIONI: No, I wouldn't say so. Because Monica Vitti is a very modern actress, so even in her theatrical career she never had those attitudes which can be defined as "theatrical." Therefore, I didn't have any great difficulty with her. And then Monica Vitti is extraordinarily expressive. This is a great quality for a film actor. Perhaps on stage this expressiveness was of less value to her; that is, if an actor does have such a quality, it is all the better, but if he does not, it doesn't really matter much; what is more important for the stage is the actor's attitude. At a distance of 100 feet, the actor's facial expression is lost, but in a film what counts the most is the actor's expressions. And Monica Vitti has an extremely expressive face.

MARIO VERDONE *(film critic and member of Centro's faculty):   Actually, what is your opinion about the contribution music can make to a film? I say actually because it has seemed to me this contribution has diminished in your last two films.*
ANTONIONI: I think music has had and can continue to have a great function in films, because there is no art form which the film medium cannot draw upon. In the case of music, it draws directly, and there-fore the relationship is even closer. It seems to me, however, that this relationship is beginning to change. In fact, the way music is being used today is quite different from the way it was used ten years ago.

At that time music was used to create a certain atmosphere in order to help get the image across to the spectator. Earlier, of course, in the period of the silent film, there was the old pianola which was originally used to hide the noise of the projecting machine and then, later, as a means to emphasize the images that passed over the screen in absolute silence. Since then, the use of music in films has changed a great deal, but in certain films today it is still being used that way, that is, as a kind of external commentary. Its function is to establish a rapport between the music and the spectator, not between the music and the film, which is its proper function. Even to this day, especially in certain films from Hollywood, a battle scene is accompanied with violent symphonic crescendoes from a full orchestra; a sad scene is always accompanied with violin music because it is felt that violins create an atmosphere of sadness. But this seems to me to be a completely wrong way to use music, and has nothing whatever to do with cinematography.

There are, of course, certain films where music is used in a more meaningful way, as a means to complement the images, to heighten and intensify the meaning of the image. And this has been done with certain scenes in *L'avventura* and in Resnais's *Hiroshima, mon amour*. And I must say that the music really worked well in these cases, that is, it expressed what the images themselves intended to express, it was used as an integral part of the image. Having said this, however, I must also say that I am personally very reluctant to use music in my films, for the simple reason that I prefer to work in a dry manner, to say things with the least means possible. And music is an additional means. I have too much faith in the efficacy, the value, the force, the suggestiveness of the image to believe that the image cannot do without music. It is true, however, that I have a need to draw upon sound, which serves an essential "musical" function. I would therefore say that true film "music" has not yet been invented. Perhaps it might be in the future. Until that time comes, however, I feel that music should be spliced out of the film and spliced into a disc, where it has an autonomy of its own.

PETRUCCI: *In connection with this, I want to bring up the entire sequence in* La notte *that takes place in the streets of Milan. It is clear that when those street sounds, those automobile horns, etc., are isolated from their corresponding images, they have no meaning in themselves. At the same time, however,*

when heard in relation to those images, their function is exclusively a
musical one.

ANTONIONI: Of course. But there must be a mutual rapport. That is,
the images cannot stand alone, without those sounds—just as those
sounds would have no meaning at all if they were detached from the
images.

VERDONE: *I seem to find a certain predilection in your films for contemporary
art. Not so much with regards to the paintings of Morandi which are seen in*
La notte *or of the abstract paintings seen in* Le amiche, *but more so in your
framing of the image itself, in your manner of seeing things, for example, a
white wall or a gravel path or some wooden boards nailed to a window. That
is, you seem to have a predilection for a kind of painting which might be called
non-painting, like that of Burri, or a sculpture by Consagra, or similar artists—
I could cite Vedova, Fontana, etc., etc. I would like to know if this is accidental (and I'm sure it's not since it seems to me nothing is accidental in your
films) or is there a definite rapport between contemporary art and your latest
films?*

ANTONIONI: I have a great love for painting. For me, it is the one art,
along with architecture, that comes immediately after film-making. I'm
very fond of reading books on art and architecture, of leafing through
pages and pages of art volumes, and I like to go to art shows and keep
in touch with the latest work being done in art—not just to be *au courant*
but because painting is something that moves me passionately. Therefore
I believe all these perceptions and this interest have been somewhat
assimilated. And, naturally, having followed modern art, my taste and
my predilection for a certain style would be reflected in my work. But
in framing a shot, I certainly don't have any particular painter or painting
in mind; that's something I avoid.

PETRUCCI: *I'd like to ask you a question about something you mentioned
before, concerning your earlier work and its particular tendency, from a technical point of view, towards using long shots, long tracks, long pans, etc. We
have not seen any widespread indication of this in your latest films. Can we
therefore assume that a change has taken place in your method of expression,
that you are now using your technical means of expression in a different way?*

ANTONIONI: When I began *Cronaca di un amore*, as I said a short while ago, I did not consciously intend to make a film in that particular way, that is, it was not a preconceived style that was evolved while sitting behind the desk. But when I started climbing on the dolly to follow the actors around in the first scene, I saw that it wasn't essential to cut right at the specified end of that scene, so I continued shooting on for a while longer. As I already said before, I felt an urge to keep the camera on the actors even after the prescribed action was completed. Evidently, I did this because I felt the best way to capture their thoughts, their states of mind, was to follow them around physically with the camera. Thus the long shots, the continuous panning, etc. Later, however, as I went along (and here I should say that even in making this film I worked quite instinctively) I became aware that perhaps this was not the best method after all, that perhaps I was concentrating too much on the external aspects of the actors' states of mind and not enough on the states of mind themselves. Perhaps it would be better, I thought, to construct the scene and try different camera movements and montage so that by setting up the camera at one level, then using a certain pan in a preceding or following shot, I could obtain the results I wanted. In short, I realized that just one specific technical approach was not enough to obtain the particular type of shot I would need to go beyond the literal aspects of the story, but that it was necessary to work more closely with the material itself, achieving my particular goals in the scene by various methods.

FRANCO BRONZI *(student of scenography):   When speaking with some of the student directors here at the Centro, there are certain times when we students of scenography meet up with some rather strange notions. We find that student directors or young directors have the feeling that scenography is not very important. It seems that as far as they are concerned, to shoot a scene against a natural wall of a building is more or less the same thing as shooting a scene against a wall constructed in a studio. According to your way of thinking, is scenography an important contributing factor in the successful realization of a film?*
ANTONIONI: I wouldn't say it isn't. It could be. It depends on the type of film you make. For example, in the next few months I'll be doing a film where I don't think I'll have any need of a studio, but immediately after that, at least if I don't change my mind and start something else,

I'll be doing another film entirely inside a studio. For it will be done in color and I want to inject my own color scheme, that is, I want to paint the film as one paints a canvas; I want to invent the color relationships, I don't want to limit myself by only photographing natural colors. In this case, scenography becomes an extremely important element. There is also something to be said for scenography when one shoots a film outdoors and wants to obtain a specific kind of background—then scenography is as important as it is in a studio. Today there are several film-makers who are working in somewhat the same way I have and will be working. Resnais, for example, is one of these, as well as several young film-makers like Godard and others. They actually intervene and change the natural setting of the environment, and even go so far as to paint walls and add trees. It's not a matter of merely selecting a place and accepting it exactly as it is. A natural setting provides you with enough of an idea of the background required for the realization of a scene, but even outdoors one should intervene and make what changes are necessary. So therefore scenography is important.

GIAN LUIGI CRESCENZI *(student of the Centro's acting school):   In the film* Le amiche, *we have the portrayal of a painter who is going through a certain crisis. In* L'avventura *we have the portrayal of an architect who neither plans nor designs but merely calculates figures and draws up estimates for construction materials. In* La notte, Mastroianni *is a writer in crisis. I would like to know if these three characterizations, which are analogous to one another, not only in terms of their professional crises but also with regard to their personal affairs, were conceived by you for the purpose of examining a certain type of individual in order to draw some conclusions about his particular situation, or was this similarity in your choice of character type simply coincidental?*
ANTONIONI: It seems rather odd that you would think it could be a coincidence. Obviously, when I select the profession of a character for one of my films, I know very well what I'm doing. I choose intellectual types mainly because they have a greater awareness of what is happening to them, and also because they have a more refined sensibility, a more subtle sense of intuition through which I can filter the kind of reality I am interested in expressing, whether it be an internal reality or an external one. Furthermore, the intellectual, more than others, is the type of person in which I can find the symptoms of that particular kind

of crisis which I am interested in describing. If I take an insensitive type, a rough and rugged type, he wouldn't have any of the particular problems I'm concerned with and the story would end right there. So I don't quite know what you mean. Do you want to know if I'm searching for a single character type that would be representative of everyman? I don't understand.

CASTELLO: *Perhaps he means to ask if there exists a certain development from one character to another; whether your ultimate objective is to create a general character who would be representative of the intellectual in crisis, or if each character is independent of the other.*

ANTONIONI: No, I don't believe the individual characters in the various films are meant to be representative of a certain type of man. Naturally, I shall make a film that will bring an end to this cycle of films which are dedicated, so to speak, to the emotions. As a matter of fact, at a certain point in the film I'm now working on—although it too is mainly concerned with the relationships of human sentiments—due to the very nature of the story itself, this particular theme is given less prominence than it had in the other films and paves the way for the introduction of other themes.

An Interview with Michelangelo Antonioni

PIERRE BILLARD/1967

PB: *What does the writing of the scenario mean for you: clarifying the dramatic line, making the visual aspect of the film more specific, familiarizing yourself with the characters?*

MA: To me, the visual aspect of a film is very closely related to its thematic aspect—in the sense that an idea almost always comes to me through images. The problem lies elsewhere. It has to do with restricting the accumulation of these images, with digging into them, with recognizing the ones that coincide with what interests me at the time.

It's work done instinctively, almost automatically, but it involves a great deal of tension. One's whole being is at stake: it is a precise moral choice.

What people ordinarily call the "dramatic line" doesn't interest me. One device is no better than another, *a priori*. And I don't believe that the old laws of drama have validity any more. Today stories are what they are, with neither a beginning nor an end necessarily, without key scenes, without a dramatic arc, without catharsis. They can be made up of tatters, of fragments, as unbalanced as the lives we lead.

Familiarize myself with characters? But the characters are not strangers that I may or may not be on intimate terms with; they emerge out of me, they are my intimate inner life.

From *L'Avventura: A Film by Michelangelo Antonioni* (New York: Grove Press, 1969). Reprinted by permission of Grove/Atlantic.

PB: *What does the fact that you work in collaboration with others on your scenario mean to you?*

MA: Every time I have tried to let others write parts of a rough script, the result, even if it was excellent from an objective point of view, was something foreign to me, something close to what I wanted without ever coinciding with it exactly. And that gave me a terrible sense of impotence. Then began the great task of selecting, correcting, even adapting—work that was as difficult as it was useless, because it inevitably led to compromise. I can never manage to be objective when I judge the work of my collaborators. The film stands between me and them. So, after trying this a few times, I ended up writing almost all the shooting scripts of my films myself.

However, I haven't ruled out collaborations altogether. I don't choose my collaborators on the basis of our affinities, but for the opposite reason. I need to have people who are very different from me around me, people with whom there can be animated, lively discussions. We talk, we discuss things for months before the film. We talk about a lot of things. Sometimes we also talk about the film, but not necessarily. What I say ricochets off them, comes back to me in the form of criticism, commentary, suggestions. After a certain time, the film becomes clear. It is only then that I begin to write the rough script. I work many hours a day, often beginning at dawn, until I'm completely exhausted.

PB: *What form does your script take in its final phase?*

MA: The shooting script is never definitive for me. It's notes about the direction, nothing more. There are no technical notations such as used to be made. The placing of the camera, the use of various lenses, the movements of the camera, all concern the phase in which the film is shot, not that in which the script is written.

I would say the same thing about dialogue. I have to hear the dialogue in the living voices of the actors, that is to say of the characters, within the scene, to decide whether or not it's right. My published scenarios, with dialogue? I rewrite them afterward, when I've already made the film and I know what I wanted to do.

And then there's another factor. I believe in improvisation. None of us has the habit of preparing for a meeting to further business, love, or friendship; one takes these meetings as they come, adapting oneself little by little as they progress, taking advantage of unexpected things that come up. I experience the same things when I'm filming.

The script is a starting point, then, not a fixed highway. I must look through the camera to see if whatever I've written on the page is right or not. In the script you describe imagined scenes, but it's all suspended in mid-air. Often, an actor viewed against a wall or a landscape, or seen through a window, is much more eloquent than the line you've given him. So then you take out the lines. This happens often to me and I end up saying what I want with a movement or a gesture.

PB: *At what point does this take place?*
MA: When I have the actor there, beginning to move, I notice what is useful and what is superfluous and eliminate the superfluous—but only then, at that moment. That's why they call it improvisation, but it's not; it's just making the film. Everything you do before consists of notes: the script is simply a series of notes for the film.

PB: *Can the choice of locations or actors influence the scenario, and if so, how?*
MA: In general, I decide upon the outdoor locations before writing the shooting script. In order to be able to write, I need to have the surroundings of the film clearly in mind. There are times too when an idea for a film comes to me from a particular place. Or more precisely, when certain locales come to mind because of the themes or characters running through my head. It's sometimes a rather odd series of coincidences.

PB: *What possibilities for improvisation do you allow for while you're filming?*
MA: Speaking of improvisation, I must add something to what I said before. If I think of the past, it's possible for me to say that I have always lived minute by minute. It's the way I live even today. Every moment of the day is important to me, every day is a new experience. And this doesn't change when I'm shooting. On the contrary, the pull of reality increases during shooting, because you're in an extremely receptive state, and because you're making new contacts, you're establishing often unexpected relationships with the crew, and these relationships are

constantly changing. All that has a definite influence on my work, and leads me to improvised decisions, and even to radical changes. This is what I mean by improvisation.

PB: *How are your relations with the crew?*
MA: Excellent. I try to create a cordial atmosphere. I like to have people laughing and joking around me. People who seem to have no problems. It's quite enough that I have problems.

I admit, however, that I am very demanding. I don't allow anybody around me to show that he doesn't know his business. Or that he's unwilling to work. There is a certain laziness about crews, it's natural, inevitable. But it's what I dislike most. When I happen to scream at someone (as all directors do, it seems), I'm railing against this sort of indifference.

PB: *What are your relations with the actors?*
MA: I've always had excellent relations with actors—sometimes too good. Hearing me say that may seem odd, but it's true. Even with Jeanne Moreau, who claims the opposite, I have never—I repeat never—had arguments during filming.

I know, however, that actors feel somewhat uncomfortable with me; they have the feeling that they've been excluded from my work. And as a matter of fact they have been. But it is precisely this form of collaboration, and no other, that I ask of them.

Only one person has the film clearly in mind, insofar as that is possible: the director. Only one person fuses in his mind the various elements involved in a film, only one person is in a position to predict the result of this fusion: the director. The actor is one of these elements, and sometimes not even the most important. There is one thing the actor can't do, and that is to see himself in the view-finder; if he could, he'd come up with a number of suggestions regarding his acting. This privilege is reserved for the director, however, who will thus limit himself to manipulating "the actor element" according to criteria and exigencies known to him alone.

There are various ways of getting certain expressions from actors, and it is of no interest to know whether or not there is a corresponding mood behind these expressions.

I have often resorted to foreign actors for practical reasons: agreements with distributors, unavailability of Italian actors, and so forth. But sometimes it was because I thought such actors were better suited to the roles than those at my disposal here.

PB: *If you go on changing scenes right through the last stroke of the clapstick, it must be rough on the actors, too. Do you think that's why some of them say it's difficult to work for you?*
MA: Who says so other than Moreau? I really don't believe that's true. I simply know what the actor's attitude should be and what he should say. He doesn't, because he can't see the relationship that begins to exist between his body and the other things in the scene.

PB: *But shouldn't he understand what you have in mind?*
MA: He simply must *be*. If he tries to understand too much, he will act in an intellectual and unnatural manner.

PB: *Do you prefer, then, not to talk to the actor about his role?*
MA: No, it's obvious that I must explain what I want from him, but I don't want to discuss everything I ask him to do, because often my requests are completely instinctive and there are things I can't explain. It's like painting: You don't know why you use pink instead of blue. You simply feel that's how it should be—pink. Then the phone rings and you answer it. When you come back, you don't want pink anymore and you use blue—without knowing why. You can't help it; that's just the way it is.

PB: *So you want your actors to do what you tell them without asking questions and without trying to understand why?*
MA: Yes. I want an actor to try to give me what I ask in the best and most exact way possible. He mustn't try to find out more, because then there's the danger that he'll become his own director. It's only human and natural that he should see the film in terms of his own part, but I have to see the film as a whole. He must therefore collaborate selflessly, totally. I've worked marvelously with Monica [Vitti] and Vanessa [Redgrave] because they always tried to follow me. It's never important for me if they don't understand, but it is important that I should have recognized what I wanted in what they gave me—or in what they proposed.

PB: *Is it true that you sometimes deliberately misdirect actors, giving them a false motivation to produce the reaction you really want from them?*
MA: Of course, I tell them something different, to arrive at certain results. Or I run the camera without telling them. And sometimes their mistakes give me ideas I can use, because mistakes are always sincere, absolutely sincere.

PB: *Have you ever worked with Method actors?*
MA: They're absolutely terrible. They want to direct themselves, and it's a disaster. Their idea is to reach a certain emotional charge; actors are always a little high at work. Acting is their drug. So when you put the brakes on, they're naturally a little disappointed. And I've always played down the drama in my films. In my main scenes, there's never an opportunity for an actor to let go of everything he's got inside. I always try to tone down the acting, because my stories demand it, to the point where I might change a script so that an actor has no opportunity to come out well. I say this for Monica, too. I'm sure that she has never given all she could in my films, because the scenes just weren't there. Take a film like *Who's Afraid of Virginia Woolf?* It offers an actress every possibility. If she's really good and has qualities like Liz Taylor, it comes out. But Liz Taylor never displayed these qualities in other films, because she never had a part like that.

PB: *Do you prefer to record the sound on the set or to dub it afterwards?*
MA: When I can, I prefer recording on the set. The sounds, the noises, and the natural voices as picked up by microphones have a power of suggestion that can't be obtained with dubbing. Moreover, most professional microphones are much more sensitive than the human ear, and a great many unexpected noises and sounds often enrich a soundtrack that's been made on the set.

Unfortunately, we are still not advanced enough technically to be able to use this system all the time. Shooting indoors it's hard to get good sound. And dubbing also has its advantages. Sometimes I find that the transformation of a noise or of a sound becomes indispensable for certain special effects. Thus in certain cases it is necessary to change the human voice.

PB: *Who decides on the exact framing and the camera movements?*

MA: I can't imagine a director who would leave that up to other people. Excluding or including detail, even an apparently secondary one, in the film image, choosing the angle of the shot, the lenses, the camera movements, are all decisions essential to the success of a film.

Technique is not something that can be applied from outside by just anybody. Practically speaking, technical problems don't exist. If style is there, it permeates technique. If style is missing, the problem disappears altogether.

PB: *Do you shoot any sequences from several angles so as to have greater freedom when you edit?*

MA: Until *Red Desert*, I always filmed with a single camera, and thus from a single angle. But from *Red Desert* on, I began using several cameras with different lenses, but always from the same angle. I did so because the story demanded shots of a reality that had become abstract, of a subject that had become color, and those shots had to be obtained with a long-focus lens.

Obviously I have the editing of the film clearly in mind during shooting. And it is only when I am led by circumstances to improvise, and consequently to shoot quickly, that I try to accumulate protection takes.

PB: *How much do you have to do with the cutting of your films?*

MA: I have always had an editor at my side on all my films. Except for *Story of a Love Affair*, this editor has been Eraldo da Roma. He is an extremely able technician with vast experience, and a man who loves his work. We cut the films together. I tell him what I want as clearly and precisely as possible, and he does the cutting. He knows me, he understands immediately; we have the same sense of proportion, the same sensibility concerning the duration of a shot.

PB: *What is the role of music and the soundtrack in your films?*

MA: I have always opposed the traditional musical commentary, the soporific function ordinarily assigned to it. It's this idea of "setting images to music," as if it were a question of an opera libretto, that I don't like. What I reject is this refusal to let silence have its place, this need to fill supposed voids.

The only way to accept music in films is for it to disappear as an autonomous expression in order to assume its role as one element in a general sensorial impression. And with color films today this is even more necessary.

PB: *Do you concern yourself with the public and its possible reactions at any stage of making your films?*
MA: I never think of the public. I think of the film. Obviously, you're always speaking to someone, but this partner in the conversation is always an ideal one (perhaps another self). If this weren't true, I wouldn't know what to base my work on, since there are at least as many publics as there are continents or human races—not to mention nations.

PB: *What phase of making a film presents the most difficulty, requires the most effort?*
MA: Each film has its own history. One will demand inhuman efforts during shooting, another intellectual tension at the scripting stage, another an iron will during the cutting or the dubbing, when you'd swear that the material you have on hand is completely different from what you wanted.
   And then we each have our private lives which are not broken off during filming; on the contrary, they acquire new point and bite, giving our work a function that is sometimes stimulating, sometimes debilitating, sometimes calming, and so forth.

PB: *Your last film,* Blow-Up, *was shot in London. Were you trying to avoid censorship troubles in Italy because of its erotic scenes?*
MA: The eroticism has nothing to do with *Blow-Up*. There are some scenes where you see nudes, but these are not what's important in the film. Italian censors have passed it with very little cutting.

PB: *Was it intentional, in the scene where the photographer has an orgy with the two girls in his studio, that pubic hair appear visible?*
MA: I didn't notice. If you can tell me where, I'll go and look.

PB: *Do you feel that moviemakers should be free to depict total nudity on the screen?*
MA: I don't think it's necessary. The most important scenes between a man and a woman don't happen when they are naked.

PB: *Is there anything you think shouldn't be shown on the screen?*
MA: There can be no censorship better than one's own conscience.

PB: *What made you choose London as the setting for* Blow-Up*?*
MA: I happened to be there by chance, to see Monica Vitti while she was working in [Losey's] *Modesty Blaise*. I liked the happy, irreverent atmosphere of the city. People seemed less bound by prejudice.

PB: *In what sense?*
MA: They seemed much freer. I felt at home. In some way, I was impressed. Perhaps something changed inside me.

PB: *How?*
MA: I'm no go good at understanding myself. But those things I knew before that interested me now seem too limited. I feel I need other experiences, to see other people, learn new things.

PB: *Was it difficult working in a foreign country?*
MA: *Blow-Up* had a rather special story, about a photographer, and I followed the work of some of the more important ones, which made it easier. Also, he moved through a limited environment in London—a minority but elite group of swingers.

PB: *Apart from its setting, how does* Blow-Up *differ from your previous films?*
MA: Radically. In my other films, I have tried to probe the relationship between one person and another—most often, their love relationship, the fragility of their feelings, and so on. But in this film, none of these themes matters. Here, the relationship is between an individual and reality—those things that are around him. There are no love stories in this film, even though we see relations between men and women. The experience of the protagonist is not a sentimental or an amorous one but, rather, one regarding his relationship with the world, with the things he finds in front of him. He is a photographer. One day, he photographs two people in a park, an element of reality that appears real. And it is. But reality has a quality of freedom about it that is hard to explain. This film, perhaps, is like Zen; the moment you explain it, you betray it. I mean, a film you can explain in words, is not a real film.

PB: *Would you call* Blow-Up, *like so many of your others, a pessimistic film?*

MA: Not at all, because at the end the photographer has understood a lot of things, including how to play with in imaginary ball—which is quite an achievement.

PB: *Then you feel that the photographer's decision to join the game and forget about the murder is a positive solution. Do you think this speaks well of the way youth deals with its problems?*

MA: Certainly. There's much talk about the problems of youth, but young people are not a problem. It's a natural evolution of things. We, who have known only how to make war and slaughter people, have no right to judge them, nor can we teach them anything.

PB: *Some people over thirty seem to feel that today's youth is a lost generation, withdrawn not only from commitment but, in the case of the hippies, from reality. Do you disagree?*

MA: I don't think they're lost at all. I'm not a sociologist or a psychologist, but it seems to me they are seeking a new way to be happy. They *are* committed, but in different way—and the *right* way, I think. The American hippies, for example, are against the war in Vietnam and against Johnson—but they combat warmongers with love and peace. They demonstrate against police by embracing them and throwing flowers. How can you club a girl who comes to you to give you a kiss? That, too, is a form of protest. In California's "lov-in parties," there is an atmosphere of absolute calm, tranquillity. That, too, is a form of protest, a way of being committed. It shows that violence is not the only means of persuasion. It's a complicated subject—more so than its seems—and I can't handle it, because I don't know the hippies well enough.

PB: *Sometimes that tranquillity you spoke of is induced by hallucinogenic drugs. Does the use of such drugs alarm you?*

MA: No; some people have negative reactions or can't stand hallucinations, but others stand them extremely well. One of the problems of the future world will be the use of leisure time. How will it be filled up? Maybe drugs will be distributed free of charge by the government.

PB: *You've always emphasized both the importance and the difficulty of communication between people in your films. But doesn't the psychedelic experience tend to make people withdraw into an inner-directed mysticism, even drop out of society altogether? And doesn't this tend to destroy communication?*

MA: There are many ways of communicating. Some hold the theory that *new* forms of communication between people can be obtained through hallucinogenic drugs.

PB: *Would you want to try some yourself?*

MA: You can't go to an LSD or pot party unless you take it yourself. If I want to go, I must take drugs myself.

PB: *Have you?*

MA: That's *my* business. But to show you the new mentality: I visited St. Mark's in Venice with a young woman who smokes pot, as do most young people in her environment. When we were above the gilded mosaics—St. Mark's is small and intimate—she exclaimed: "How I'd like to smoke here!" You see how new that reaction is? We don't even suspect it. There was nothing profane in her desire to smoke; she merely wanted to make her aesthetic emotions more intense. She wanted to make her pleasure giant-sized before the beauty of St. Mark's.

PB: *Does this mean you believe that the old means of communicating have become masks, as you seem to suggest in your films, that obscure communication?*

MA: I think they become masks, yes.

PB: *Is alienation, then—from one's self and from others—the subject of your films?*

MA: I never think in terms of alienation; it's the others who do. Alienation means one thing to Hegel, another to Marx, and yet another to Freud; so it is not possible to give a single definition, one that will exhaust the subject. It is a question bordering on philosophy, and I'm not a philosopher or a sociologist. My business is to tell stories, to narrate with images—nothing else. If I do make films about alienation—to use that word that is so ambiguous—they are about characters, not about me.

PB: *But your characters do have difficulty communicating. The industrial landscape in* Red Desert, *for example, seems to leave little room for human emotion. It seems to dehumanize the characters.*

MA: Nothing regarding man is ever inhuman. That's why I make films, not iceboxes. I shot some of *Red Desert* along a road where half the horizon was filled with the pine trees that still surround Ravenna— though they are vanishing fast—while the other half of the skyline was taken up with a long line of factories, chimneys, tanks, grain silos, buildings, machinery. I felt that the skyline filled with things made by man, with those colors, was more beautiful and richer and more exciting for me than the long, green, uniform line of pinewoods, behind which I still sensed empty nature.

PB: *Most of the men in your films seem to cope very easily with this new technological reality, as far as their work relationships are concerned. But in their love relationships, they tend to be incapable of achieving or sustaining an emotional involvement. Compared with your female characters, they seem weak, lacking in initiative.*

MA: What do you mean—that there exists an ideal relationship between man and woman? Do you really think that a man must be strong, masculine, dominating, and the woman frail, obedient, and sensitive? This is a conventional idea. Reality is quite different.

PB: *Is that what you meant when you said once that women are the first to adapt themselves to an epoch, that they are closer to nature and thus stronger?*

MA: I said women are a finer filter of reality. They can sniff things.

PB: *You also said that you understand them better than men. Why?*

MA: It's only natural. I've had intimate relations with women but not with men.

PB: *Are the Italian women you've known different from those of other nationalities?*

MA: Yes, of course.

PB: *How?*

MA: This is becoming frivolous. It leads to such platitudes as that French women are calculating; Italian women, instinctive; English women, hot.

The women I like, no matter what nationality, all seem to have more or less the same qualities. Perhaps this is because one goes looking for them—that is, you like the type of woman and then look for her. I've always dreamed of getting to know the women of other countries better. When I was a boy, I remember, I used to get angry at the thought that I did not know German or American or Swedish women. I hope the women in my films have at least a minimal common denominator with the women of other countries, because, after all, the problems are more or less the same.

PB: *Your heroines tend to be mature in years. Do you find older women more attractive than young girls?*
MA: It depends upon the age of the woman you're in love with.

PB: *What do you find most attractive sexually in a woman?*
MA: A woman's sex appeal is an inner matter. It stems from her mental make-up, basically. It's an attitude, not just a question of her physical features—that arrogant quality in a woman's femininity. Otherwise, all beautiful women would have sex appeal, which is not so.

PB: *Do you think there can be love without eroticism between a man and a woman?*
MA: I believe it's all the same thing. I can't imagine love without a sexual charge.

PB: *In your films, though, you imply that love is more complex, that even when two people are attracted to each other, they have to struggle to keep their love alive. Why?*
MA: That love is conflict seems to me obvious and natural. There isn't a single worthwhile work in world literature based on love that is *only* about the conquest of happiness, the effort to arrive at what we call love. It's the *struggle* that has always interested those who produce works of art—literature, cinema, or poetry. But I can't give any absolute definition of what love is, or even whether it ought to exist.

PB: *Love seems to bring little happiness to your characters. Has this been true of your own life?*
MA: I read somewhere that happiness is like the bluebird of [Maurice] Maeterlinck: Try to catch it and it loses its color. It's like trying to hold

water in your hands. The more you squeeze it, the more the water runs away. Personally, I know very little about love.

PB: *How do you feel about marriage?*

MA: I'm more or less skeptical about marriage, because of family ties, relations between children and parents—it's all so depressing. The family today counts for less and less. Why? Who knows—the growth of science, the Cold War, the atomic bomb, the world war we've made, the new philosophies we've created: certainly something is happening to man, so why go against it, why oblige this new man to live by the mechanisms and regulations of the past?

PB: *What about religion? Do you agree with those who say that God is dead?*

MA: I remember a character, in a Hemingway story, who was asked: "Do you believe in God?" And he answered: "Sometimes, at night." When I see nature, when I look into the sky, the dawn, the sun, the colors of insects, snow crystals, the night stars, I don't feel a need for God. Perhaps when I can no longer look and wonder, when I believe in nothing—then, perhaps, I might need something else. But I don't know what. All I know is that we are loaded down with old and stale stuff—habits, customs, old attitudes that are already dead and gone. The strength of the young Englishmen in *Blow-Up* lies in their ability to throw out all such rubbish.

PB: *What besides marriage and religion would you throw out?*

MA: The sense of nation, "good breeding," certain forms and ceremonies that govern relationships—perhaps even jealousy. We're not aware of all of them yet, though we suffer from them. And they mislead us not only about ethics, but also about aesthetics. The public buys "art"—but the word is drained of its meaning. Today, we no longer know what to call "art," what its function is, and even less what function it will have in the future. We know only that it is something dynamic—unlike many ideas that have governed us.

PB: *What sort of ideas?*

MA: Take Einstein; wasn't he looking for something stable and change-less in that enormous, constantly changing melting pot that is the universe? He sought fixed rules. Today, instead, it would be helpful to find all those rules that show how and why the universe is *not* fixed—how this dynamism develops and acts. Then maybe we will be able to explain many things, perhaps even art, because the old instruments of judgment, the old aesthetics are no longer of any use to us—so much so that we no longer know what's beautiful and what isn't.

PB: *Do you feel that the language of film has evolved, and to what extent do you think you have contributed to this evolution?*
MA: My contribution to the formation of a new cinematic language is a matter that concerns critics. And not even today's critics, but rather those of tomorrow, if film endures as an art and if my films resist the ravages of time.

PB: *But many critics have called you one of the foremost directors in the search for a new aesthetic, in changing the "grammar" of the cinema. Don't you feel you've brought any innovations to the screen?*
MA: Innovation comes spontaneously. I don't know if I've done anything new. If I have, it's just because I had begun to feel for some time that I couldn't stand certain films, certain modes, certain ways of telling a story, certain tricks of plot development, all of it predictable and useless.

PB: *Was it the old techniques that bothered you—or simply the old story lines?*
MA: Both, I think. The basic divergence was in the substance, in what was being filmed—and this has been determined by the insecurity of our lives. A particular type of film emerged from World War II, with the Italian neorealist school. It was perfectly right for its time, which was as exceptional as the reality around us. Our major interest focused on that and on how we would relate to it. Later, when the situation normalized and post-war life returned to what it had been in peacetime, it became important to see the intimate, interior consequences of all that had happened.

PB: *Doesn't your own interest in the interior of external events, in man's reaction to reality, date back to before the war? Your first film venture, a documentary, was shot in a mental hospital in Ferrara. Why did you choose that subject?*
MA: As I suffer from nervous tics, I had gone for consultation to a neurologist who was in charge of this mental home. Sometimes I had to wait, and found myself in contact with the insane, and I liked the atmosphere. I found it full of poetic potential. But the film was a disaster.

PB: *Why?*

MA: I wanted to do it with real schizophrenics, and the director of this hospital agreed. He was a bit mad himself—a very tall man who demonstrated reactions of mad people to pain by rolling about on the floor with the rest of them. But he provided me with some schizophrenics and I chatted with them, explaining how they were supposed to move in the first scene. They were amazingly docile and they did everything in rehearsal as I asked them. Everything was fine—until we lit the klieg lights and they came under a glare that they'd never seen before. All hell broke loose. They threw themselves on the ground; they began to howl— it was ghastly. We were in a sea of them and I was absolutely petrified. I hadn't even the strength to shout "Stop!" So we didn't shoot the documentary: but I've never forgotten that scene.

PB: *You left Ferrara to attend the University of Bologna. What made you decide not to return to Ferrara? Didn't you like it there?*

MA: I enjoyed myself tremendously in Ferrara. The troubles began later. But I didn't like university life much in Bologna. The subjects I studied—economics and business administration—didn't interest me. I wanted to make films. I was glad when I was graduated. Yet it's odd; on graduation day, I was overcome with a terrible sadness. I realized that my youth was over and now the struggle had begun.

PB: *And you went to Rome?*

MA: Yes; and the first years there were very hard. I wrote reviews for a film magazine; and when they fired me, I was penniless for days. I even stole a steak from a restaurant. Someone had ordered it but was away from the table when it came; so I put it in a newspaper and ran out. My father had money—he was then a small industrialist—and wanted me back in Ferrara. But I refused and lived by selling tennis trophies; I had boxes full of them that I'd won in tournaments during college days. I pawned and sold them all. I was miserable, since I'd won them myself.

PB: *How did you switch from film criticism to film directing?*

MA: I went to the Centro Sperimentale di Cinematografia in Rome; but I stayed only three months. The technical aspect of films—by itself alone—has never interested me very much. After you've learned two or three basic rules of cinema grammar, you can do what you like—including breaking those rules.

PB: *Then you began to direct?*
MA: No, it wasn't that easy. At first I wrote filmscripts. I did one with Rossellini, called *Un pilota ritorna* [*A Pilot Returns*, 1941–42]. I'll never forget Roberto. In those days he lived in a big empty house he'd found in Rome and was almost always in bed, because it was the only piece of furniture he had. We worked on his bed, with him in it. From this I moved on to other things, until I was drafted into the army. The hell began then.

PB: *Because of army life?*
MA: No, the nightmare was to work on the set of a film I had helped write—*I due Foscari*, with Enrico Fulchignoni directing—and still show up as a soldier. I used to sneak out of camp at night and crawl back at dawn, over a wall or sometimes through a hole under a hedge. It was freezing and I was paralyzed from this and from sheer exhaustion.

PB: *Why did you keep going back over the wall?*
MA: Because of the excitement of working on a film, although only in a small way as an assistant. They let me experiment and I learned a lot, especially about camera movement and how to relate the movement of actors to the field of your lens.

PB: *Did you work on any other films while you were in the army?*
MA: Michele Scalera [head of Scalera films] called me in one day and asked me if I'd like to go to France to work with Marcel Carné—as his codirector—on a picture being coproduced by Scalera. I couldn't believe it—codirect with this man who was the greatest of his day—and I said yes. I had to pull strings all over Rome to get leave from the army. Then, when I got it, I was stopped at the French border. It was maddening. When I finally got to Paris, it was Sunday and I found Carné shooting in the suburbs. He looked at me as if I had brought the plague. Finally, he said: "You've got eyes, my friend. Look." After that, he said nothing more to me. I didn't dare tell him I was supposed to be his codirector. I merely said I was to be his assistant; but I was never even that. We went to Nice for some exteriors and the train was so crowded I rode on the car steps,

hanging on for my life. Carné spoke to me again, then—obviously scared I'd get hurt and he'd have to pay for it. At Nice we stayed at the Negresco [Hotel], where I began to enjoy myself a bit. I met the nurse-maid of a rich family and made some notes for a film on the life of a great hotel, seen from the back rooms. Somewhere along the line, I eventually lost the notes, but I'll never forget Carné. Scalera had wanted me to stay on in France and work with [Jean] Gremillion and [Jean] Cocteau, but my leave ran out and I had to hurry back to the army in Italy.

PB: *Mussolini's regime collapsed shortly afterward. How did this affect you?*
MA: It forced me into a hand-to-mouth existence. During the German Occupation of Rome, cinema didn't exist. I earned a little money by doing translations—Gide's *La Porte étroite,* Morand's *Monsieur Zero.* But then I became involved with the Action party and the Germans looked for me. I escaped to the Abruzzi hills, but they followed me there and I had to escape once more. Finally, when the Allies took Rome, we could begin again.

PB: *Did that lean period color the political or social outlook of your later films?*
MA: That had already begun, long before. When I was a boy, we often went with friends to swim in the Po, which flows near Ferrara. There were *barconi,* great river boats towed by men dragging them from the towpath. Men pulling five or six boats, against a river's current, made a tremendous impression on me. I returned time and again to stare at them and at the people who lived on them, with their family and chickens, and washing hung out; the boat was their home. It was there that I got my first glimpse of the bad distribution of wealth. Later I began to make *People of the Po Valley.* It was my first documentary and the first time I ever handled a cinecamera.

PB: *Yet, your first feature—*Story of a Love Affair, *in 1950—caused a sensation by breaking with the neorealist school's penchant for portraying the working class. This film and most of those you've made since are about the affluent middle class. Why?*
MA: I've made films about the middle classes because I know them best. Everyone talks about what he knows best. The struggle for life is not only

the material and economic one. Comfort is no protection from anxiety.
In any case, the idea of giving "all" of reality is overly simple and absurd.
I take a subject and I analyze it, as in laboratory. The deeper I can go in
the analysis, the smaller the subject becomes—and the better I know it.
This doesn't prevent a return from the particular subject to the general,
from the isolated character to the entire society. But in *Story of a Love
Affair,* I was interested in seeing what the war had done more to the
mind and spirit of individuals than to their place in the framework of
society. That's why I began to make films that the French critics described
as "interior neorealism." The aim was to put the camera inside the
characters—not outside. *The Bicycle Thief* was a great film in which the
camera remained always outside the characters. Neorealism also taught us
to follow the characters with the camera, allowing each shot its own real
interior time. Well, I became tired of all this; I could no longer stand real
time. In order to function, a shot must show you only what is useful.

PB: *Why couldn't you stand real time?*
MA: Because there are too many useless moments. It's pointless to
describe them.

PB: *Your insistence on paring the superfluous from your films is also
reflected in the sparseness of your dialogue. Is that why you prefer to establish
the dark, cold mood of your films with a background of gray, cloudy skies?*
MA: In the early days, the films I shot in black and white were fairly
dramatic, so the gray sky helped create an atmosphere. *Story of a Love
Affair,* for example, was set in Milan in winter—which was correct for
climate and mood. But the sun also limits movements. At that time,
I used very long shots, turning up to 180°; it's obvious that the sun will
stop you from doing that sort of thing. So, with a gray sky you move
ahead faster, without problems of camera position.

PB: *In your last two films, you've switched to color. You've kept the gray
skies, but you've been known to change the colors of roads and buildings for
effect. What don't you like about real colors?*
MA: Wouldn't it be ridiculous if you asked a painter that same question?
It's untrue to say that the colors I use are not those of reality. They *are* real:
The red I use is red; the green, green; blue, blue; and yellow, yellow. It's a

matter of arranging them differently from the way I find them, but they are always real colors. So it's not true that when I tint a road or a wall, they become unreal. They stay real, though colored differently for my scene. I'm forced to modify or eliminate colors as I find them in order to make an acceptable composition. Let's suppose we have a blue sky. Who knows if it's going to work? Or, if I don't need it, where can I put it? So I pick a gray day for neutral background, where I can insert all the color elements I need—a tree, a house, a ship, a car, a telegraph pole. It's like having a piece of white paper on which to apply colors. If I begin with a blue sky, half the picture is already painted blue. But what if I don't happen to need blue? Color forces you to invent. It's more than just a challenge, though. There are practical reasons for working in it today. Reality itself is steadily becoming more colored. Think of what factories were like, especially in Italy at the beginning of the nineteenth century, when industrialization was just beginning: gray, brown, and smoky. Color didn't exist. Today, instead, almost everything is colored. The pipe running from the basement to the twelfth floor is green because it carries steam. The one carrying electricity is red, and that with water is purple. Also, plastic colors have filled our homes, even revolutionized our taste. Pop art grew out of that and was possible because of this change in taste. Another reason for switching to color is world television. In a few years, it will all be in color, and you can't compete against that with black-and-white films.

PB: *Besides the switch to color, have your methods of filming a picture changed much from the early days?*
MA: I've never had a method of working. I change according to circumstances; I don't employ any particular technique or style. Some people believe I make films with my head, a few others think they come from the heart; for my part, I feel as though I make films instinctively, more with my belly than with my brain or my feelings.

PB: *In general, where does the original idea for your films come from?*
MA: It seems to me that no one engaged in creative activity can answer that question in good faith. Lucidity is not one of my outstanding qualities. I look at everything, avidly, and I also think I listen a great deal.

One thing is certain: ideas come to me unexpectedly. But I'm not really interested in getting to the bottom of such a question.

PB: *But I am. How does the process begin? Please, tell me.*

MA: With a theme, a small idea that develops within me. The idea for the next film, which I want to make in America, came to me from something I can't tell you about fully, because it would mean telling the story of the film. But someone told me of an absurd little episode, saying: "Just think what happened to me today. I couldn't come for this and that reason." I went home and thought about it—and upon that small episode I began to build, until I found I had a story, growing out of a small event. You put in everything that accumulates inside you. And it's an enormous quantity of stuff—mostly from watching and observing. The way I relax, what I like doing most, is watching. That's why I like traveling, to have new things before my eyes—even a new face. I enjoy myself like that and can stay for hours, looking at things, people, scenery. Do you know, when I was a boy, I always had bumps on my head from running into mailboxes because I was always turning around to stare at people. I also used to climb into window sills to look into houses—yes, I was crazy—to peek at someone I'd seen in the window. So around the kernel of an idea or an episode, you instinctively add all you have accumulated by watching, talking, living, observing.

PB: *And then you begin to write the script?*

MA: No, that's the last thing I do. When I'm sure I have a story, or the makings of one, I call my collaborators and we begin to discuss it. And we conduct studies of certain subjects to make sure of our terrain. Then, finally, in the last month or two, I write the story, or—in light of what I said earlier—the outline, what some call the treatment.

PB: *How long does this gestation period last?*

MA: Perhaps six months. Then I start shooting.

PB: *It's said that you insist on being left alone on the set for fifteen or twenty minutes before beginning to shoot. True?*

MA: Yes. Before each new setup, I chase everyone off the set in order to be alone and look through the camera. In that moment, the film seems quite easy. But then the others come in and everything becomes difficult.

PB: *When do you pick your actors?*

MA: When you work on a character, you form in your mind an image of what he ought to look like. Then you go and find one who resembles him. For *Blow-Up,* I began with photographs sent by agents, throwing them out one by one. Then I went around looking into theaters. I found David Hemmings in a small London production.

PB: *Some directors claim it's difficult to direct a woman they love. Is this true with Monica Vitti?*

MA: I have no difficulty, because I forget about the relationship between myself and any actress when working with her.

PB: *Would you number Monica among the most gifted actresses you've ever seen?*

MA: Monica is certainly the first who comes to mind. I can't think of another as good as Vanessa, as strong as Liz Taylor, as true as Sophia Loren, or as modern as Monica. Monica is astonishingly mobile. Few actresses have such mobile features. She has her own personal and original way of acting.

PB: *What about directors? Have you any favorites?*

MA: They change, like favorite authors. I had a passion for Gide and Stein and Faulkner. But now they're no use to me anymore. I've assimilated them—so, enough, they're a closed chapter. This also applies to film directors. Also, when I see a good film, it's like a whiplash. I run away, in order not to be influenced. Thus, the films I liked most are those I think least about.

PB: *Are you an admirer of Ingmar Bergman?*

MA: Yes; he's a long way from me, but I admire him. He, too concentrates a great deal on individuals; and although the individual is what interests him most, we are very far apart. His individuals are very different from mine—but he's a great director. So is Fellini, for that matter.

PB: *What do you do between films? Do you feel the same emptiness as Fellini when you're not working?*

MA: I don't know how it is with Fellini. I never feel empty. I travel a lot and I think about other films.

PB: *Are you ever bored?*
MA: I don't know. I never look at myself.

PB: *Have you ever known anyone who has understood you?*
MA: Everyone has understood me in his own way. But I would have to understand myself first, in order to judge—and so far, I haven't.

PB: *Have you many friends?*
MA: The close friends remain fairly fixed. The older I get, the more I like the people whom we call *mezzi matti*—half crazy. I like them best because they fit into my conviction that life should be taken ironically: otherwise it becomes a tragedy. Fitzgerald said a very interesting thing in his diary: that human life proceeds from the good to the less good— that is, it's always worse as you go on. That's true.

PB: *You've said your films always leave you unsatisfied. Isn't that true of the work of most creative artists?*
MA: Yes, but especially for me, since I've always worked under fairly disastrous conditions economically.

PB: *Have all the lost years—the time wasted fighting against incomprehension from producers—left you bitter?*
MA: I try not to think about it. I dislike judging myself, but I will say I would be wealthy today if I had accepted all the films that have been offered to me with large sums of money. But I've always refused, in order to do what I felt like doing.

PB: *Have you ever been tempted?*
MA: Yes, often.

PB: *As far as wealth goes, didn't the success of* Blow-Up *make you rich?*
MA: I'm not rich and maybe I'll never be rich. Money is useful—yes— but I don't worship it.

PB: *What's your next film? Do you intend to continue working outside Italy?*
MA: Quite frankly, I'd like to but don't know if I'll have the strength. It isn't easy to understand the lives of people different from your own.

I'm thinking about doing a film in the United States, as I mentioned earlier, but I don't know if it will come off.

PB: *Have you ever considered making an autobiographical film, like some of Fellini's?*

MA: My films have always had an element of immediate autobiography, in that I shoot any particular scene according to the mood I'm in that day, according to the little daily experiences I've had and the settings I've inhabited—but I don't tell what has happened to me. I would like to do something more strictly autobiographical, but perhaps I never will, because it isn't interesting enough, or I won't have the courage to do it. No, that's nonsense, because it isn't a question of courage. It's simply that I believe in the autobiographical concept only to the degree that I am able to put onto film all that's passing through my head at the moment of shooting.

PB: *Have you ever thought about retiring?*

MA: I'll go on making films until I make one that pleases me from the first to the last frame. Then I'll quit.

Zabriskie Point

MARSHA KINDER/1968

Antonioni's sympathy with the young radicals was very apparent. When I asked him what kind of a reception he had received from them, he replied:
They didn't trust me at the beginning, and they were right. First of all, I walked in and said I was working for MGM, for the establishment. But after many, many meetings, and after I had started working with Fred Gardner, who is one of them, and after he explained to them what I was trying to do, they became much more open. And they allowed me to use the initials of their group, SDS [Students for a Democratic Society], which is important.

But this sympathy does not mean that he is uncritical of the movement or unaware of the problems it faces. He seemed very sensitive to the differences between student radicals in America and elsewhere.
The student movement in America is different because they are less together. There are many, many groups. They can't work together yet. You know this country is so big, so contradictory, that it is more difficult here for them to do something important. When something happens in Paris, it is happening in France. When something happens in Rome, it is happening in Italy. And the same thing for Berlin in Germany. Not here. When something happens in Los Angeles, it doesn't matter for New York—it has nothing to do with New York. What happened at Columbia University was important here, but as an echo. They don't have any relationship. They get in touch sometimes, but they don't work together. At least, that is what they themselves admit.

From *Sight and Sound*, vol. 38, no. 1 (Winter 1968–1969). Reprinted by permission of the British Film Institute.

It would be misleading to overemphasize the political aspects of this film. Despite rumour, Antonioni sees it as a film about interior feelings.
I think that this film is about what two young people feel. It is an interior film. Of course, a character always has a background.

The contemporary context, the young central characters, and the setting seem crucial. I wonder which came first and how he had decided to make this particular film.
I took two trips to America (the first in the spring of 1967 and the second in autumn). I had this idea to do a film here because I wanted to get out of Italy and Europe. Nothing was started in Europe yet, I mean this movement of youth. When I came to America, the first thing that interested me was this sort of reaction to the society as it is now—not just to the society, but to the morality, the mentality, the psychology of old America. I wrote some notes, and when I came back I wanted to know if what I had written down, the intuition, was true or not. My experience taught me that when an intuition is beautiful, it is also true. When I came back I realized that what I had in mind *was* true. I decided on this story when I came to Zabriskie Point. I found that this particular place was exactly what I was looking for. I like to know where the story is placed. I have to see it somewhere to write something. I want a relationship between the characters and the place; I can't separate them from their milieu.

But their milieu was not Antonioni's. I wondered whether he could really feel comfortable in making a film about this world which was essentially foreign to him and in foreign language.
I wrote this story, the story is mine. I called in Tonino Guerra, whom I have worked with before; but he doesn't speak English and it was difficult for him to help me get in touch with people, so Tonino went back. When the script was in the synopsis stage (without dialogue or an indication of dialogue), I started to look for someone else because I could not write dialogue in Italian. You can't translate dialogue. An American answers in a different way from an Italian or Frenchman. I wanted to write the dialogue in English. I started to read a lot of plays and books, and I found Sam Shepard, who started to work on the dialogue for the film. I did the first version of the script with him. I did many versions of the script, and

then I got in touch with Fred Gardner, who is one of these young people and very cooperative. The last version of the script was written with him, but I am still changing as I am shooting.

The process of change was very apparent on location. For example, it had been reported that the following week Antonioni was importing hundreds of people from San Francisco, Salt Lake City, and Las Vegas to shoot a love-in, but on the day of the interview he changed his mind.
It was just an idea, but I never saw this idea as something real. I didn't have the image, I couldn't find the key to doing it. I saw lots of love-ins in America—with groups playing and people smoking or dancing or doing nothing, just lying on the ground. But I was looking for something different—something which was more related to the special character of Zabriskie Point, and I couldn't find this relationship. I'm going to put it in the film anyway, but in a different way—just a few people and the background almost empty.

Last-minute changes have always been an essential part of Antonioni's method of working. He has never been tied to a script before, and this film is no exception. When asked how he decided a change had to be made, he replied:
A film is not one thing after another, everything in it is related. I know immediately when something is wrong. And if something is wrong here, the consequence is that it is also wrong later in the script. So if I have to change something here, I have to change something else. I can't judge a line until I hear the line said by the actor at the moment of shooting. Sometimes I shoot two versions of the same scene. I did this on one of the Mobil scenes. I shot one version and wasn't quite happy. I wanted something more ironic, so I did another version of the scene. Maybe you hear a suggestion, you see a particular place, or going to the set in the morning you have an idea and you have to explore it.

The Mobil scene to which he referred is a sequence that takes place in Los Angeles. Antonioni constructed an expensive set high up atop the Mobil Building in downtown Los Angeles, which is supposed to be the plush offices of the Sunny Dunes Real Estate Company. In one shot he simultaneously has in focus a TV commercial for these land developers, the action inside the office, and the view of downtown L.A. outside the window.

When asked about his impressions of Los Angeles, Antonioni commented on the billboards:

The billboards are an obsession of Los Angeles. They are so strong that you can't avoid them. Of course, there is the danger of seeing Los Angeles as a stranger. To us the billboards are so contrary, but for people who live there they are nothing—they don't even see them. I am going to show them in the film, but I don't yet know how.

Apparently, he chose Los Angeles as a location because of its proximity to Death Valley.

This story should start in a city that is not so far from the desert. It is easy for someone from Los Angeles to come here. The desert is something very familiar to people who live in Los Angeles.

Yet there seemed to be a more meaningful connection between the two sites. When we were on location in Lone Pine looking at the dry lake bed below Mount Whitney, Antonioni observed that it had been drained because Los Angeles needed the water. It occurred to me that this was another example of Los Angeles as the consumer society. Los Angeles forces upon you an awareness of the materialistic culture; you are constantly confronted with objects to be desired, pursued, and replaced. It is both physically and emotionally draining. But Death Valley with its stark beauty merely exists without forcing anything upon you.

When I first heard that Antonioni was shooting in Death Valley, I immediately thought of the settings in The Cry, L'avventura, *and* Red Desert, *and assumed it would be linked to sterility. But once I got there and observed its beauty, I began to suspect that he might not fulfill these conventional expectations, that it might be used in a more complex way. In Lone Pine he casually remarked that Death Valley contains both the highest and lowest points in the United States. It is vast, cosmic, and varied. When I asked him specifically how he intended to treat Death Valley, he answered:*

When I came here, I had these two young people in mind. It seemed to me the best place to have them *out* of their milieu—to be free. Zabriskie Point was perfect; it was so primitive, like the moon. I'm not going to explore this landscape in the film in the same way that you see it when you come here. I want to put it in the background because otherwise it would be too strong.

This particular setting will undoubtedly affect Antonioni's use of color, for he seemed to use it quite differently in Red Desert *and* Blow-Up.

In *Red Desert* it was subjective. For the most part of the film, the reality was seen from the view of the woman who was neurotic, so that's why I changed the color of the backgrounds, the streets, everything. In *Blow-Up* my problem was completely different. I knew London because I had shot there before on one of the episodes in my second film. But when I went back to London, I found it so different. When I am visiting a town I have thousands of impressions and images. The problem for *Blow-Up* was that I had just a few exterior scenes of London, and I had to concentrate all my impressions in these few scenes. So I had to decide, more or less, what was the color of London—not for others, but for me. I changed the colors of the streets according to the story, not according to the real London. For *Blow-Up* it wasn't really London; it was something *like* London. But I didn't change the colors very much. In this new film I don't change colors; I try to exploit the colors that I have.

The changes in style are not limited to the use of color. Antonioni predicted there would be many changes, mainly because he is working in Panavision for the first time.

The technique for this film is different from *Blow-Up*. I am shooting in order to have the possibilities for choosing a style at the end in the cutting stage. I am shooting in different ways. I am talking primarily about the use of lenses. This is the first time I am shooting in Panavision, and Panavision forces you to use different techniques because the lenses are different. As soon as you get familiar with them, you have to exploit this difference. For example, I am using the sides much more than I did before because in this way you have a stronger relationship between the character and the background.

Since one of the main stylistic changes in Blow-Up *was the faster pace, I wondered whether this trend would continue in* Zabriskie Point.

In *Blow-Up* it was fast, very fast, because the character was lively and needed this sort of pace. I don't know here. In this film the plot is not so precise. In *Blow-Up* there was a beginning, and then something happens, and then you go straight to the end. Not here. The plot is much less strong in this film. The beginning of this film will be almost documentary. No plot at the beginning—but a mosaic of many things. And then the characters come out from this mosaic. So I don't know yet how fast the pace or beat will be. While I'm shooting I never think of that.

Since this is Antonioni's first experience of working in America, I was curious to discover whether there were any problems, especially in his relationship with MGM. Although he did not feel any restrictions on his autonomy, he did express uneasiness about problems connected with the budget.

My autonomy, I would say, is complete. They leave me free to do what I want. The only thing now is that they are starting to be worried about the budget. They ask me why the film is so expensive, but that's what I'm going to ask them. I don't know why it's so expensive, I really don't know. I have a crew that is only half the size of what is usual in America because I don't want a big crew.

It was clear that he considered the fact that they were over-budget the fault of the Americans and not his. In fact, he was horrified by the American tendency to waste money.

It seems to me I'm seeing such a waste of money. It seems to be almost immoral. I feel bad sometimes. For instance, they threw away a piece of gelatin that we used and the piece was still new. There is also a waste of film. If I am shooting with two or three cameras and I need this camera only in the middle of the scene, in Italy I would start with that camera just at that moment. Not here. They start from the beginning. It is a waste of film! They are consumers. They are used to wasting something— goods, materials, food, everything. And I'm *not* used to this.

Ironically, this tendency toward conspicuous consumption and waste seems to be one of the American characteristics under attack in Zabriskie Point. *Antonioni's crew was unusual not only because it was small, but also because it was surprisingly young for a Hollywood film. For many this was there first assignment on a feature, and most of them were very enthusiastic about working with Antonioni. The first assistant director, Bob Rubin, is only twenty-seven and his only experience is in television. Although Harrison Starr was associate producer on* Rachel, Rachel, *this was his first assignment as an executive producer. The still photographs on the set were being shot by Bruce Davidson, a talented and noted artist in his own right. The press agent, Beverly Walker, who is very knowledgeable about cinema, came right from a job with the New York Film Festival. One of the electricians, Jerry Upton, is an avid film buff who has seen most of Antonioni's films several times. Since this kind of crew is unusual in Hollywood, I wondered whether Antonioni had selected it purposely. He admitted that he had tried to get as many young crew members as possible, but added:*

I have some elements of this crew who are not so young—some older people who worked, for instance, on the first film of Greta Garbo, on the first *Ben-Hur*, on Stroheim's *Greed*. It's very amusing to talk to them about these things.

His problems were not limited to age; they also involved the unions. For one thing, he had tried to hire some black cameramen to shoot a sequence that takes place in a Negro ghetto but was unsuccessful because he couldn't find any black men in the union. Some of the problems with the unions were also linked with age.

I had a lot of problems with unions, and in Hollywood this is much more difficult than in New York. The unions are so strong. There are lots of old people. You can't find what you are looking for. I needed some cameramen and some assistant cameramen—some young people used to shooting in the modern way, people who can zoom without your having to tell them the exact distance from the actors to the camera, people who can make changes on their own and who can sometimes do what they want. I *want* them to do that, to do something different from the script, maybe. At that critical moment, the assistant cameraman has to make the decision, but the American cameraman can't do this. That's why I was forced to bring some people from Italy.

Antonioni links these difficulties not only to the unions, but also the national character. He finds it much more difficult to work in America than in England.
I don't know why, but English people are much more familiar to me. At the time I was making *Blow-Up*, at least, they were so mad—in a positive and very pleasant way—that they were almost Neapolitan (that's a joke). I like them, I like English people much more than Americans. I mean I find myself closer to them. The Americans are so cool sometimes. They need to know exactly what they are doing. Sometimes they are like

Germans—fastidious, precise. This makes me upset because I like to
have people around me who are more spontaneous.

*This difficulty did not seem to apply to his relationship with his two leading
actors—Mark Frechette, a twenty-year-old carpenter from Boston who is interested in founding an underground newspaper and who has never worked in a
film before; and Daria Halprin, the 19-year-old daughter of Ann Halprin, head of
the experimental San Francisco Dance Workshop. Daria is an anthropology
major at Berkeley. She reminded me of a miniature Sophia Loren, with plenty
of vitality, warmth, and guts. In the particular sequence I watched them shoot,
Daria was in a car being buzzed by a plane (supposedly flown by Mark). The
stunt pilot came so close in one pass that the plane scraped the radio antenna
of the car. In the next shot the plane chased Daria as she was running across
the desert and came within five feet of her head. She was scared but kept
her cool.*

 *Antonioni seemed to select these non-professionals for their naturalness
and spontaneity—which he couldn't find among actors.*

I saw a lot of young people—actors and students in acting school, but I
couldn't find the right people. And so I started to look for them out of
the schools—out of the usual milieu of young actors; and I saw Daria in
a film. She wasn't acting. There was a ballet in this film, and Daria was
one of the girls dancing. I saw this face coming out from the back, and I
was impressed. We made a test, and she was extraordinary. She had the
best qualities for an actress. She is so sincere, she can communicate
anything, everything. Finding Mark was much more difficult because I
made a lot of tests of young people, students and actors before I could
find anyone. One of these tests was Mark's.

*He felt it was particularly fitting to use non-professionals like Mark and Daria
for this film "because this story could have happened to them. They use their
own names—first names and family names—in the film because the story is
about them." In an attempt to preserve their naturalness, Antonioni is not
allowing them to be interviewed or to see the rushes, which is probably a wise
decision. The one time I saw Mark and Daria ruffled was when they read
their first publicity. At first they were excited to see their names and pictures
in print, but when they read the article they were angered by what was said.
The writer didn't understand their respect for Antonioni, their attitude toward*

the film, or their sense of humour. Starring in a movie has not yet destroyed their "authenticity." And they know they are not just in any movie, but a movie by Antonioni (although Mark Frechette had never heard of Antonioni when he was first offered the part). They seem to be aware of why he chose them for their roles. Thus, they appear casual on the set while at the same time they realize the implications of what it means to be acting in this film. They probably both will become stars, but this will probably be the high point of their careers.

And for Antonioni Zabriskie Point *looks as though it will also be a high point. For it deals with some of the most vital contemporary issues, it is visually exciting, and it continues his experimentation with the medium.*

Michelangelo Antonioni

CHARLES THOMAS SAMUELS/1969

SAMUELS: *You are quoted as saying. "Once one has learned the two or three basic rules of cinematographic grammar, he can do what he likes—even break these rules." What rules were you referring to?*

ANTONIONI: The simplest ones: cross-cutting, making the actor enter from the right if he had previously exited to the left of the frame, etc. There are hundreds of such rules which are taught in cinema schools and which have value only until you actually begin making films. Often I have shot something simply to show myself how useless they are. You break one and no one notices, because the audience only sees the result of your "error." If that works, who cares about rules!

S: Cronaca di un amore, *your first feature film, has more inventive and innovative camera work than your second film,* La signora senza camelie. *For example, in* La signora *you regularly track into a character when he moves toward the camera, which is certainly playing according to the rules, whereas in* Cronaca, *as in your later films, you are seldom so orthodox. Why is this so?*

A: I can't answer that question. When I am shooting a film I never think of how I want to shoot something; I simply shoot it. My technique, which differs from film to film, is wholly instinctive and never based on a priori considerations. But I suppose you are right in saying that *La signora* seems more orthodox than the earlier *Cronaca* because when I was shooting the first film, I made very long takes, following the actors with my camera even after their scene was finished. But, you know, *Cronaca* isn't more innovative than what comes after. Later I break the rules much more often. Look at *L'avventura* and particularly *Blow-Up*.

S: *Blow-Up is the most cinematographically unorthodox of all your films. But I was interested to notice precedents for the camera work of* Blow-Up *in your short documentary* L'amorosa menzogna, *which is about making* fumetti, *or live-action comic strips, and which contains almost as many trick shots as the later work. I think, for example, of the shot of a* fumetti *scene reduced to its reflection in the camera. Isn't it more than a coincidence that the two films which contain your most complex shooting are the two that concern photography?*

A: You are right to say that *Blow-Up* is my most unorthodox film, but it is unorthodox in montage, as well as photography. At the Centro Sperimentale they teach you never to cut a shot during its action. Yet I continually do that in *Blow-Up*. Hemmings starts walking to a phone booth—snip go a few frames—in a flash, he is there. Or take the scene in which he photographs Verushka; I cut many frames during that action, doing what the teachers at the Centro regard as utterly scandalous.

S: *Is the rhythm of this scene meant to suggest the photographer's emotions?*

A: Up to a point. I wanted to give the audience the same sensations as the photographer feels while shooting. However, this sort of thing is fairly common in the cinema today. I began taking liberties a long time ago: now it is standard practice for most directors to ignore the rules.

S: *Your cutting in the Verushka scene has now become a sort of cliché in TV commercials.*

A: Yes?

S: *It doesn't disturb you, eh? Well, let's get back to this question of camera technique. Why do you so rarely use reverse cutting in dialogue scenes?*

A: Because it is so banal that instinctively I find it irritating. But occasionally I do use it, even as late as *Zabriskie Point*. Normally, however,

I try to avoid repetitions of any shot. It isn't easy to find one in my films. You might, I suppose, see something twice, but it would be rare. And then, you know, every line requires its own kind of shot. The American method of shooting one actor continuously, then moving to the other, then intercutting both—this method is wrong. A scene has to have a rhythm of its own, a structure of its own.

S: *Progressively during your career, you seem to efface the precise moment of cutting and to avoid obvious transitions, almost as if you wish to keep the spectator from relaxing. In view of the fact that your later films tell slow, deliberate stories, aren't you trying to achieve briskness in the way you cut?*
A: If so, it is instinctive. I don't do anything deliberately.

S: *That's not true. You told Rex Reed that all your films were made with your stomach, except* Blow-Up, *which was made with your head.*
A: In *Blow-Up* I used my head instinctively!

S: *Checkmate. When you were interviewed by* Bianco e Nero *in 1958 you said that modern directors had eliminated the "problem of the bicycle."*
A: What could I have meant by that?

S: *I supposed you to mean sociological motivation for the character's behavior, and you certainly concentrate on the power of personality, of self rather than society. However, even though your characters aren't caused by society, they are embedded in a specific social context, which is what gives your films their extraordinary richness. Therefore, I think that 1958 statement indicates what is really a false distinction.*
A: You know what I would like to do: make a film with actors standing in empty space so that the spectator would have to imagine the background of the characters. Till now I have never shot a scene without taking account of what stands behind the actors because the relationship between people and their surroundings is of prime importance. I mean simply to say that I want my characters to suggest the background in themselves, even when it is not visible. I want them to be so powerfully realized that we cannot imagine them apart from their physical and social context even when we see them in empty space.

s: *Because of your telling eye for detail, you do relate your characters to their background. In fact, as one goes through your films, he sees you relying less and less on dialogue and more and more on the physical environment to establish your characters.*

A: Yes.

s: *What did you mean in the Cannes manifesto that accompanied* L'avventura *when you said that man is burdened on the threshold of space by feelings entirely unsuited to his needs?*

A: I meant exactly what I said: that we are saddled with a culture that hasn't advanced as far as science. Scientific man is already on the moon, and yet we are still living with the moral concepts of Homer. Hence this upset, this disequilibrium that makes weaker people anxious and apprehensive, that makes it so difficult for them to adapt to the mechanism of modern life.

s: *That much I understand, but I'm puzzled about some implications. Do you mean to imply that the old moral baggage must be thrown away? If so, is that possible? Can man conceive of a new morality?*

A: Why go on using that word I loathe! We live in a society that compels us to go on using these concepts, and we no longer know what they mean. In the future—not soon, perhaps by the twenty-fifth century—these concepts will have lost their relevance. I can never understand how we have been able to follow these worn-out tracks, which have been laid down by panic in the face of nature. When man becomes reconciled to nature, when space becomes his true background, these words and concepts will have lost their meaning, and we will no longer have to use them.

s: *Let me match your statement with a moment in one of your films. By the end of* L'avventura, *Sandro recognizes that his promiscuity is harmful—to Claudia, with whom he has had the one intense relationship of his life, so far as we know. Do you mean us to believe that his ensuing guilt (inspiring him to tears) is an error because what makes him feel this guilt are conceptions of romantic love and personal responsibility that have become irrelevant burdens?*

A: Sandro is a character from a film shot in 1960 and is therefore entirely immersed in such moral problems. He is an Italian, a Catholic, and so he is a victim of this morality. What I said awhile ago is that such moral dilemmas will have no right to exist in a future that will be different from the present. Today we are just beginning to glimpse that future, but in 1960 we lived in a country with the Pope and the Vatican, which have always been extremely important to all of us. There isn't a school in Italy still, not a law court without its crucifix. We have Christ in our houses, and hence the problem of conscience, a problem fed to us as children that afterward we have no end of trouble getting rid of. All the characters in my films are fighting these problems, needing freedom, trying to find a way to cut themselves loose, but failing to rid themselves of conscience, a sense of sin, the whole bag of tricks.

s: *I don't think you're proposing something that's only a matter of time. Would it indeed ever be good to dispense with the bag of tricks, as you call it? I wonder if we shouldn't be more proud of this tradition going back to Homer than of the trip to the moon. Speaking only for myself—no, I'm sure I speak for others, too—the ending of* L'avventura *is so powerful because Sandro has the conscience to regret what he has done. To feel such regret, one has to believe in the supreme importance of human responsibility, and I can't conceive of art without that belief.*

A: I would like to make clear that I speak only of sensations. I am neither a sociologist nor a politician. All I can do is imagine for myself what the future will be like. Today we find ourselves face to face with some curious facts. For example, today's youth movement was born under the sign of anarchy. It has made anarchy point to a new society which will be more flexible, based on a system that can, by degrees, concur with contemporary events, facts, necessities. On the other hand, these youths structure themselves in mystic groups, and I must confess this rather disturbs me. I don't know what to think about it anymore. . . . I don't want what I am saying to sound like a prophecy or anything like an analysis of modern society . . . these are only feelings I have, and I am the least speculative man on earth.

s: *The implication of what you've been saying as far as* Blow-Up *is concerned intrigues me. Aren't you suggesting that you meant to depict the young people in that film positively?*

A: Yes, *Blow-Up* is favorable to the youth of that particular moment and place. I don't know how I would feel if I were to start studying certain groups in Italy, for example, about which I must admit only the vaguest knowledge.

s: *But I find the film critical, and so do others. For example, recall the peace-march scene, where the young people walk by with placards reading "Go," "On, on," "Forward." That's parody, yet you say you intended it to be favorable.*

A: When a scene is being shot, it is very difficult to know what one wants it to say, and even if one does know, there is always a difference between what one has in mind and the result on film. I never think ahead of the shot I'm going to make the following day because if I did, I'd only produce a bad imitation of the original image in my mind. So what you see on the screen doesn't represent my exact meaning, but only my possibilities of expression, with all the limitations implied in that phrase. Perhaps the scene reveals my incapacity to do better; perhaps I felt subconsciously ironic toward it. But it is on film; the rest is up to you.

s: *Last week I saw for the first time your documentary on the superstitions of Calabrese peasants, and I was struck by the similarities between these peasants and the hippies in whom you have such faith.*

A: What similarities?

s: *The hippies are also superstitious. The peasants have their magus, the hippies their guru. Hippies wear talismans, just like the Calabrese. Are they really the future? Aren't they bearing baggage even older than the moral tradition you find so burdensome?*

A: I believe these similarities derive from the hippies' desire not to reform present society, but to destroy it and, in destroying it, return almost to antiquity, to a purer, more primordial life, less—less mechanical . . . not based on the same principles as present life. Therefore, they return to the original source, and their gurus resemble the wizard in *Superstizione*. But I don't believe that if they ever reach a position of power, these young people would reconstruct society along antique lines, for that would be absurd. They need to rethink society, and nobody knows the answers yet.

S: *Therefore, both in* Blow-Up *and* Zabriskie Point *you aren't so much admiring their present behavior as hoping that they will produce something better?*

A: More or less. They believe in the possibility of life; that is what they show in their primitive communities. But I think that technology will one day shape all our actions. I don't think this can be helped, and there will be no chance to resist.

S: *I'm still puzzled. You say that the future must be technologically controlled and, moreover, that you desire that. But so far as I can see, your films suggest a revulsion against technology. In* Red Desert, *for example, there's a scene where Corrado talks to Giuliana's husband in front of a factory. The noise makes it impossible to hear, and the smoke makes it impossible for them to see each other. Soon the smoke envelops them so that we don't see them either. On the other hand, you painted the factory pipes so that they become rather attractive. On the one hand, you show that technological modern life is bad; on the other, you're saying it's good.*

A: But I'm not saying that technology is bad, something we can do without. I'm saying that present-day people can't adapt to it. These are merely terms of a conflict: "technology" and "old-fashioned characters." I'm not passing judgment, not at all. Ravenna, near the sea, has a stretch of factories, refineries, smokestacks, etc. on one side and a pine forest on the other. Somewhere I've written that the pine forest is much the more boring feature. Look at this, for example. I find these components of a television circuit absolutely marvelous. Look! They're wonderful. So you see, I'm an admirer of technology. From an outsider's view the insides of a computer are marvelous—not just its functioning but the way it is made, which is beautiful in itself. I f we pull a man apart, he is revolting; do the same thing to a computer and it remains beautiful. In *2001*, you know, the best things in the film are the machines, which are much more splendid than the idiotic humans. In *Red Desert*, I also confronted this technology and these machines with human beings who are morally and psychologically retarded and thus utterly unable to cope with modern life.

S: *You mean, then, that it is man's fault and not the fault of the environment that he can't adjust, is miserable, etc.?*

A: Yes. Modern life is very difficult for people who are unprepared. But this new environment will eventually facilitate more realistic relationships between people. For example, that scene, that great puff of—not smoke—steam that blasts out violently between the two characters. As I see it, that steam makes that relationship more real, because the two men have nothing to say to each other. Anything that might crop up would be hypocritical.

s: *OK. But isn't it also possible to say that they can't speak to each other because their environment deprives them of an inner life to communicate?*
A: No. I don't agree. In that case. . . . Wait, let me think it over a moment. I think people talk too much; that's the truth of the matter. I do. I don't believe in words. People use too many words and usually wrongly. I am sure that in the distant future people will talk much less and in a more essential way. If people talk a lot less, they will be happier. Don't ask me why. In my films it is the men who don't function properly—not the machines.

s: *That isn't what we're discussing; we're discussing the cause. Is this something unavoidable in man's soul or something located in a specific moment of history.*
A: You are trying to make me into some sort of philosopher of modern life—which is something I absolutely cannot be. When we say a character in my films doesn't function, we mean he doesn't function as a person, but he does function as a character—that is, until you take him as a symbol. At that point it is you who are not functioning. Why not simply accept him as a character, without judging him? Accept him for what he is. Accept him as a character in a story, without claiming that he derives or acquires meaning from that story. There may be meanings, but they are different for all of us.

s: *There is a difference between an anecdote and a story. It is interesting to hear the director whose films are most like stories and least like anecdotes asking me to take his characters as if they were anecdotal, people who are shown doing things without obvious significance.*
A: I'm not saying that they have no significance. I am saying that this mustn't be extracted from the film according to a preestablished scale of values. Don't regard my characters as symbols of a determined

society. See them as something that sparks a reaction within you so that they become a personal experience. The critic is a spectator and an artist insofar as he transforms the work into a personal thing of his own.

s: *What if I transform the film into something wrong?*
A: There is nothing in the film beyond what you feel.

s: *Ah, that's Berkeley: If a tree falls and no one sees it, it didn't fall. You believe that?*
A: No.

s: *Then the film is an objective fact and as such can be misapprehended. Unless you're willing to grant a meaning that the film forces or should force you to understand, you've got to accept every silly thing anyone has to say.*
A: What can I say? I saw a film made by a friend of mine that was panned by all the critics and withdrawn by the censor. So I wrote to the newspapers explaining why it was a good film. But I am the only one who liked it, the only person in Italy!

s: *But you're talking about evaluation, which is subjective. I'm talking about objective meaning. For example, is Sandro in* L'avventura *a weak or a strong character? Sandro is a fact, and the fact equals weakness. Right?*
A: No, not right. In a way, he is a strong character.

s: *In what way?*
A: He is capable of giving up something he had never believed he would have the power to give up. You need strength for that sort of renunciation.

s: *Why does he cry at the film's end?*
A: For several reasons. A man who kills people during a war—which is an act of strength and courage—can also have a crisis and break down and cry. But it doesn't last long. Ten minutes later he will probably have stopped crying. But perhaps the crying will have released him from his crisis. Who knows?

S: *If you think that Sandro's crying doesn't compromise him as a courageous character, I presume that you think that others of your characters possess courage. Yet most of them cry in the final shot.*

A: Where?

S: *The heroine cries at the end of* Cronaca—

A: No? Yes.

S: *—and that's the way one episode ends in* I vinti, *and* Il grido *means the outcry, which is what concludes the film. . . .*

A: And Nene in *Le amiche. . . .*

S: *And Sandro—and Vittoria in* Eclipse. . . .

A: No. That is a very optimistic film.

S: *Optimistic? Why, the lovers don't even see one another again, or do they?*

A: No. They never meet.

S: *If you wanted us to be so certain of this (let's leave the question of optimism aside for the moment), why does our last glimpse of Piero indicate a change in his character? Whereas he is frantic and agitated throughout the film, at the end we see him refusing to answer his phones, leaning back in his chair and smiling, while the breeze (which has such important symbolic overtones) ruffles his hair.*

A: There are people like that living all around me, full of contradictions, with weak and strong points, etc. My characters are ambiguous. Call them that. I don't mind. I am ambiguous myself. Who isn't?

S: *Well, then, what of your statement that the film is optimistic? You once said that it illustrated these sentiments of Dylan Thomas': "There must, be praised, some certainty, if not of loving, well then, at least of not loving." Isn't it stretching things to call that optimistic?*

A: No. If these characters can give up an affair that is just beginning, it is because they have a certain confidence in life. Otherwise, to speak in ugly old words, if they thought they could not survive the grief of having lost love, they would not have renounced each other but would have met again.

S: *But the film begins with a renunciation (when Vittoria leaves her first lover) which is one of the unhappiest scenes in your films. Why is that so unpleasant and the later renunciation a sign of optimism?*

A: Because the last scene is Vittoria's refusal to relive the first. That is, she doesn't want to suffer again the pangs of love. That is more or less the sense of it—put into words.

S: *What about the ending? Doesn't it symbolize the end of the world: that house which will never be finished, those bricks lying on the ground, the rainwater pouring out of the barrel, the headline "Peace is weak"?*

A: That only shows the error of this way of looking at films, because if we go back there, we will see that the house was finished!

S: *All right. Let's change the subject. In America, the pace and rhythm of* Blow-Up *were surprising to audiences used to your previous films. Do you think, albeit subconsciously, that you made* Blow-Up *a briskly paced film in response to criticism of your "slowness"?*

A: Absolutely not. The film was cut that way because I felt that this story needed such a rhythm; these characters moved nervously. I never at any time thought of the critics because I rarely read them.

S: *What is the function of the neon sign in* Blow-Up *that can't be understood since it isn't a word?*

A: I didn't want people to be able to read that sign; whether it advertised one product or another was of no importance. I placed it there because I needed a source of light in the night scenes. Furthermore, I liked having the sign near the park. It is there for an obvious reason: to break up the romantic atmosphere.

S: *Are you disturbed by critics who want to go beyond that level of explanation?*

A: No, because, as I've said, every object in a film is an experience of the viewer's. After all, what does the director do? He conveys what he thinks he has seen. But, good Lord, the meaning of reality, living as we do enclosed in ourselves, isn't always clear to us. We could discuss for hours an episode or even an object found on the street. And the same thing is true of a filmed episode or object. Except that I never ask explanations from what I see in real life, but with a film I ask the director. But the director is only a man. Very often I cannot give an explanation because I see only images, and images are what I transfer to the screen. Very often these images have no explanation, no *raison d'être* beyond themselves.

s: *A moment ago you said you read criticism rarely. Are there no critics who seem important to you?*

A: Sometimes I pick up a magazine and read a piece of film criticism—to the end only if I like it. I don't like those which are too free with praise because their reasons seem wrong and that annoys me. Critics who attack me do so for such contradictory reasons that they confuse me, and I am afraid that if I am influenced by one, I will sin according to the standards of the other.

s: *I'd like to get back to* Blow-Up. *In the so-called orgy sequence one sees two men in the background behind the models. Why?*

A: There is no reason for it. They are two cameramen whom I did not notice and so forgot to cut.

s: *It seems to me that a statement you make in the introduction to the Italian edition of your screenplays has a particular relevance to* Blow-Up: *"We know that under the image revealed there is another which is truer to reality and under this image still another and yet again still another under this last one, right down to the true image of that reality, absolute, mysterious, which no one will ever see or perhaps right down to the decomposition of any image, of any reality."*

A: I would say that this applies more to the finale of *Eclipse* than to *Blow-Up*, but it applies to *Blow-Up* as well. In the final scene of *Eclipse*, I was trying for a sort of decomposition of things.

s: *You are quoted as saying that the two main components of your technique are the camera and the actors.*

A: I never said such a thing. Where did you read it?

s: *I forget.*

A: People are always misquoting me.

s: *Like Rex Reed?*

A: He made that whole interview up. I've never said what you report. I've always said that the actor is only an element of the image, rarely the most important. The actor is important with his dialogue, with the landscape, with a gesture—but the actor in himself is nothing.

s: *Indeed, your films are vulnerable on this ground. For example, why do you use so many foreign actors whose voices need to be dubbed into Italian? Why do you use an actor like Richard Harris, who, in my opinion, is so inexpressive?*

A: You must bear in mind that a director isn't a painter who takes a canvas and does what he likes with it. We are more like painters in past centuries who were ordered to paint frescoes to specific measurements. Among the people in the fresco may be a bishop, the prince's wife, etc. The fresco isn't bad simply because the painter used for models people from the court of the prince who ordered and paid for it. At the moment I made *Red Desert* the Italian actor I wanted wasn't free, or asked for too much money, or didn't have an important enough name. Harris wasn't right—but not because he was foreign. Still, I chose him, and the mistake is mine. But for the voice: Why shouldn't cinema make such a change? The voice I dubbed in suited the role better than Harris' own voice, which is soft, toneless. I needed a stronger voice to match the image of Harris' figure. But I must repeat, when we find ourselves up against practical obstacles that can't be overcome, we must go forward. You either make the film as you can or don't make it at all.

s: *Let's talk about the camera now. How much independence do you give your cameraman? That is to say, does Di Venanzo or Di Palma etc. impose his style on the film he shoots?*

A: No. I have always imposed my wishes on the cameraman. Moreover, I have always picked them at the outset of their careers and, to a certain extent, have formed them myself. I used Di Venanzo, for example, in my segment of *L'amore in città*. I remember that at the time he wasn't used to handling photofloods, photospots—that type of lighting—he was still using projected lighting. I got him to use the other sort, to shoot in reduced zones, and to use a special bulb that produced just the quality I wanted. He was using the wrong sort of film until I made him use Kodak.

Now he indicates in his contracts that he will shoot only with Kodak; I had to impose that choice on him, though he went on to make it his own style. Scavarda, the man who shot *L'avventura*, has never made another film that was as well photographed. In my short documentary *N.U.* I used Ventimiglia. His photography was superb. But I chose the shots, even the moments at which they should be taken. I would say, "We will start at twelve twenty and finish at twelve thirty-two, because after that the light won't be any good." Everything depends on what you put in front of the camera, what perspectives you create, contrasts, colors. The cameraman can do great things, provided he is well grounded technically. If a person hasn't the raw material, I obviously couldn't do anything with him. But all I ask of a cameraman is technical experience. Everything else is up to me. I was amazed to find that in America cameramen are surprised that this is the way I work.

S: *In the interview you had with Alberto Moravia about* Zabriskie Point *you said that America was made up of two populations: two-thirds old and awful; one-third young and fine. Is that what you feel?*

A: Well, perhaps I got the proportions wrong. Two-thirds and one-third is too absolute a statement, and I don't know the whole of America well enough to say that. Obviously, in America as elsewhere, one finds contrasts in the populations, but because it is such a violent country, the contrasts stand out. That is why I have said that Wallace and the hippies are brothers: They are each children of a country that runs to extremes.

S: *You once said that critics should not speak of documentary elements in your feature films but rather of narrative elements in your documentaries. If you could, would you prefer dispensing with narrative?*

A: No. I always want to tell stories. But they must be stories that evolve, like our own lives. Perhaps what I seek is a new kind of story. In my next films I am going to change the kinds of stories I tell and the way I tell them.

S: *Do you find that being a famous director causes you to have difficulties with other people?*

A: Yes. There are times when my being an observer changes the scene. The moment I appear, people feel a little intimidated, and that intimidates me. Because I would like to feel part of the natural atmosphere. Often I have had to resort to tricks so as to be able to see things in their natural state. But difficulties remain, and I find them very annoying.

S: *Your films show a familiarity with Italian high life. Do you enter this world out of choice or to get material?*

A: It is very hard to make a distinction. One doesn't enter groups of people simply because one wants or needs to. One has an infinite number of opportunities that occur for no particular reason. Sometimes you feel a sudden unexpected pleasure at being where you find yourself. The reason may be frivolous—well, why not? I'm not the cold-blooded sort who carries a little notebook around and jots down phrases from the conversations he hears. I try to live an easygoing, natural life. What remains inside me is what I'll need to draw on.

S: *In an interview I had with him, John Updike said something that fascinated me: "Being an artist is dangerous because it allows one to turn one's pain too quickly to profit."*

A: I couldn't use that phrase today—"being an artist"—as if that were something exceptional. And if somebody transmutes his pain into profit, very good. I find that the most wonderful way to kill pain.

S: *Why do you say "today"? Could you have used the phrase "being an artist" in some other period?*

A: Yes, of course. I think that during the Renaissance everything was influenced by art. Now the world is so much more important than art that I can no longer imagine a future artistic function.

S: *But today what is the function?*

A: I don't know.

S: *You don't know?*

A: Do you?

S: *Yes.*

A: Then tell me.

s: *You want* me *to tell* you *what the function of art is! No, you tell me what you think of François Truffaut.*

A: I think his films are like a river, lovely to see, to bathe in, extraordinarily refreshing and pleasant. Then the water flows and is gone. Very little of the pleasant feeling remains because I soon feel dirty again and need another bath.

s: *Do you mean his films pass away because their images aren't memorable?*

A: Yes, that's part of it. No. His images are as powerful as those of Resnais or Godard, but his stories are frivolous. I suppose that's what I object to.

s: *But I thought you weren't too concerned about the significance of a story.*

A: René Clair told light stories, too, but they touch me more. I don't know why Truffaut's leave me unmoved. I'm not trying to say that he has no significance. I only mean that the way he tells a story doesn't come to anything. Perhaps he doesn't tell my kind of story. Perhaps that's it.

s: *Do you dislike his way of working because it so emphasizes tricky camera effects?*

A: There is never an image that gives me a blow in the stomach. I need these punches. Godard, on the other hand, flings reality in our faces, and I'm struck by this. But never by Truffaut.

s: *Let me get back to your films for a moment. At the end of* L'avventura *do you mean us to believe that Sandro and Claudia are drawn closer together by their experience?*

A: No. I don't mean to say anything at that moment except what the moment itself says: Her are two people who have their own stories—rather dissimilar ones—but who are, for the moment, rather close. What their future is I don't know. I couldn't say anything about it and wouldn't be interested in the subject.

s: *When I ask you about the last scene of* L'avventura, *you say you can't tell me anything beyond it. Yet earlier, when I made a statement about the end of* Eclipse, *you countered me with a fact occurring in the real world after the film was finished. In one case, you're insisting that the work of art stops*

and we only know so much as it tells us: in the other, you speak of the work
as if its life flowed on into the life from which it came.

A: [Silence.]

S: *All right, I'll go back to* L'avventura. *Let me tell you what I think the*
end means. Now Claudia has looked at Sandro, and she knows him
completely. That's all.

A: Yes. And it has no significance, no necessary effect on their future.
Time and time again we bind ourselves to people whose limitations we
know all too well, and so what? You are absolutely right. The story is over.

S: *Why does Anna leave behind her the Bible and* Tender Is the Night?
Did you choose the latter simply because you like Fitzgerald, or is the book
supposed to point to Anna's relationship with her father?

A: No. I merely thought that Scott Fitzgerald was an author that a girl
like that would read.

S: *There are a number of long shots in the film that don't seem objective,*
that rather suggest the perspective of an onlooker. For example, at one point
Sandro's car is in a piazza. Claudia and Sandro are seen moving around. Then
we cut to a distance shot taken from the end of a street leading into the piazza,
and we track into them. Is this supposed to suggest that Anna may be there?

A: That is the most ambiguous shot in the film. I think it is impossible
to explain. I don't know why I wanted it. I don't believe Anna was there;
I shouldn't say so, at least. But it is a great effort for me to recall the mood
I was in when I shot that. I felt the need for mystery, which the tracking-in
produces. That's what you feel, and that's why you wonder about the way
it moves. I knew that shot would create puzzlement. I don't know what
mystery was created, but some mystery was what I needed.

S: *Whether or not you shoot a scene instinctively—*

A: I always know where I want to go.

S: *Yes. You've some sense of a desired effect for the spectator. What I'm*
trying to get at is the effect produced. Look, the spectator is discovering in
L'avventura *that Sandro and Claudia aren't really searching for Anna, right?*

A: They're searching for her at the beginning, but, little by little, they
forget her.

s: *Exactly. Now, if that's true, the spectator has to become aware of the widening discrepancy between their action and its ostensible purpose. We've got to keep feeling that they're not doing enough, that they're going through the motions but don't really want to find her. So in the shot we're talking of, the track-in makes us feel "Maybe Anna's there. Why don't they walk down the street and—"*

A: Why should she be there?

s: *Why not? We don't know where she went. She could be anywhere.*

A: Somebody told me that she committed suicide, but I don't believe it.

s: *I'd like to ask just one question about* La notte. *Even among critics sensitive to your work I've heard derogation of the last scene. They say they find it implausible that Mastroianni should be able to listen to so much of Moreau's reading without realizing that she is reading his own letter. Moreover, even if plausible, the point made about the marriage has already been demonstrated and the letter-reading is redundant. What do you think about this?*

A: Nothing at all. The letter gives a precise portrait of the writer. It's a modestly written letter, showing how correct he was to think his talent unsatisfactory. Perhaps I should have had it read so that the words could not be understood. But then one might have had the impression that it was a very beautiful letter, whereas it wasn't even a nice one. And it is needed for the rhythm of the final sequence, which ends in a squalid, unnecessary act of lovemaking. Without the letter—the emotion it provokes—without the proof that he had forgotten it, that he was so drained of feeling, the action would have been too brutal and would have had a different significance.

s: *Talking about* La notte, *I'm reminded of another subject I wanted to bring up: the question of repeated moments in your films. At the end of* La notte *the camera leaves the couple in the sand trap and pans to a new day dawning, with obvious irony. The same effect occurs in your first feature film,* Cronaca di un amore, *when the lovers meet in the planetarium. At precisely the moment when we first realize the hopelessness of their relationship, the lights go on, signaling a new day.*

A: Not at all. It is only the light going on because the performance is finished.

s: *What about ending both* Blow-Up *and the English episode of* I vinti *with a tennis court?*

A: People play tennis all over England. The two scenes have different purposes.

s: *Why did you use the tennis court in* I vinti?

A: Because it was near the courthouse and because I wanted to show this sort of life continuing while a man was condemned to death. A frivolous game.

s: *But you've just pointed to a similarity of meaning. In both cases a murder has occurred, and yet we end up with a frivolous game.*

A: It's not frivolous. The game is serious.

s: *Without a ball?*

A: Yes, in a way.

s: *In what way?*

A: I don't know in what way, but I know that it is serious. I shot it seriously.

s: *I'd like to get your reaction to a criticism that has been made of your films from* La notte *on. For example, Dwight Macdonald, who was one of your most devoted admirers, eventually came to feel that you show effects in characters without detailing their causes. What do you say about this?*

A: Is it important to show why a character is what he is? No. He is. That's all.

s: *I agree with that for all of your films except* Red Desert. *In the others we see normal characters at a certain moment, and all our questions are about that moment. But Giuliana is sick, and sick people always make us want to know how they got that way.*

A: To answer that question, I should have had to make another film. How someone becomes neurotic is a long, complicated story.

s: *But doesn't the film show that her ambience is, in some sense, the cause of her neurosis?*

A: Yes, but nobody becomes neurotic if they haven't a—I mean, neurosis attaches itself to a fertile ground where it can flourish. There is always a physical basis so that the environment plays its part only to the degree that the physical makeup of the person is susceptible to its influence. It doesn't interest me to go into the origins of neurosis, only its effects.

s: *But there are characters in* Red Desert *who resist their environment and don't become neurotic. What typifies their makeup and is absent from Giuliana's?*

A: I don't know, but Giuliana was more important to me than the others because she represents an extreme version of them. When I was searching locations for *Red Desert* I found myself among whole families of neurotics. One of them, for example, lives near an electric works whose turbines were going day and night. I found that noise almost unbearable, so that by the end of the day I thought I was losing my mind. However, the woman of that family never complained. Yet when we started up our generators, she came to the door and began to scream at us. Our generators were nothing compared to the turbines, but you see, they produced a new noise. That woman was a neurotic without knowing it. One day she will explode, just like Giuliana. In her, there is that basis for the environment to work on. Who knows why? Hereditary defects, maternal or paternal? There are a thousand reasons why a person is neurotic. Then one day the neurosis explodes. That explosion is what interests me.

s: *In this film, am I right in thinking that the color represents Giuliana's state of mind?*

A: Yes. It is transfigured from the point of view of a neurotic.

s: *But there are problems. For example, in the hotel scene, the plants etc. are white before she enters the lobby. That is, we see color distortions that don't seem to be the result of her perspective.*

A: It strikes me as an oversimplification to claim that all the shots from her point of view must be transfigured and those from anybody else's not. The whole world around her is transfigured.

s: *For us as well?*

A: Not for us. I mean that she is aware of the whole world crowding in around her.

S: *Let me pose a similar question about another shot. In your interview with Godard, he asked you about the sequence when Corrado is telling the workers about Patagonia. Suddenly we cut from him to the wall, and the camera pans, tilts up, etc. You said this was Corrado's mind wandering to Giuliana. I find this difficult to accept. There is no other shot in the film from his perspective, and there is no reference to Giuliana made in his dialogue. How can the audience know that he is thinking of her just from seeing the shot of the wall?*

A: I only said that he was distracted as he spoke and that he might have been thinking of Giuliana. Later he exits; what for? It seems likely that he is thinking of this love affair that has only just begun. After all, what does a man in love think about? It goes without saying that I could not insert a cut to Giuliana. Godard might have done that. I never could.

S: *Why does the ceiling change colors in the seduction scene?*

A: You mustn't ask me to explain everything I do. I can't. That's that. How can I say why at a certain moment I needed this. How can I explain why I needed a confusion of colors?

S: *Recalling the end of* Il grido, Red Desert *opens with a strike. Why did you start the film this way?*

A: Perhaps because I wanted to show that when a man is absorbed in his personal problems, he can ignore everything else.

S: *But you're talking about* Il grido. *I asked you about* Red Desert.

A: They are totally different.

S: *But the strike—*

A: There is no strike in *Red Desert*.

S: *Yes. At the beginning.*

A: Ah, at the beginning. But the situation is different. She isn't a person from the factory; she's only the wife of one. These problems are far from her concern.

S: *That's what I've said. In both cases a strike is going on so that we can see how little concerned with it the central character is.*

A: Well, so what! [We both laugh.]

S: *Well, you are right in a way. Because the scene in* Red Desert *contains one implication missing from* Il grido: *a contrast between workers and the bourgeoisie. Because Giuliana is not only a neurotic, but also a bourgeoisie. In your film both seem forms of incapacity.*

A: Okay. But I would never be able to make this comparison.

S: *There is so much evidence for it in the film. Remember the woman whose apartment Giuliana and Corrado visit. They offer her husband a well-paying job, but she won't let him leave her. That scene depicts an obvious contrast between the familial feelings of the workers and the bourgeois characters who have already embarked on the road to adultery. Or remember that worker to whom Giuliana talks near the antennas.*

A: [Silence.]

S: *In the preface to the Italian edition of your screenplays you say, "The greatest danger for those working in the cinema is the extraordinary possibility it offers for lying." What did you mean?*

A: To give an interpretation that we know is untrue to life. Because at that moment it is more interesting or amusing to put something in, to forget the real sense of what we are doing in our amusement with the medium.

S: *Here you are speaking of a standard outside yourself; usually you say your only standard is what pleases you.*

A: Whenever I make a film, I have inside me a certain truth—"truth" is a bad word. Here inside, rather, I have a confusion in the pit of my stomach, a sort of tumor I cure by making the film. If I forget that tumor, I lie. It is easy to forget, even if I subconsciously realize I am forgetting. Very easy.

S: *Do you mean lying so as to please the audience?*

A: No. Suppose I have to film a character coming down those stairs. I want to focus on his face because his expression while seeing a second character is very important in this moment. So I make him come down, but then my fancy is caught by that Lichtenstein. I like that, too. So I make the character stand for a moment before the Lichtenstein, with its glowing greens and whites. I like that. I'm tempted by it, but it is a mistake. It means making the painting important at the very moment that the only important thing is the character.

S: *You've been quoted as saying that Aldo in* Il grido *is an admirable character because he seeks to break out of his unhappiness. Is that what you believe?*
A: No.

S: *So far as I can see, he's a sort of egoist of grief. All the women he meets are much braver than he.*
A: I agree.

S: *Am I correct in believing that you did not write the commentary that introduces* I vinti?
A: I had a fight with my producers, and because of that, I was helpless. They insisted on an introduction and conclusion. I worked on it a little, but it isn't mine.

S: *Did you learn anything of value from your apprenticeship to Carné?*
A: I was in general disagreement with him for temperamental reasons and because we came from such different backgrounds. His poetic world never interested me. Perhaps what he taught me was a certain method of framing at which he was especially good. But I think time has dealt badly with his films.

S: *I was surprised to read that you like Andy Warhol's films. Could you tell me why?*
A: I can't say I like his films—some yes, the others no. I like his freedom. He does what he wants to and is fundamentally contemptuous toward cinema, which is usually taken too seriously. But I don't mean to say that he is contemptuous toward his own films. He makes more films than paintings now, so he must like his films. What I admire are his means: his characters do and say what they want to and are, therefore, wholly original in contemporary films.

S: *Who are your favorite Italian directors?*
A: Fellini and Visconti. The only young man who seems very promising to me at the moment is Bellocchio. There are others who

have possibilities—Maselli, for one—but they haven't yet realized them. But I know all these men personally and so prefer not to discuss them.

s: *Do you think any American directors belong in the front rank?*

A: I don't have any favorite directors, in truth. My taste changes according to my current interests. I was, however, very impressed by *Easy Rider*. There are many young men today who are breaking the rules of American cinema, and they interest me. I've noticed in their work the influence of underground films; this shows how fruitful that movement has been.

s: *With the exception of* Blow-Up *each of your films is about a woman who loses something for having placed her faith in some man. Why do you keep returning to this plot?*

A: You are making me think of this just now. It's very difficult to explain what I do. It is much more instinctive than you realize; much, much more. For example, I was amused by the articles I read about Joseph Losey, for I know how he works. He reads a book; if he likes it, he makes a film. But if a producer says, "Make another film," he drops his own choice. For me, of course, it is different, but even for me, the reasons that make me interested in a subject are, how shall I say, fickle. Many times I have chosen, among three stories, one for reasons that are entirely accidental: I get up and think this one will be stupendous because the night before I had a certain dream. Or perhaps I put it better by saying that I had found inside myself reasons why this particular story seems more valid.

s: *Joseph Losey is a dreadful director. You see this in* Accident, *which is a veritable parody of Antonioni, in which he does things you do but for no discernible reason. Now are you trying to tell me—leave the selection of stories aside—that when you film a story, you are as unconscious of motives as he seems to be? Or is it simply that you don't wish to explain your motives?*

A: I always have motives, but I forget them.

s: *Sometimes you'll explain something in your films and at other times you refuse.*

A: You make me look for a reason. I had none.

s: *But in some cases. . . .*

A: Maybe what I told you so far is completely wrong.

s: *Sometimes you are willing—*

A: I am never willing.

s: *But you do—*

A: Only when I am forced. Otherwise, I would prefer not to.

Antonioni Discusses *The Passenger*

BETTY JEFFRIES DEMBY AND
LARRY STURHAHN/1975

BETTY JEFFRIES DEMBY: *Did you do the screenplay for* The Passenger*?*
MICHELANGELO ANTONIONI: I have always written my own scripts, even if what I wrote was the result of discussions with my collaborators. *The Passenger*, however, was written by someone else. Naturally I made changes to adapt it to my way of thinking and shooting. I like to improvise— in fact, I can't do otherwise. It is only in this phase—that is, when I actually see it—that the film becomes clear to me. Lucidity and clearness are not among my qualities, if I have any.

LARRY STURHAHN: *In this case, were there any major changes in the screenplay?*
MA: The whole idea, the way the film is done, is different. The mood is changed—there is more of a spy feeling, it's more political.

LS: *Do you always adapt a piece of material to suit your particular needs?*
MA: Always. I got the idea for *Blow-Up* from a short story by Cortázar, but even there I changed a lot. And *The Girlfriends* was based on a story by Pavese. But I work on the scripts by myself with some collaboration, and as far as the act of writing is concerned, I always do that myself.

LS: *I have often felt that the short story is a better medium to adapt to film because it's compact and about the same length as a film.*

From *Filmmakers Newletter*, no. 8 (9), July 1975.

MA: I agree. *The Girlfriends* was based on a short novel, *Among Women Only*. And the most difficult pages to translate into images were the best pages as far as the novel and the writing were concerned. I mean the best of the pages—the pages I liked the most—were the most difficult. When you have just an idea it's easier. Putting something into a different medium is difficult because the first medium was there first. In a novel there's usually too much dialogue—and getting rid of the dialogue is difficult.

LS: *Do you change the dialogue even further when you're on the set?*
MA: Yes, I change it a lot. I need to hear a line pronounced by the actors.

LS: *How much do you see of a film when you're looking at the script? Do you see the locations? Do you see where you're going to work with the film?*
MA: Yes, more or less. But I never try to copy what I see because this is impossible. I will never find the exact counterpart of my imagination.

LS: *So you wipe the slate clean when you're looking for your location?*
MA: Yes. I just go and look. I know what I need, of course. Actually, it's very simple.

BJD: *Then you don't leave the selection of location up to your assistants?*
MA: The location is the very substance of which the shot is made. Those colors, that light, those trees, those objects, those faces. How could I leave the choice of all this to my assistants? Their choices would be entirely different from mine. Who knows the film I am making better than me?

BJD: *Was* The Passenger *shot entirely on location?*
MA: Yes.

BJD: *I believe most of your other films were, too. Why do you have such a strong preference for location shooting?*
MA: Because reality is unpredictable. In the studio everything has been foreseen.

BJD: *One of the most interesting scenes in the film is the one which takes place on the roof of the Gaudí cathedral in Barcelona. Why did you choose this location?*

MA: The Gaudí towers reveal, perhaps, the oddity of an encounter between a man who has the name of a dead man and a girl who doesn't have any name. (She doesn't need it in the film.)

BJD: *I understand that in* Red Desert *you actually painted the grass and colored the sea to get the effects you wanted. Did you do anything similar in* The Passenger?
MA: No. In *The Passenger* I have not tampered with reality. I looked at it with the same eye with which the hero, a reporter, looks at the events he is reporting on. Objectivity is one of the themes of the film. If you look closely, there are two documentaries in the film, Locke's documentary on Africa and mine on him.

BJD: *What about the sequence where Nicholson is isolated in the desert? The desert is especially striking, and the color is unusually intense and burning. Did you use any special filters or forced processing to create this effect?*
MA: The color is the color of the desert. We used a filter, but not to alter it; on the contrary, in order *not* to alter it. The exact warmness of the color was obtained in the laboratory by the usual processes.

BJD: *Did shooting in the desert with its high temperatures and blowing sand create any special problems for you?*
MA: Not especially. We brought along a refrigerator in which to keep the film, and we tried to protect the camera from the blowing sand by covering it in any possible way.

BJD: *How do you cast your actors?*
MA: I know the actors, I know the characters of the film. It is a question of juxtaposition.

LS: *Specifically, why did you choose Jack Nicholson and Maria Schneider?*
MA: Jack Nicholson and I wanted to make a film together, and I thought he would be very good, very right for this part. The same for Maria Schneider. She was my understanding of the girl. And I think she was perfect for the role. I may have changed it a bit for her, but that is a reality I must face: you can't invent an abstract feeling. Being a "star" is

irrelevant—if the actor is different from the part, if the feeling doesn't work, even Jack Nicholson won't get the part.

LS: *Are you saying that Nicholson acts like a star, that he's hard to work with?*
MA: No. He's very competent and a very, very good actor, so it's easy to work with him. He's intense, yet he doesn't create any problems—you can cut his hair (I didn't,) he's not concerned about his "good" side or whether the camera is too high or too low; you can do whatever you want.

BJD: *You once said that you see actors as part of the composition; that you don't want to explain the characters' motivations to them but want them to be passive. Do you still handle actors this way?*
MA: I never said that I want the actors to be passive. I said that sometimes if you explain too much, you run the risk that the actors become their own directors, and this doesn't help the film. Nor the actor. I prefer working with the actors not on an intellectual but on a sensorial level. To stimulate rather than teach.

First of all, I am not very good at talking to them because it is difficult for me to find the right words. Also, I am not the kind of director who wants "messages" on each line. So I don't have anything more to say about the scene than how to do it. What I try to do is provoke them, put them in the right mood. And then I watch them through the camera and at that moment tell them to do this or that. But not before. I have to have my shot, and they are an element of the image—and not always the most important element.

Also, I see the film in its unity whereas an actor sees the film through his character. It was difficult working with Jack Nicholson and Maria Schneider at the same time because they are such completely different actors. They are natural in opposite ways: Nicholson knows where the camera is and acts accordingly. But Maria doesn't know where the camera is—she doesn't know anything; she just lives the scene. Which is great. Sometimes she just moves and no one knows how to follow her. She has a gift for improvising, and I like that—I like to improvise.

LS: *Then you don't preplan what you are going to do on the set? You don't sit down the evening before or in the morning and say, "I'm going to do this and this"?*
MA: No. Never, never.

LS: *You just let it happen as you're on the set?*
MA: Yes.

LS: *Do you at least let your actors rehearse a scene first, or do you just go right into it?*
MA: I rehearse very little—maybe twice, but not more. I want the actors to be fresh, not tired.

BJD: *What about camera angles and camera movement? Do you carefully preplan in this area?*
MA: Very carefully.

LS: *Are you able to make decisions about print takes very soon, or do you—?*
MA: Immediately.

LS: *Then you don't shoot a lot of takes?*
MA: No. Three. Maybe five or six. Sometimes we may do fifteen, but that is very rare.

LS: *Would you be able to estimate how much footage you shoot per day?*
MA: No.

LS: *Just whatever you can accomplish?*
MA: In China I made as many as eighty shots in one day, but that was very different work; I had to rush.

LS: *How long did it take to do the final scene of* The Passenger?
MA: Eleven days. But that was not because of me but because of the wind. It was very windy weather and so difficult to keep the camera steady.

BJD: *One critic has said that the final seven-minute sequence is destined to become a classic of film history. Can you explain how you conceived it?*
MA: I had the idea for the final sequence as soon as I started shooting. I knew, naturally, that my protagonist must die, but the idea of seeing him die bored me. So I thought of a window and what was outside, the afternoon sun. For a second, just for a fraction—Hemingway crossed

my mind: "Death in the Afternoon." And the arena. We found the arena and immediately realized this was the place. But I didn't yet know how to realize such a long shot. I had heard about the Canadian camera, but I had no first-hand knowledge of its possibilities. In London, I saw some film tests. I met with the English technicians responsible for the camera and we decided to try. There were many problems to solve. The biggest was that the camera was 16 mm and I needed 35 mm. To modify it would have involved modifying its whole equilibrium since the camera is mounted on a series of gyroscopes. However, I succeeded in doing it.

LS: *Did you use a zoom lens or a very slow dolly?*
MA: A zoom was mounted on the camera. But it was only used when the camera was about to pass through the gate.

LS: *It's interesting how the camera moves toward the man in the center against the wall but we never get to see him, the camera never focuses on him.*
MA: Well, he is part of the landscape, that's all. And everything is in focus—everything. But not specifically on him. I didn't want to go closer to anybody. The surprise is the use of this long shot. You see the girl outside and you see her movements, and you understand very well without going closer to her what she's doing, maybe what her thoughts are. You see, I am using this very long shot *like* closeups; the shot actually takes the place of closeups.

LS: *Did you cover that shot in any other way or was this your sole commitment?*
MA: I had this idea of doing it in one take at the beginning of the shooting and I kept working on it all during the shooting.

LS: *How closely do you work with your cinematographer?*
MA: Who is the cinematographer? We don't have this *character* in Italy.

LS: *How big a crew do you work with?*
MA: I prefer a small crew. On this one I had a big crew—forty people—but we had union problems so it couldn't be smaller.

LS: *How important is your continuity girl to your work?*
MA: Very important. Because we have to change in the middle, we can't go chronologically.

BJD: *How closely do you work with your editor?*
MA: We always work together. However, I edited *Blow-Up* myself and the first version of *The Passenger* as well. But it was too long and so I redid it with Franco Arcalli, my editor. Then it was still too long, so I cut it by myself again.

BJD: *How closely does the edited version reflect what you had in mind when you were shooting?*
MA: Unfortunately, as soon as I finish shooting a film I don't like it. And then little by little I look at it and start to find something. But when I finish shooting it's as if I haven't shot anything. Then when I have my material—when it's been shot in my head and on the actual film—it's as if it's been shot by someone else. So I look at it with great detachment and then I start to cut. And I like this phase.

But on this one I had to change a lot because the first cut was very long. I shot much more than I needed because I had very little time to prepare the film—Nicholson had some engagements and I had to shoot very quickly.

LS: *So you didn't have time before the shooting to cut your screenplay down to size.*
MA: Right. I shot much more than was necessary because I didn't know what I would need. So the first cut was very long—four hours. Then I had another that ran two hours and twenty minutes. And now it's two hours.

LS: *Do you shoot lip sync—record the sound on location?*
MA: Yes.

LS: *What about dubbing?*
MA: A little—when the noise is too much.

BJD: *The soundtrack is an enormously important part of your films. For* L'avventura *you recorded every possible shading of the sound of the sea. Did you do anything similar for* The Passenger?

MA: My rule is always the same: for each scene, I record a soundtrack without actors.

BJD: *Sometimes you make critical plot points by using sound alone. For instance, in the last sequence we have only the sound of the opening door and what might be a gunshot to let us know the protagonist has been killed. Would you comment on this?*

MA: A film is both image and sound. Which is the most important? I put them both on the same plane. Here I used sound because I could not avoid looking at my hero—I could not avoid hearing the sounds connected with the actual killing since Locke, the killer, and the camera were in the same room.

BJD: *You use music only rarely in the film, but with great effectiveness. Can you explain how you choose which moments will be scored?*

MA: I can't explain it. It is something I feel. When the film is finished, I watch it a couple of times thinking only about the music. In the places where I feel it is missing, I put it in—*not* as score music but as source music.

LS: *Whom do you admire among American directors?*

MA: I like Coppola; I think *The Conversation* was a very good film. I like Scorsese; I saw *Alice Doesn't Live Here Anymore* and liked it very much—it was a very simple but very sincere film. And you have Altman and *California Split*—he's a very good observer of California society. And Steven Spielberg is also very good.

LS: *I have the impression from your films that your people tend to just appear full-blown in a particular situation, that there's not much of a past to your characters. For instance, we find Nicholson in an alienated place with no roots behind him. And the same for the girl; she's just there. It's as though people are just immediately in an immediate present. There's no background to them, as it were.*

MA: I think it's a different way of looking at the world. The other way is the older way. This is the modern way of looking at people. Today everyone has less background than in the past. We're freer. A girl today can go anywhere, just like the one in the film, with just one bag and no thoughts for her family or past. She doesn't have to carry any baggage with her.

BJD: *You mean moral baggage?*
MA: Precisely. Moral, psychological luggage. But in the older movies people have homes and we see these homes and the people in them. You see Nicholson's home, but he's not tied down, he's used to going all over the world.

BJD: *Yet you seem to find the struggle for identity interesting.*
MA: Personally, I mean to get away from my historical self and find a new one. I need to renew myself this way. Maybe this is an illusion, but I think it is a way to reach something new.

BJD: *I was thinking of the television journalist like Mr. Locke getting bored with life. Then there's no hope for anything because that's one of the more interesting careers.*
MA: Yes, in a way. But it's also a very cynical career. Also, his problem is that he *is* a journalist—he can't get involved in everything he reports because he's a filter. His job is always to talk about and show something or someone else, but he himself is not involved. He's a witness, not a protagonist. And that's the problem.

LS: *Do you see any similarity between your role as a film director and the role of Locke in the film?*
MA: In this film it may be, yes; it's part of the film. But it's different in a way. In *The Passenger* I tried to look at Locke the way Locke looks at reality. After all, everything I do is absorbed in a kind of collision between myself and reality.

LS: *Some people think of film as being the most real of the arts and some think it's purely illusion, a fake, because everything in a movie is still pictures. Can you speak a bit about this in relation to* The Passenger?
MA: I don't know if I could speak about it—if I could do the same thing with words I would be a writer and not a film director. I don't have anything to *say* but perhaps something to *show*. There's a difference.

That's why it's very difficult for me to talk about my films. What I want to do is make the film. I know what I have to do. Not what I *mean*. I never think about the meaning because I can't.

LS: *You're a film director and you make images, yet I find that in your films the key people have a problem with seeing—they're trying to find things or they've lost something. Like the photographer in* Blow-Up *trying to find reality in his own work. Are you, as a director working in this medium, frustrated at not being able to find reality?*

MA: Yes and no. In some ways I capture reality in making a film—at least I have a film in my hands, which is something concrete. What I am facing may not be the reality I was looking for, but I've found someone or something every time. I have added something more to myself in making the film.

LS: *Then it's a challenge each time?*

MA: Yes! I fight for it. Can you imagine? I lost my male character in the desert before the ending of *Red Desert* because Richard Harris went away without telling me. The ending was supposed to be all three of them—the wife, the husband, and the third man. So I didn't know how to finish the film. I didn't stop working during the day, but at night I would walk around the harbor thinking until I finally came up with the idea for the ending I have now. Which I think was better than the previous one—fortunately.

BJD: *Have you ever wanted to make an autobiographical film?*

MA: No. And I'll tell you why: because I don't like to look back; I always look forward. Like everyone, I have a certain number of years to live, so this year I want to look forward and not back—I don't want to think about the past years, I want to make *this* year the best year of my life. That is why I don't like to make films that are statements.

BJD: *It's been said that in a certain sense a director makes the same film all his life—that is, explores the different aspects of a given theme in a variety of ways throughout his pictures. Do you agree with this? Do you feel it's true of your work?*

MA: Dostoevski said that an artist only says one thing in his work all through his life. If he is very good, perhaps two. The liberty of the paradoxical nature of that quotation allows me to add that it doesn't completely apply to me. But it's not for me to say.

Antonioni Speaks . . . and Listens

RENEE EPSTEIN/1975

MY INTERVIEW WITH MICHELANGELO ANTONIONI was
at 10 A.M. I walked down through Central Park. The animals in the Zoo
were enjoying their early morning moments of privacy. The white polar
bear was bathing himself. He seemed more like an overweight child
performing aquatic tricks than a caged animal.

Antonioni's suite was on the twenty-second floor of the Sherry-
Netherland Hotel. He invited me to see the view from his window.
Looking at the city from this height, I felt like a stranger. The city was
unrecognizable to me. Antonioni smiled and said, "It's beautiful, isn't it?"

ANTONIONI: I think that it would be interesting for this interview to
take the form of long statement-questions and short answers. It is also
the only possible form. I cannot use words. A director in some way is a
man of action even if this action is intellectual. My life is divided into
two kinds of experiences, practical and intellectual. They both push me
to do something and behave in some way, but I don't know why. It is
something unconscious. I can't explain. You know Pirandello? Pirandello
was once asked, "Why does that character behave like that?" He replied,
"I don't know why, I'm only the author."

EPSTEIN: *In thinking about the film this morning, I had the feeling that I
had seen certain scenes before. I realized that it was in Camus's* The Stranger.
Standing by the window one Sunday, Meursault records in his apathetic voice,

From *Film Comment*, vol. 11, no. 4, pp. 7–8 (July/August 1975). Copyright © 1975 by the
Film Society of Lincoln Center. All rights reserved.

so like Jack Nicholson's, life as it passes by in the street. Also, for the first time, the murder of the Arab achieved a clearer reality for me. I understood Meursault's explanation about the five bullets: it was the sun, it was the fact that he was there at that particular moment.

M.A.:   Someone else also made this comparison. I think that it is fundamentally wrong. Meursault has "existential" problems, abstract problems. My character, David Locke, has very concrete problems. He is frustrated with his life. His marriage is a failure. He is not completely satisfied with his job even if done successfully. He is unable to be more committed politically and he does not know why. Locke's situation is not the same as the Stranger's.

R.E.:   *One of the things that struck me about the characters in* The Passenger *is that these people live at a distance—from themselves and from each other. We are told that Locke and Rachel have a child. However, we never see the child, and there is no reference made to this child by them. Language seems to describe the character, but the character listening to the words is a stranger to that description.*

M.A.:   This is deliberate. Rachel is critical of her husband because of this. At the end of the film she says that she never knew him. Well, perhaps, he never really knew her. They thought of each other in certain terms, but they may have been mistaken.

R.E.:   *I find myself making cross-associations with your film. Are you familiar with the photographs of Edward Weston?*

M.A.:   I know him and have seen some of his work.

R.E.:   *I think that what instinctively leads me to make this connection is that both you and Weston are interested in the perceptual relationship between the viewer and the represented world of the cinematic frame and the photograph. When I look at a Weston photograph, I often have the uneasy feeling that a human being is present but not immediately visible. I find myself searching the landscape, at first with the intention of restoring the human figure's central position within it, and then rather ashamedly, allowing the elements to be seen as they are in their relationship to one another.*

M.A.:   Every audience is tied to certain habits in the way that they look at film. If they don't have the same articulation of a scene, they get lost. This makes me crazy. Your problem in viewing Weston's photographs is the same question of habit.

When I see *The Passenger* now, I ask myself why I did a particular scene in that particular way. Only after the completion of the film could I explain why I chose that solution to a given sequence. However, while I am shooting, it is instinct that I follow. The only need that I had was to be free with my camera. Usually we follow one person, or the camera moves between two people in dialogue. In this film, I did not want to maintain one style. I wanted the technical solution to each problem to come to me intuitively without any preconceptions. There isn't any unity of style. The unity of the film comes from inside the film, itself, from the relationship between me and the world and between me and my characters.

R.E.:   *You have initiated the audience into a way of perceiving. We become aware that there is a functional similarity between the eye of the audience and the eye of your camera. As we sit stationary in our seats staring into the world of your film, so your camera fixes itself on a particular space, seemingly unconcerned with the movements of the people operating within that space. The camera no longer has a subordinate relation to character or plot. It becomes a character with a dynamic power of acting upon the audience.*

Your camera can be very humorous in its disengagement. For example, the sequence where Nicholson and Schneider are having lunch in a sidewalk café. You open with a car moving from right to left and another car moving from right to left and another car moving from left to right. The camera then moves back and reveals the bordering sidewalk where the two of them are seated, two people in a busy street scene. I found myself surprised at seeing them, surprised that they were there at all.

Or the sequence when Nicholson walked down a street, moving from the center of the screen and disappearing around the corner of the celluloid. I was tempted to peer behind the screen in order to find out where he was going. The camera is totally detached from its own world.

M.A.:   This was an idea that I had. Sometimes, I realized that I was following this same idea after the sequence was shot. This means that the idea was inside me and not theoretically formulated.

This is a film about someone who is following his destiny, a man watching reality as reported, in the same way that I was watching him, in the same way that you are pursuing me. You could go back and find another camera watching me and another one watching the other camera. It's surrealistic, isn't it?

R.E.:   *What hope is there to get beyond the images? We see countless photographs in the newspapers of mutilated bodies, of starving children. We hear the news repeated over and over again, every fifteen minutes on the radio. We titillate ourselves nightly with violence and commercials offered by television.*

We are confronted in you film with an execution.

M.A.:   This is a very ambiguous piece of film. Locke is doing a documentary film on a guerrilla movement within an African country. He is trying to get more and more politically involved. We can think that he chooses to shoot the execution because he knows that it will be visually impressive. He may have chosen to use it for sensationalism but perhaps not. We don't know, and perhaps he, himself, did not know what he wanted. I begin the sequence with a full screen as though it was happening that moment. And then we see it viewed by the television producer on the moviola for his documentary of David Locke's life as a journalist. This is another way that I was able to be free with my camera. I recorded the execution twice so that the audience's perception of that event would be different each time that they watched it. The format on the screen was different from the format on the moviola. It was as though I was filming the execution myself. And then it was watched by Knight and Rachel on the moviola as film shot by Locke.

This was a film of an actual execution. Please don't ask me anything about it. I cannot tell you.

R.E.:   *You often make the audience unexpectedly adjust the levels of their involvement. The tone of your characterizations and the apparent disinterest of the camera as it records events create an atmosphere of distances between the characters and their world, and our personal relation to that projected reality. And then the execution scene.*

Is it a real execution or is it staged by the film company? It is left to the audience to choose. We see at first the archetypal image of the martyr. It is only when we see the final shuddering of his body on the film replayed in the moviola that the horror of this man's death touches us. The reality strangely assumes proportions that defy the perimeters of the moviola. The reel is suddenly stopped, and Knight apologizes for upsetting Rachel.

M.A.:   My intention was to show something that shocked Locke.

R.E.:   *But was it not you that was shocked? How do we know what effect that shooting had on Locke? We know very little about these people. The camera has more of an effect on us than the people.*

M.A.:   You have to believe that scene. You have to imagine that Locke was shocked. He is of course a very conventional interviewer and this is what Rachel accuses him of. We are following Rachel, who is trying to know him better.

We are in the same position as Rachel. We know no more. We have to imagine.

R.E.:   *But why do we have to imagine? You are probing levels of reality. You are dealing with many minds including the audience's trying to get beyond appearances that we offer each other day by day, that condition us through the media, through the language that we use to describe reality. And then you say that these people are coming closer in their understanding of one another. Your film closes with Rachel and the girl making statements about the dead man on the bed. That man for me lost his identity as David Locke. He had become as exchangeable as the original Robertson, as disengaged from his name as he was from his former life. Was this your intention?*

M.A.:   Yes. Things are what they are, they are what you see. We work with images, not with words. I cannot use words. That is my problem.

R.E.:   *Dialogue is secondary in your film. Language that is used to describe what these people see and feel only achieves a reality when we are visually presented with that world. For example, the last seven minutes of the film. The girl asks, "What would it be like to be blind?" and Locke tells the story of the man who regains his sight. I thought to myself, why is he doing this, it's so tired and flat. And then suddenly the clichés of our lives became very new, after we have lived through the concluding moments of the film. The words, themselves, don't say very much about the world. Then we see that world and the language becomes vital and truthful.*

This is one of the interesting ironies. I am trying to use words to re-create your world when your world exists so completely on its own terms, visually.

M.A.:   Yes.

R.E.:   *In the film you say that men don't change, only places. Although there was extreme contrast in topography, it seemed as if it was one unfolding landscape. If man does not change, and if places are more or less alike, then what can we say about the future?*

M.A.:   The future? My God! I have nothing to say, I am waiting. I can imagine but I can say nothing.

Antonioni after China: Art versus Science

GIDEON BACHMANN/1975

There is a difference between seeing and proving, and it is this difference
which divides art from science. To the artistic observer, the scientist who
seeks proof seems a pitiable wretch, and conversely, the use of mere
perception as the source of knowledge seems highly suspicious to some
scientists.

—Konrad Lorenz

"I WANT THE CHINESE TO KNOW THIS: during the war, as
a member of the Resistance, I was condemned to death!"

Antonioni's need to make this statement, polemically and publicly,
in discussing the Chinese attempts to sabotage, the world over, the
screening of the documentary he shot in China, indicates the bitterness
in the man. A bitterness, undoubtedly, which cannot but reflect on his
works which follow. In fact, Maria Schneider, who plays in it, told me
that *The Passenger*, his latest film, seemed to her, during its production,
his most desperate. A film, she says, without any form of optimism. He
had gone to China full of optimism.

There he produced 220 minutes of calm, poetic footage. A documentary that gives no facile answers, provides no scientific analysis. A
work of perception that calls upon your sensibilities, even your endurances.

From *Film Quarterly*, vol. 28, no. 4 (Summer 1975), pp. 26–30. © 1975, The Regents of the
University of California. All rights reserved. Reprinted by permission of University of
California Press and Gideon Bachmann.

Certainly not one of those which to its claim of objectivity adds a dose of attitude. (That, in fact, is evidently what the Chinese resent most.)

Even if Antonioni's "other side" is less easily defined today than it was in 1943, when even anti-fascism seemed a simpler concept, with enemies more readily identified, it is certainly not Antonioni who has changed barricades. It is precisely the lack of the simplistic, "scientific" attitude requested by the Chinese, precisely that openness and lack of bias, which for the thinking viewer represents the film's greatest value. *Chung-Kuo* is a film made with love, not with opinion.

In *The Passenger* (originally entitled *Profession: Reporter*) Jack Nicholson plays a man given the chance to change identity midway in life. Based on an idea by Mark Peploe, it shows what disasters follow this attempt at self-liberation. It is basically a film about the uselessness of human individuality and of the strive for quality in one's expressions. It is the first time that Antonioni has filmed the idea of another, but after initial perplexity he found in the story elements which intrigued him in terms of his own experience. He denies that it is an autobiographical study. But the spirit of the work is the spirit of Antonioni.

BACHMANN: *Your films are similar inasmuch as they have always shown the world to be in decline, but you have always seemed to say that we must live in it, as best we can, anyway. This seems the first time you depict the attempt at escape. Are you less confident now?*

ANTONIONI: I have only tried to be more objective, even if this word seems ambiguous. A journalist sees reality with a certain consistency, the ambiguous consistency of his viewpoint, which to him, and only to him, seems objective. Jack in the film sees things in his way, and I, as the director, play the role of the journalist behind the journalist: I again add other dimensions to reproduced reality.

B: *So "objectivity" isn't something you seek . . .*

A: No, the dialectic of life would be missing. Films would become boring. Pretending to be objective, you annul yourself. Others talk through you but you remain extraneous. What sense would life have, then? When I say that I have tried to be more objective, I mean it in a technical way. I no longer want to employ the subjective camera, in other words the camera that represents the viewpoint of the character.

The objective camera is the camera wielded by the author. Using it I make my presence felt. The camera's viewpoint becomes mine.

B: *Did going to China, where you were forced to use the camera as an observer, prepare you for this?*
A: Certainly; this is one of the reasons why the China project was so interesting for me. I had to shoot very quickly: 80 shots a day, my absolute record. We had five weeks and an enormous itinerary. I could not do what I had done in the period of my early documentaries, where I studied the light for every shot, and picked the best hours of the day for shooting. I couldn't prepare much. While my early documentaries prepared me for features, this Chinese experience has prepared me for the new way in which I have used the camera in *The Passenger*. I am not really a good son of neorealism; I'm rather the black sheep of its family, and with this film even more so. I have replaced my objectivity with that of the camera. I can direct it any way I want; as the director, I am God. I can allow myself any kind of liberty. Actually, the liberty I have achieved in the making of this film is the liberty the character in the film tried to achieve by changing identity.

B: *So it is your own story in a way?*
A: Only inasmuch as it is my story as an artist, as a director—without wanting to sound presumptuous. In my own life, I don't know whether I shall succumb. I don't mean to the temptation to change identity; we all have that. But to destiny, since each one of us carries his destiny within himself. I do not know whether I shall succumb to that, to all those acts which at the end of a life come together to make up one's destiny. Some succumb and some don't. Perhaps changing one's identity one commits an error, one succumbs to life, one dies, in essence. It depends on the acts one commits, having appropriated to oneself that other identity. It's a presumptuousness that probably puts one in conflict with life itself.

B: *Of all the species, only man seems overly concerned with his identity. We seem to have done, as a species, what you describe.*
A: We have created a structure that produces doubts. We are all dissatisfied. The international situation, politically and otherwise, is so

unstable, that the lack of stability is reflected within each individual. But I'm used to talking in pictures, not words. This conversation doesn't create images; I prefer to remain more concrete. When I talk of man, I want to see his face. In China, when I asked them what they felt was the most important thing in their revolution, they said it was the new man. That is what I tried to focus on. Each individual, each one creating his own little revolution, all those little revolutions which together will change humanity. That's why I insist upon a personal viewpoint, concretizing it with the camera; every change in history has always started from individuals. You can't change facts: it's the human mind that creates human action.

B: *Aren't we losing this faith in the industrial age?*
A: When this age began, it enlarged the definition of the individual. As it also enlarged the conflict between the individual and society, the social conflict, which obviously was born in an industrial context. Perhaps Marx today should be corrected a little. Not his drive to change society, but the ways of doing it. We are back to discussing identity. It is a question of the usefulness of individuality in a given social context. In an antheap identity was lost since it no longer served a practical purpose. It was replaced by the individuality of the group. In my work, too, the usefulness of art is changing, and its utility to society, but I think that the product we call art will continue to exist. The human being needs to express himself in some way, in community with others. That is the search for identity: the desperate need to participate in society.

B: *Thus you create a personal cinema, a viewpoint cinema, in order to participate in society?*
A: Films are seen by this mass of people, all together. Thus a minimum of contact, for those seeking it, is produced. It is important to find the common denominator, even if this can lead to misunderstandings. As in the case where the common denominator is the political ideal. But I don't think cinema will remain so complicated much longer; the future lies in videotape. People will use film cameras as they use still cameras today; they will express themselves. And when television comes to present—as it has barely begun doing in a few countries—a more

stimulating product than the cinema, the cinema will lose out. But we are still very much behind. In Italy, for example, until we have color television, I will not work for TV. What I would really like to do is make a feature film with television cameras, that is my dream. That is what I had planned on doing with *Technically Sweet*, the film I had hoped to make before this one. It was to be based on a story by Calvino, the Italian poet who lives in Paris. Telecameras offer a very free working method. You can paint your images. You can change the colors. Since the colors are electronic, this is easy, as it is for a painter. I had tried to do this in the cinema, with *Red Desert*, but I want to carry this technique even further. What counts, is the reality that ends up on the screen. My reality.

B: *So "objective" reality doesn't exist?*
A: Certainly not. But it exists inasmuch as we exist.

B: *What does this film represent, finally, in your career?*
A: It's an important stage for me, mostly because it's not based on a story I wrote myself. When it was first suggested to me that I should direct a film based on this script of Mark Peploe's, I was somewhat taken aback, but then, rather instinctively, I decided for it, feeling that after all there was something in this story which reminded me of I-don't-know-what. I began to shoot, to work, before I even had a final script, because there wasn't much time, due to Jack Nicholson's other commitments. So I started working with a certain feeling of distance. A feeling of being somewhat removed from the story itself. For the first time I found I was working more with the brain than, let's say, with the stomach. But during the shooting of the film's beginning, the certain something that this story contained began to interest me even more. In this journalist, as in every journalist, there co-exists the drive to excel, to produce quality work, and the feeling that this quality is ephemeral. The feeling, thus, that his work is valid for a fleeting moment only.

B: *In an age of rapid consumption, that is a feeling shared by all those working in art or in communication.*
A: In fact no one can understand such a feeling better than a film director, since we are working with a material, the film stock, which is

itself ephemeral, physically short-lived. Time consumes it. In my film, when Jack feels saturated to the gills with this sentiment, after years of work, a moment arrives when there is a break in his inner armor, when he feels the need for a personal revolution. Add to this, frustrations for other motives: a failed marriage, an adopted son whose presence did not have the expected effect upon his life, and another, ethical need, which becomes stronger as he progresses. You will understand, then, how this character, in the moment when the occasion arises, takes the opportunity to change identity, fascinated by the promise of the liberty that he expects will follow. That, in any case, was my point of departure. What the film tells, is the story of what happens to him after this change of identity, the vicissitudes that he encounters, perhaps the disappointments.

B: *So the film is in a way also the story of itself?*
A: Only indirectly, because I have been able to apply a technique which resembles that of the journalist in the film. I shot the film with the same eye the journalist uses in his viewing of reality, using this "objective" kind of camerawork I described. Two or three "subjective" shots have remained in the film, but for the rest of it the camera was free to abandon the characters, to precede them where they were headed, to shoot that which was interesting for me, the reporter of my reporter, to watch, to fix, to record. I have thought a great deal about this, because in my previous films I had never quite felt this liberty.

B: *How would you define the technical differences between this work and your preceding ones?*
A: This way of looking at things has permitted me to return to the *piano-sequenza* [the "sequence-shot" or very long camera take, in which events change and grow within the frame, rather than using a short-take-based "montage" technique.—G.B.], which I had abandoned quite some time ago. But even that is not true for the whole film; actually every sequence in the film uses its own particular technique. I can't even say whether there is a coherent, uniform style for the whole; if there is, it is an *internal* style. I felt the need to present myself, afresh, in a free way, in confrontation with every new part of the film. In shooting, this system has allowed me a feeling of great joy.

B: *You said China prepared you for this. There, too, you had gone with joy.*
But you seem to have carried those experiences to fruition more in The
Passenger *than in* Chung-Kuo. *Was that because you had more control?*
A: My experiences in China must be divided into two clear and
separate ones. The first one was that of the shooting, of visiting certain
parts of China—unfortunately not many, but more was not allowed me.
That experience, I must say, was of an absolutely positive nature. I
found myself facing a people, a country, which showed clear signs of
the revolution that had occurred. In seeking out the face of this new
society I followed my natural tendency to concentrate on individuals,
and to show the new man, rather than the political and social structures
which the Chinese revolution created. Because in order to understand
those structures, one would have to stay in a country much longer.
These five weeks permitted only a quick glance; as a voyager I saw
things with a voyager's eye. I tried to take the film spectator with me, to
take him by the hand, as it were, and have him accompany me on this
trip. Also, social and political structures are abstract entities which are
not easily expressed in images. One would have to add words to those
images, and that wasn't my role. I had not gone to China to understand
it, but only to see it. To look at it and to record what passed under
my eyes.

B: *Had it been your idea to go there?*
A: No. This was not a documentary planned by me. The project was
born of a relationship which Italian television (RAI) had initiated with
the Chinese Embassy in Rome. I had not been informed beforehand.
One day they called me and asked if I wanted to shoot a documentary
in China. I responded enthusiastically, because the matter obviously
interested me greatly.

B: *You said your experiences in China must be divided into two parts . . .*
A: When the film was finished, the first persons, outside of my
collaborators, to whom it was shown, were some representatives of the
Chinese Embassy in Rome. The ambassador didn't show up. There was
the director of the New China Agency and two or three others. At the
end of the screening these persons expressed themselves positively.
"You," they said, "Signor Antonioni, have looked at our country with a

very affectionate eye. And we thank you." That was the first reaction of certain responsible Chinese people. I don't know what happened after that. I have no idea why they changed their opinion. I can only imagine why, but it would be a useless subject for discussion.

B: *From what I've read, it doesn't seem to me that the objections were on an artistic or filmic level at all.*

A: I am accused of having associated myself with Lin Piao in denigrating the Chinese revolution. It has been said that I did not sufficiently appreciate what the socialist system and the dictatorship of the proletariat in China have constructed. I reject in the most decisive manner that this is true of my documentary. Seeing it you will realize this. It has been said that I am being paid by Russian revisionists. Who these Russian revisionists are supposed to be, I truly do not know; or rather I suppose that I do know, because, after all, I live on this planet and not on another, and thus what happens in other countries does interest me. It has been said that I purposely denigrated China in many other ways; one of these is supposed to be the fact that I have used a "cool" color tone in order to eliminate the real colors of China and of the Chinese landscape. It has been said that I've denigrated Chinese children, I really don't know why. I made shots of those children while they were singing their little songs, of their delicious little faces. They are really beautiful, Chinese children, and if I could, I would adopt one. I don't see how I could have denigrated them. I have been told that I showed the bridge in Nanking in a diminished way, not triumphal enough. I must say that in fact the day I went to shoot it, it was a foggy day and I asked to be allowed to return another day. There is a long shot of the bridge left in the film, I think, but it doesn't show the bridge in a very expressive way. I had to limit myself to take shots of the bridge from closer by, and naturally, passing underneath it, the bridge appears slightly deformed. But that is our way of looking at things, from an individualistic viewpoint. That is the point of departure that our own social context creates. When certain aspects of reality fascinate me, my first instinct is to record them. We, as descendants of Western civilization, point our cameras at things that surround us, with a certain trust in the interpretative capacities of the viewer.

B: *Is there anything that could fall under this definition that you were actually kept from shooting?*

A: Well . . . I remember when we were in the center of China, in Hunan province, we came through a village where a free market was going on, a thing apparently widely tolerated in China. I asked to get off, but the driver wouldn't stop. I made something of a fuss; I said to the driver, look, let me off, and I opened the door of the car, and he stopped. But the people who were there to accompany me—and in this case they were eight—didn't tell me "don't shoot." They just said, "You may shoot, if you wish, but it displeases us." You will see this scene in the film. What would another Italian director have done in my stead? Obviously I started shooting; then I saw that their displeasure was indeed great, and I stopped. What I want to say is that everything I did in China was done in complete accord with the people who were there to accompany me. Usually there were eight of them. In Nanking there were fourteen. Thus I never did anything that wasn't allowed and I never shot anything without their being present. I don't see what they are accusing me of now. It is really unheard of. May I add that the vulgar language of their accusations really hurts me. And that is what I mean by my second experience of China; not the experience in China itself, which was positive. The negative experience concerning China is this one, this lurking about in the undergrowth of politics. Their going to the Foreign Ministry to try and stop the projection here. Their going to Sweden, as they did, to try to blackmail the Swedish government by threatening to cease having cultural relations with Sweden if Swedish TV presented the film. Their going to Greece—mind you, while the colonels were still in power—and asking the colonels not to show the film, which happened. Their going to Germany to try and do the same thing; the Germans, unlike the Greeks, refused. Their going to France to try and do the same thing again. It is this method they use which seems so small-minded to me. This way they have of insulting me personally, calling me a charlatan, a *buffone*—that is the word, I can't tell you the Chinese original, I only read the papers in Italian. I have been accused of being a fascist! Of having fought with the fascist troops! I want the Chinese to know this: during the war, as a member of the Resistance, I was condemned to death. I was on the other side! I must say these things, once and for all, because it can't go on that these people go around insulting me in this way and I can't even find anyone to defend me, because . . . because, after all, we do like the Chinese people, and I like them too. What I don't like is those who insult me without even knowing who I am, this business of allowing people like those fools of "Italia-China" [a Maoist Italian youth organization.—G. B.] to say whatever idiot things they want to. I have nothing else to say.

An Interview with
Michelangelo Antonioni

AMERICAN
CINEMATOGRAPHER/1976

MICHELANGELO ANTONIONI, one of the most famous of Italy's motion picture directors, was honored at the IVth Tehran International Film Festival by a retrospective presentation of fourteen of his films. In the following interview, excerpted from his press conference at the Festival, Mr. Antonioni expresses his views on film-making.

QUESTION: *Mr. Antonioni, you have said somewhere—in reference to your latest film,* Profession: Reporter—*that if you had known there was a similarity between your story and a story written by Pirandello, you would not have made this film. Is that so?*

ANTONIONI: I have never said such a thing. I should be a fool to say that if my story is like something that Pirandello has written, I would not make a film about it. This would be foolish—especially since I had already read the work. It is a part of the Italian culture; therefore, there was no question of my not having known that Pirandello had written this story. Actually there is a great difference between what Pirandello wrote and what I have made as a film. The difference may seem rather subtle—at first glance it may not be apparent—but then, if you delve into the question, you will find that they are so totally different, these

From *American Cinematographer,* vol. 57, no. 2 (February 1976), pp. 158–59, 173 Reprinted by permission of *American Cinematographer.*

two things. So the difference is great and subtle at the same time. The problem of the character in Pirandello's story is that of finding an identity which is to be given to him by the society, whereas, what the character in my film is seeking is more personal. There is a crisis of identity within himself. What he is seeking is from his own insides. That is what he is looking for—so that is quite a difference.

QUESTION: *As somebody who comes from India, I must say that we have noted that the characters in your films often choose renunciation. They give up. They go away. The reporter in your latest film gives up his profession and almost renounces what he is. Your characters often give up what they have— their positions, their wives—in order to go after what they are looking for, in order to find their own salvation. Now, to me this has an almost mystical quality. Is that deliberate on your part? Does this indeed have some mystical meaning?*

ANTONIONI: No mystical meaning. There are no mystical concepts behind my ideas and my way of presenting my thoughts, because I don't believe in a sort of mystical state—in something other than what I am involved with personally. Behind my films there is only me— myself. The films might have the appearance of being pessimistic— indeed, there are some pessimistic trends in them—but if you really look into them deeply, you will find there is a man with hope. There is actually hope behind them. It is possible to come to some constructive conclusions even through pessimism. But you should not think that I am—as a man who makes these films—mystical-minded, a man who believes in mystical possibilities. To be a pessimist would obviously mean that you should say "no" to everything. But to say "no" to some things means also to say "yes" to other things—so there would seem to be a sort of balance between the negative and the positive side.

QUESTION: *What is your method of arriving at how you will express yourself in terms of cinematic concepts?*

ANTONIONI: As you may know, I have never been to a film school. I mean, I have never studied the cinema in any particular school. In dealing with this matter of cinema, I give myself up to my instincts and my feelings. I follow my instincts and my feelings—and I don't bother to sit down and think and work out schemes for doing things.

QUESTION: *How much liberty do you give your cameramen, in terms of expressing their creativity?*

ANTONIONI: I believe that I give my chief cameraman a lot of liberty—and they believe I don't give them any freedom at all. As you all know, the chief cameraman is very important, one of the major elements of film-making. He is the person who is closest to the director, but the ideas of the chief cameraman should pass through the filter of the director's knowledge. There is no doubt about this, because the director is the only one who knows what is the final result that he wants to produce. He is the fellow who is in charge and is responsible. He is to direct the film in such a way that he will get the result that he had designed originally.

QUESTION: *In comparing two masterpieces, don't you think it's an unfair thing to try to compare them in order to give a prize to one or the other? Which brings us to the question of film festivals; do you believe that such festivals are justified when they are competitive?*

ANTONIONI: I think this is a very relevant question. I believe that a masterpiece comes from a unique poetic channel. Therefore, two masterpieces come from two different poetic channels belonging to different natures. They express two different ways of thinking, two different attitudes. For this reason, they are not comparable—if they are masterpieces. Therefore, it would be unfair to try to compare one to the other, and to try to give one a prize over the other. For this reason—even though people like Mr. Daryoush and his colleagues who set up film festivals do it with a lot of dedication, love, and perseverance and do a very good job—I still believe that competition at a festival is not a just thing.

QUESTION: *As some of us know, Mr. Antonioni, at the end of your latest film,* Profession: Reporter, *there is a very long, long moving camera shot that has everything in it. The continuity is all in one, without a cut. Many questions have been asked about the manner in which this shot was produced, but you have not actually disclosed the secret of it. Yet, you have promised that one day you would disclose the secret of how it was done. If you would be willing to do that now, we would be delighted to hear it.*

ANTONIONI: The idea of doing this classic shot occurred to me at the beginning of the shooting of the film, but I kept asking myself how I would be able to realize it, because it seemed impossible. In order to achieve what I had set out to achieve, I considered many solutions, many different ways of doing it, but I found that all of these methods were rather common, ordinary, clichéd ways of doing cinema work. They were things which had already been done and none of them actually served my purpose. I tried harder and harder to find a way.

Then I went to London in order to shoot some of the scenes for the film, and it was there that I encountered a camera that had been made by Canadians. It was a new movie camera and I found that the possibilities presented by this camera might help me to achieve what I had set out to achieve.

As you know, at the beginning of this sequence we are inside a bedroom. Then the camera begins gently to move forward. It very slowly reaches the window and then goes through the window to the outside. This movement is not achieved in the normal way of putting the camera on an ordinary track on the ground. The rail is actually installed on the ceiling, and the camera is suspended from the rail.

The rail installed on the ceiling actually continues for a distance of one meter outside the window into the open. When the camera reaches the window, in order to avoid the grill which is outside the window, there is a gentle zoom to put the grill out of the frame. As the camera continues to move outside, the window grill gently opens (without our seeing it) and we are now outside the room, with the camera suspended from the end of the rail. But the camera movement is supposed to continue. In order to achieve this, a high crane has been positioned behind the building in such a way that a hook at the end of a cable hanging down from the crane-boom is level with the end of the rail from which the camera is suspended.

Now, the problem at this moment is to transfer the camera from the fixed rail to the hook hanging from the end of the cable—which is not so fixed. We had two operators, two experts, sitting there waiting to take the camera from the rail and put it on the hook suspended by cable from the end of the boom. Now, how to solve the problem of avoiding a jump or jerk in transferring the rail to the cable?

It is here that the special camera which has been made in Canada comes to my aid, because it has gyroscopic setups and cushions in it which are shock-proof, vibration proof. They actually absorb shock and allow a certain latitude in movements and jerks without those movements showing on the screen. This setup does the work of a Dynalens, without using a Dynalens, and it is the thing which helped me take the camera from the rail and hook it onto the cable without showing a jerk or jump.

Now we are at the point where the camera has been installed at the end of the cable hanging from the crane boom. The camera has certain special handles installed on it so that it can be held steady, and there is a camera operator waiting there to hold onto these special handles. Now the movement continues and the camera moves around the square following the various characters. In the meantime, the grill in front of the window has been closed again, so that by the time the camera has done its complete movement around the square and has gotten back to this window, we see that the grill is closed.

Now, how did I guide the movements of the camera and the actions of the cameraman? I was inside a van in which there was a monitoring screen—a sort of closed-circuit television monitor—on which I could see exactly what the cameraman could see in his viewfinder. Through a microphone I could give orders to the actors, controlling their movements, and I could also give instructions to the camera operator, who would then follow and do exactly as I wanted him to do.

The whole process took 11 days because of the precise nature of the operation and the delicacy of the camera, which, in spite of all the shock absorbers and gadgets, is a very sensitive camera and has to be handled very carefully. It was especially sensitive in this case, because, in order for it to be able to go through the window grill, we had to take it out of the big, box-like blimp which ordinarily protects it. Otherwise, it could not have gone through the grill.

Another major problem was the wind, which blew all the time and caused movement of the cable, which, in turn, disturbed the movements that we had in mind. Therefore, we had to wait for "windless" moments when we could actually go on with our business.

After we had spent 11 days shooting this scene and had finally gotten what we wanted, on the twelfth day there was a cyclone which destroyed the whole setup—the village, the building, everything!

QUESTION: *Mr. Antonioni, I know that your films are very personal, but are they also autobiographical to some degree?*

ANTONIONI: I never sit down and look inwards and decide that whatever I have inside me I am going to disgorge. This I never do. Every day when I am working, I am affected by whatever is happening on that particular day, and what is reflected in my work is my reaction to what I have observed on that particular day. Therefore, even if somebody wants to think of what I do as autobiographical, it's a daily "autobiographic" which is different from day to day. Each day differs; things change. Therefore, the combination of things that actually make my work is constantly variable. I can't say that there is one set of things I would just let out—and that is me.

I'd like to make that more clear. Every morning going from my hotel to the set I have some experiences. I listen to some speeches. I notice how the light is that day. I see everything, and it influences me and it creates in me a certain mood. This mood I try to put into my sequence. It influences me in my shooting.

QUESTION: *Mr. Antonioni, your film* Zabriskie Point *stirred up tremendous controversy in the United States. American audiences, in general, felt that it was extremely biased in its depiction of American life. Therefore, for many of them, it lacked credibility and they refused to take it seriously. Do you feel that there is any justification to this charge that the film's point of view was one-sided?*

ANTONIONI: *Zabriskie Point* was a sort of reaction to an emotion that was produced in me by coming face to face with America. Now, this is how I felt—but what the Americans felt was a matter for the Americans to feel. It had nothing to do with how I reacted personally.

Of course—and I must make this point clear—at the time when I made this film, there were movements and incidents in America which did contribute toward the sort of pessimism that was produced in me. There were the student movements and social upheavals caused by the Vietnam War that we all know about. So, at that time I felt that American society itself was in a state of turmoil.

However, now we see that there is a sort of tranquility. All those movements and protestations have stopped. We no longer see them. Mr. Tom Hayden has married Jane Fonda and withdrawn his protests. He's even trying to become a Democratic senator. This means that there was justification for the pessimism that I felt at the time. Now we see that all the people who led those movements have, in one way or another, been digested into the system. They have become a part of the Establishment and are participating in the leading of American society in an orthodox way.

QUESTION: *Don't you think, Mr. Antonioni, that this trend is universal, something that happens in every country? Young people who begin to protest, after a while stop protesting and other young people begin this protestation— and it goes on and on like that.*

ANTONIONI: This is a disease which is the disease of life. In that sense, it is universal. I must make it clear at this point that I have absolutely no hostility towards any movement by any people, young or old, in any part of the world. I think everyone must do what he feels is right for the betterment of society. But it happens that *Zabriskie Point* was my reaction, at that point in history, to what was happening in the United States.

QUESTION: *Mr. Antonioni, in your films you place some of your characters in front of nature and other characters in front of architectural edifices. What is the significance of this?*

ANTONIONI: Depending upon the mood of the moment, I just put my characters into whatever situation that mood requires. This question is an illogical question and you can't give a logical answer to it. If I were to get into explaining why I put some characters in nature and others in front of architecture, I would have to go into detail explaining how the story was developed and why these characters were developed, and so on. Therefore, you should look for yourself and you will find out the reason. This is not an answerable question.

Film Is Life: An Interview with Michelangelo Antonioni

BERT CARDULLO/1978

THE FOLLOWING INTERVIEW TOOK PLACE in June 1978 at the Plaza Hotel in New York City, shortly before Antonioni was to return to Italy to begin shooting *The Oberwald Mystery.*

BC: *How do you like New York, Signor Antonioni?*
MA: Well, I have been here a number of times, but still, I have a sense of unreality whenever I am in this city—it's as though I'm living in a film. I have never made a movie in New York, but I am ready to do so the day the screen becomes vertical.

BC: *I know that you are going to return to Italy soon to begin shooting* Il Mistero di Oberwald (The Oberwald Mystery), *so, aside from a few general questions, I'd like to concentrate today both on this upcoming work and on the three feature films you made prior to it, all of them outside your own native country:* The Passenger, Zabriskie Point, *and* Blow-Up. *The last film you made in Italy was* Red Desert, *right?*
MA: Yes, that is correct. And after three films abroad, I have to say, I feel rootless. I don't think it is useful to stay out of your own country for so long. I need to shoot a film in Italy, to which I now feel I can go back and not repeat myself. I need to hear Italian. I'm fed up with hearing only English. Most people are blind in their own country; they

---

Previously unpublished. Printed by permission of Bert Cardullo.

can't see at all. What does a Roman know of Rome? Only his own itinerary. But I am trained to *look*, to use my cultural baggage and education in a creative way—not to speak English.

BC: *Your English isn't so bad*
MA: You miss my point. As Brecht used to say about his English, "I say what I can say, not what I want to say." I have to complicate my thoughts in a foreign language; I have to change my nature and think in American or British terms. It must be something similar for an actor who has to play many parts and who therefore has to change many times.

In any event, whatever language I am using, I am not a man of words. A film director is in some way a man of action even if this action is intellectual. Words are symbols, whereas images are what they are. And I may be someone who is successful—I don't know, perhaps—with something to show, not something to say. I can't find the right words; I'm not a writer, and I'm not a speaker, either.

BC: *Do you do a lot of research before you start shooting a picture?*
MA: Yes. If I didn't do so much research for my films, my work would then be a lie. I must always start from more or less scientifically proven data. The biggest danger and temptation of cinema is the boundless possibility it gives movie directors to lie.

BC: *When did you first put your eye behind a camera?*
MA: "When" is not so important, but what happened at that moment was. The first time I got behind a camera was in a lunatic asylum. I had decided with a group of friends to do a documentary film on mad people. We positioned the camera, got the lamps ready, and disposed the patients around the room. The insane obeyed us with complete abandon, trying very hard not to make mistakes. I was very moved by their behavior and things were going fine. Finally, I was able to give the order to turn on the lights. And in one second, the room was flooded with light . . .

I have never seen again, on any actor's face, such an expression of fear, such total panic. For a very brief moment, the patients remained motionless, as if petrified. That lasted literally only a few seconds, followed by a scene really hard to describe. The men and women started having convulsions, then they screamed and rolled on the floor. In one instant, the room turned into a hellish pit. All the mad people were trying to escape from light as if they had been attacked by some prehistoric monster.

We all stood there, completely stunned. The cameraman didn't even think to stop the camera. Finally, the doctor shouted, "Stop, cut off the lights!" Then, when the room was dark and silent again, we saw piles of corpses, slightly shaking as if they were going through their final death throes. I have never forgotten that scene, and it is one of the reasons I keep making films.

BC: *Research aside, how mentally prepared are you when you arrive on a set to shoot?*
MA: Just as an actor, in my view, must arrive on the set in a state of mental virginity, so, too, must I. I force myself not to overintellectualize, and I force myself never to think the night before of the scene I'll be shooting the next morning. I have a lot of confusion in my head, a real mess—lots of thoughts, lots of ideas, one of which cancels out the other. That's why I can't think about what I'm doing. I just do it.

Once on the set, I always spend a half hour alone to let the mood of the set, as well as its lighting, prevail. Then the actors arrive. I look at them. How are they? How do they seem to feel? I ask for rehearsals—a couple, no more—and then shooting starts. It's while I'm shooting that everything, so to speak, becomes real. After a shot is finished, I frequently continue to shoot the actors, who don't know that I am doing this. The after-effects of an emotional scene, it had occurred to me, might have meaning, too, both for the actor and for the psychological progression of his character. Once shooting really stops, sometimes it takes me fifteen minutes of complete silence and solitude to prepare for the next scene. What I still cannot do, however, is concentrate when I feel the eyes of a complete stranger on me, because a stranger always interests me. I want to ask him questions.

BC: *Could you say something about your work with actors, about how you work with them?*
MA: An actor does not have to understand; he has to *be*. Somebody will object that in order to be, you have to understand. I don't think so.

If that were so, the most intelligent actor would also be the best. In reality it is quite otherwise, indeed the complete contrary. It was so from Duse to Garbo. Intelligence is a brake on an actor, and to use it is equivalent to putting on the brakes. For me the secret is this: to work, not with psychology, but with imagination. It is no use trying to turn it on automatically. Our imagination has no switches which fingers can flick when we wish.

In the cinema, an actor must make the effort to follow what the director tells him as a dog does his master. If you change your direction and take a different street from usual, your dog will raise his head and look at you in surprise, but at a signal he will come along behind you. The method that I prefer to use is to provoke certain results through a "secret process": to stimulate the actor by playing on those chords of his being which he himself doesn't, perhaps, know. One must excite his instincts, *not* his brain. One mustn't justify, but rather illuminate.

BC: *Giovanni Fusco, who composed the music for* L'avventura *and* Red Desert, *among other films of yours, has complained of the difficulty of working with you. He once said, "The first rule for any musician who intends to collaborate with Antonioni is to forget that he is a musician." What, then, is your view on the use of music in films, since directors sometimes use it to buttress a weak or at least less than scintillating performance?*
MA: Even though I have studied music ever since I was a boy, every time I have music in films it means a terrible sacrifice for me. In my opinion, the image is not enriched but rather is interrupted, even, I'd dare to say, vulgarized. The image loses its purity. If I could, if a producer would let me, I'd assemble a soundtrack with only natural noises, in which noise itself would be the music. And I'd get a conductor to orchestrate the sounds for me.

BC: *But in* Blow-Up, *for the first time, music played a significant role in the story. And the same was true of* Zabriskie Point.
MA: The rock music you're referring to was natural at the time—it was a kind of new language for young people. But even in these instances I was hesitant, suspicious, because rock music in the end—and especially in America—has less to do with rebellion or even revolution than big business.

BC: *Where do you get your ideas for films?*

MA: How can I say it? It's one of my failings that everything I read or
see gives me an idea for a film. Fortunately, I can't do them all. If I could,
maybe they would all be very bad. One thing I can say: until I edit a
film of mine, I have no idea myself what it will be about. And perhaps
not even then. Perhaps it will only be the reflection of a mood; perhaps
the film will have no plot at all in the conventional sense. I depart from
my shooting script constantly, so it's pointless beforehand to release a
synopsis of the film's action or to discuss its meaning. In any case, my
scripts are not formal screenplays, but rather dialogue for the actors and
a series of notes to the director—myself. When shooting begins, there is
invariably a great degree of change. I may film scenes I had no intention
of filming, for example, since things suggest themselves on location
and you improvise. Only in the cutting room, when I take the film and
start to put it together—only then do I begin to get an idea of what it is
all about.

Usually I write the original stories of my films myself, but I never start
out with an idea that afterwards turns into a story. Most of the stories
which go through my hands in search of form are simply germs which
have been breathed in as from the air. If, when the film is finished, it
turns out to be saying something, it has happened *a posteriori*, and that
is natural enough. I am a human being and I am not lacking in perceptions about the people and affairs of this world. If I make the film in all
sincerity, then these perceptions will inevitably reveal themselves.
However, it is the story which fascinates me most. The images are the
medium through which a story can be understood. To be a lover of
form for me means being a lover of substance.

BC: *Are you ever satisfied with any of your films?*

MA: Sometimes I think *L'eclisse* is my best work, other times I like
L'avventura better. The other day I screened *La notte* again and thought
it was pretty good. But I don't think *Blow-Up* is one of my best pictures,
and I don't know why. I guess I am never really satisfied; I amuse myself
by experimenting. Even though my experience is deeper now, and technically I am more mature—everything I have to say comes out fluently—
I'm not happy after I complete a film. I'm not even happy while I'm
shooting it. Again, I don't know why. Still, I don't look back, or at least

I try not to. These are the best years because they are the only years. You can't afford to look back; you have to make the best of the present, whatever it may send your way—and however, finally, you may respond.

BC: *You clearly respond to urban landscapes in your cinema.*

MA: True, but in *Zabriskie Point*, for example, there were two locations: Los Angeles and the desert, the desert and the city. In the United States people can go into the desert—in Southern California, it is only an hour or two away by car. Yet it is so different. And it is nothing, an enormous area of nothing. We do not have spaces like that in Europe. Perhaps the existence of such great spaces so close to the city says something to me about America. You see, this is how I work: putting things together and seeing what the result is. I try to compress my feelings about a subject.

I have to say, though, that I love cities above all. I have never felt salvation in nature. An urban landscape with its masses of concrete and steel, and even of flowers and grass, which repeat themselves indefinitely—the repetition makes me dizzy; and it is exactly this repetition that can make reality so fleeting at times, and the thinking, feeling, aware man consequently so insecure. And such a cityscape—I like the word—takes away all the meaning of nature, which becomes like a word you repeat too often. The static immobility of nature is what really scares me. Take a tree: nothing weighs heavier on me than an old tree. Look at it: it goes on aging for centuries without having ever really lived, without ever changing. The Empire State Building doesn't change, either, but the people around it are changing all the time. An urban landscape, you see, is in a state of perpetual transformation. And when I am far away from the city, I feel I have left the world and detached myself from the struggle of life. What progress there is, goes on in the cities, and I want to be present.

BC: *Your films often deal with lonely or isolated characters in such a landscape.*

MA: Yes, and I think that the theme of most of my films is loneliness. Often my characters are isolated, as you say; they are individuals looking for social institutions that will support them, for personal relationships that will absorb them. But most often they find little to sustain them. They are looking for a home—and "looking for a home," in a wider sense, could be said to be the subject of all my films. That said, I never think in terms of a conflict between the solitary individual and the masses. I'm not a sociologist, and I never propound political theses. If I place a character against a landscape, however, there is naturally a relationship, and I would prefer that my meaning derive implicity from such a visual juxtaposition.

BC: *You say that you never propound political theses in your films, and I agree with you. But you yourself obviously have political views, right?*

MA: Yes and no. For example, I have a view of technology, and *Red Desert* was among the first films, if not the very first one, to deal directly with the destructive relationship between people and industrial technology in their environment. And other films of mine have dealt, if only indirectly, with the issue of technology and communication. In my view, technology doesn't help communication. It hinders it. The fact that you are forced to be a specialist to be successful: that in itself works against communication, because everyone is a specialist and knows little else. I don't see how you can communicate in a world of technological specialities. Technology forces people to adapt to it, rather than adapting itself to people.

But none of this means that I'm a Communist, which is how some critics describe me. It's just not so at all. My only political wish is to see the Italian bourgeoisie crushed. It is the curse of Italy, the worst such class in the entire world, the most hypocritical, the laziest, and the most cowardly. I hate it. And I speak with some authority: the experience that has been most important in making me the director I have become is that of my own middle-class background. It is that world which has contributed most to my predilection for certain themes, certain conflicts, certain emotional or psychological problems; and in that very general sense, my pictures are autobiographical. With an obstinacy that can only be called pathetic, we persist in our allegiance to an aging morality, to outworn myths, to ancient conventions, and the bourgeoisie is the reason why.

Once there was what I would call the Ptolemaic fullness of the individual in a God-centered world; then, after Copernicus, Renaissance man found himself thrown into an unfamiliar universe, even if at first its unfamiliarity was not acknowledged. We are still there, with all our fears and hesitations, loaded down with baggage and pushed by forces that condition our situation without helping it, that get in our way without offering a solution—all courtesy of the puniness of the middle class.

Let me end here by putting the matter of my, or my films', politics another way: I would say that my films are political, but they are not about politics. They are political in their approach, that is—they are made from a definite point of view. And they certainly may be political in the effect they have on people.

BC: *Of the great film directors now at work, you are arguably the most contemporary. In expressing your chief thematic preoccupation—modern man's often crushing feeling of alienation—you have evoked a profound sense of recognition in a number of your films, most notably* L'avventura, Blow-Up, *and* The Passenger. *Moreover, as you yourself have noted, you communicate as much as possible through images rather than through words—stark images of desolation and despair that, paradoxically, could scarcely be more dazzlingly beautiful. You have described your art as "narrating with images," in contrast to traditional literary cinema's focus on language, as being concerned with non-verbal communication and with abstracted emotions. And some commentators have even called your films "interior realism" because, as you well know, you are concerned more with the inner lives of your characters than with worldly or physical action.*

Yet, as you also know, many critics and viewers find your work pretentious, boring, and needlessly perplexing. They say that your films are intentionally ambiguous, so much so that the motivations of your characters become obscure and even inexplicable. For instance, David Locke's casual abandonment in The Passenger *of his own identity in order to take on the identity of a man whom he knows virtually nothing about, but whom he chances remarkably to resemble. What is your response to this negative perception of your films?*

MA: My films are mirrors of life, and life itself is ambiguous. Indeed, if life were not ambiguous, if everything in life were unmysterious and fully explained, we would all be miserable to the point of wanting to die. In any event, I find that Americans—who make up the preponderance of the critical spectators you are talking about—take films too literally. They are forever trying to puzzle out "the story" and to find hidden meanings where there are perhaps none. For them, a film must be entirely rational, without unexplained mysteries. But Europeans, on the other hand, look upon my films as I intend them to be looked upon, as works of visual art, to be reacted to as one reacts to a painting, subjectively rather than objectively. For Europeans, "the story" is of secondary importance, and they are not bothered by what you have described as "ambiguity."

BC: *Let me follow up with an additional criticism made of your films: that they are so slow-paced and, for the most part, without dramatic incident—filled with long stillness and rambling, seemingly pointless conversations. Any comment?*
MA: Again, my films mirror life, and life is lived mainly from day to day without unusual incident, without melodrama, without moments of bombast and high emotion. More than anything, I hate melodrama, as in the films of a director like Luchino Visconti. Melodrama is the easiest thing in the world to do—the scene of the drunken whore or the brutal, shouting father—and it is the cheapest thing to do, too. And so not worth doing. Far more difficult, more complicated, and thus more artistically challenging is to make a film that reflects the true rhythms of life. Of course, cinema cannot create an exact portrait of reality. The best it can hope to do is create a personal reality. I began, you know, as one of the first exponents of neorealism, but by concentrating on the internals of character and psychology I do not think that I deserted the movement. Instead, I pointed the way to extending its boundaries. Unlike early neorealist filmmakers, I am not trying to show reality—I am attempting to recreate realism. In fact, while I mean in no way to suggest that we are comparable artists, you must think when looking at my films of Proust's novel *A Remembrance of Things Past*—I like the literal translation of the French title better, *In Search of Lost Time*—rather than of other films. That is, my films are indeed "slow-paced" and "without dramatic incident," but in the same way as Proust's stellar fiction is.

BC: *You mentioned Visconti in your last response, and I think it would be helpful to contrast your work with his and also with Fellini's.*
MA: Let me do so by speaking of three films: *L'avventura*, Visconti's *Rocco and His Brothers*, and Fellini's *La Dolce Vita*. All three films deal

with a certain condition of society today. But while in *La Dolce Vita* and *Rocco* the analysis is directed towards the actions of the characters, in *L'avventura* the emphasis is on the inner world of the individual, particularly in relation to that individual's feelings. There is also a fundamental difference of style among these films. While Visconti tends to dramatize his material to a maximum degree, and Fellini carries his dramatic tension to the extreme in visual terms, my intention is the opposite: I try to remove the external drama from my characters and create a situation in which the conflict remains inside. Both *La Dolce Vita* and *Rocco* are "outer" dramas in this sense, while *L'avventura* is an interior narrative.

BC: *Over the years, you have been very outspoken on the subject of love. I remember that, when* Blow-Up *was released, you had a few things to say about the subject.*

MA: Yes, the very quality of the emotion has changed. Indeed, we live in a world where nothing is stable anymore—even physics has become metaphysical. The young people among whom *Blow-Up* is situated live in a world that has finally broken down all barriers between one individual and another. Especially now, you can talk with anyone about anything. If you like to smoke marijuana, you can say so without fear. If a girl likes sex, she is not afraid to admit it. *Blow-Up*'s generation, and the generations to follow, have sought a certain aimless freedom from restrictions of all kinds. And, to be sure, the pursuit of such freedom can give man his most exciting moments. But once it is achieved, once all discipline is discarded, then you have decadence—and decadence without any sign of change in sight.

Sexual freedom also means freedom from feelings, and that means I don't know whether young people can ever love again the way my generation loved. They must suffer, I guess, but I'm sure they suffer for reasons very different from those of people my age—and never romantic ones. They have taken leave of all norms, all traditions, and there is a price to pay for that. Eroticism, you see, is the most obvious symptom of an emotional sickness. There would not be this eroticism if eros were still in good health. And by good health, I mean perfectly in harmony with the measure and condition of man.

Let me give an example of the weakness or paleness of Eros, or love, from the time of *Blow-Up*, which is when I began to notice the decadence of this emotion. When the Soviet cosmonaut Titov came back from his flight among the stars, he was asked by the press whether from the heights he had reached he'd once thought about his wife. "No," said Titov quietly, before returning to live with her.

BC: *Some critics faulted you less for your depiction of the quality or nature of love in* Blow-Up *than for your embroidering the set design, if you will.*
MA: Yes, when I was making *Blow-Up*, there was a lot of discussion about the fact that I had a road and a building painted. Antonioni paints the grass, people said. To some degree, all directors paint and arrange or change things on a location, and it amused me that so much was made of it in my case. I did it in *Red Desert*, too, and in *Zabriskie Point* I did some set painting again. An airport runway, some hangars, and some other things. And I put up some billboards on the front lawns of the houses across the street from the airport. When I do something like this, it is not so much to make the scene more attractive visually—it is to compress. I can only show so much. In *Blow-Up* there were only so many scenes, and yet there were many things I wanted to show. So by painting a house or a road, I was able to compress, to show more in fewer shots.

BC: Blow-Up, *one could say, was about the feel of London in the 1960s, just as your earlier trilogy—consisting of* L'avventura, La notte, *and* L'eclisse—*had examined the state of Italian society in the late 1950s. Similarly, was* Zabriskie Point *about the condition of American society around 1969 or 1970?*
MA: How could it not have been, when America—the location of this film—was constantly changing or transforming at the time, even physically, and therefore demanded that such change be reflected on the screen?

BC: *Is there a certain visual quality that represents America in your eyes, and were you trying to express that in* Zabriskie Point?
MA: No. Not in the way I had in the past, as with *Red Desert* and *L'eclisse*. The only place where I tried to have the landscape play an

equal role to that of the characters was in Death Valley, especially around Zabriskie Point. In that portion of the film I needed to surround the characters with a lunar-type landscape, to suggest solitude. Otherwise, I was not using American architecture symbolically in this film.

BC: *What do you think of revolutionary or at least experimental theater of the kind once represented by the Living Theater and the Open Theater? You were obviously once interested in it, since you chose Sam Shepard to help with the script of* Zabriskie Point.

MA: I liked the experiment of the Living Theater, but I was never able to see all of their work. I feel much closer to the work of the Open Theater—it and Joe Chaikin are part of the cast of *Zabriskie Point*, you will recall. They didn't use the word; they used the *sound* of the word. Of course, I don't agree with those old-fashioned critics who say that theater is the word, that it is essentially or primarily verbal. That's ridiculous. And one of the ways in which the Open Theater, and the Living Theater, de-emphasized the word was by always attempting to involve the audience in the *experience* of the action and not the *idea* of the drama. They even sold tickets to their rehearsals, less to see the "show" than to experience the rehearsal process.

BC: *You made* Zabriskie Point *for MGM but it is obviously an Antonioni film, not a Hollywood product.*

MA: Yes, I made *Zabriskie Point* in the United States, but, as you suggest, my way of working was, and remains, diametrically opposed to the way things are done in that enormous bureaucratic machine known as Hollywood. Of course, I'm not talking just about opposite working methods, but about an opposite approach to life itself, a refusal to accept embalmed ideas and clichés, affectation and imitation.

It was in 1967 that I started work on *Zabriskie Point*, when I went across the United States and saw a good many things. Then I went back to Rome and looked over my notes and gradually decided to do a film about two young Americans. In August, just before we were going to begin shooting, I went to Chicago for the Democratic National Convention. What I saw there—the behavior of the police, the spirit of the young people—impressed me as deeply as anything else I had seen in

America. To some degree, *Zabriskie Point* was influenced by what happened in the streets of Chicago. Not directly, you understand; the film is not about Chicago, or the politics of the convention—inside or outside. But my ideas about young Americans were shaped by what happened in Chicago, and I hope that somehow those ideas were expressed in the film.

BC: *Filmmakers and other creative people often go through life as you did in Chicago: looking, recording, and interpreting, rather than participating.*
MA: That's true, and the film I made after *Zabriskie Point—The Passenger*—deals in part with this very theme: in it a journalist stops being an onlooker and becomes a doer, even though he isn't sure what he is doing. I myself was a kind of onlooker when I accepted the assignment of directing *The Passenger*. It is the first time that I agreed to make a film from someone else's script entirely—Mark Peploe's in this case—so I got involved with this project in a cool, detached way. I had to use my brain at first, not my instinct, though eventually my instinct took over and I had to change the script somewhat according to my own nature.

BC: *Jack Nicholson played David Locke in* The Passenger, *and, as you well know—and I guess you knew at the time—this is not the kind of role he normally performs.*
MA: No, you are right, but the thing I discovered in Jack was that he was very different from what I had expected. In some way he was humble with me—and he's not in life particularly. He is very intelligent. He immediately finds a way to deal with someone.

He had to do everything in a most natural way in *The Passenger*. I didn't give him any opportunities to do something his way. This journalist, Locke, was not an extraordinary man. This was a most difficult character to play, for Jack somehow had to find a way not to do anything. He usually acts more, and here everything was almost static.

BC: *So, to continue the metaphor of the onlooker versus the insider or initiator, Nicholson had to play Locke from the outside in, instead of the way an American actor—particularly one of Nicholson's magnetism—usually plays a character: from the inside out.*

MA: Yes, I think that is a fair assessment. You know at the time of *The Passenger*'s release, a lot of people thought that, though breathtaking to look at, the film didn't seem, upon reflection, to make sense. What, they wondered, had been the meaning of Locke's change of identity, of his travels, and of his ultimate death? But the theme of this film is not so hard to determine: I was trying to investigate the myth of objectivity, the idea that looking at something from the outside is better than looking at it from the inside. As an onlooker, or someone maintaining that pose in his life as in his work, David Locke was frustrated: his marriage was a failure; he had failed in his relationship with his adopted child; and he wasn't as committed to his job as he would have liked to be. Hence he sought to make a change—and a drastic one at that.

BC: *Is the camera itself an outsider at the end, traveling in circles?*
MA: You could put it that way. I didn't want to show the actual killing of Locke, which is how it's usually done in suspense melodramas. I didn't want to film the death of a man, Locke, who, having assumed the identity of a dead man, was in a sense already dead himself—doubly so, as a matter of fact. So I used the Westcam—a camera mounted in a ball and stabilized with gyroscopes, which can shoot 360-degree pans when further stabilized from a crane—to shoot a seven-minute take that proceeds out of Locke's room, through a wrought-iron grill on to a dusty Spanish plaza, and then finally returns to the room where Locke now lies dead. The "objective" camera had its back turned, you could say, while inside his hot, airless hotel room Locke was murdered for being someone he wasn't—or for not being who he really was. A subjective, ambiguous moment—like life itself.

BC: *Your upcoming picture will offer you several firsts with which to end the 1970s, or begin the 1980s, won't it?*
MA: Yes, in addition to my working in Italy for the first time since 1963, *The Oberwald Mystery* will also be the first time I have worked with Monica Vitti since I made *Red Desert* in the same year. Above all, it will be the first time I have worked with television cameras, and with magnetic tape that will later have to be transferred to film.

BC: *This is your first film adapted from a play as well, right?*

MA: Yes, I adapted the screenplay from Cocteau's *Two-Headed Eagle*, which was a romantic vehicle for Edwige Feuillère and Jean Marais, first on stage and then on the screen. But I have to say that this is one of the worst things Cocteau ever did for the screen.

BC: *Why Cocteau's play in particular?*

MA: I thought of *The Two-Headed Eagle*, not because it was a work that appealed to me particularly but because it seemed as good a vehicle as any for trying out television cameras, which for years I had wanted to do. In addition, the play offered me a chance for intellectual non-commitment. It is a novelettish story, this tale of an anarchist who infiltrates the queen's castle and ends by killing her for love rather than ideology. Of course I don't care a damn about this queen and the anarchist. Somebody will perhaps enjoy reading some contemporary significance into it, connections with the terrorist Red Brigades and all that. However, I won't try to camp it up, which is something that doesn't come naturally to me. I'll try to be neutral. If the film becomes camp it will be because the subject matter is what it is. One cannot achieve miracles with the camera if you are bound to a text like this. I don't think anybody's capable of miracles these days, not even the Almighty.

BC: *How will Miss Vitti adapt to a romantic tale like this?*

MA: The part is very declamatory, very theatrical. And Monica comes from the theater, you know. I myself am not used to big set-speeches in my films, but with this play it's difficult to avoid them.

BC: *So, in the end, the television cameras are what interested you most in this project? How different do you think shooting will be from what you are used to?*

MA: Well, of course I will have to take into account that the format for the two screens is different. Close-ups on television's square screen require different compositions from the cinema screen. Consequently, I will often compose the image in two different ways for the same scene. An example is a scene where the anarchist whips a table-cloth off a table and all the objects fall to the floor. For the cinema, I would compose the frame with the female figure in the background, the man in the center and the objects in the foreground. For television, I will lose either the female figure or half the objects on the floor I want in the shot, so I'll have to start the shot on the objects and pan up to take in the characters. You are limited by space, by the presence of other cameras, and by the wall behind you. Where the operation becomes interesting is in the use of color. Certainly it can change everything for you, even the faces of the actors. The subtle use of different shades of light and dark is possible, but it's a complicated technical process on TV. What is fascinating about it is that you can make corrections afterwards, even violent ones.

BC: *Are there technical problems in transferring the magnetic tape to film?*
MA: Yes, it isn't at all easy. In Italy it's impossible. I've decided to have it done in California. I'm not completely satisfied with what they can do there but I'll go over myself and personally supervise the printing.

BC: *It'll be seen first on television?*
MA: Yes, it was made for Rete 2, the Second Channel, for which the Taviani brothers' *Padre Padrone* was also made. I should add that I don't pretend that I will resolve all the problems of the relationship between cinema and television. Don't expect anything particularly revolutionary in terms of technique. Probably the differences between the cinema and television, except in the case of obvious effects, will not be discernible. You will find close-ups according to TV and close-ups according to the cinema. The novelty consists only in the fact that I will film both versions with electronic means yet shoot each one in a different way. With a script like this with so much dialogue, you are limited anyway in creative visual terms. It will remain a theatrical *pièce* even if my co-adaptor Tonino Guerra and I try to make it as cinematic as possible.

BC: *What would you have done, may I ask, had you not become a film director?*
MA: If I had not become a director, I should have been an architect, I suspect, or maybe a painter. *Seeing* for a filmmaker is a necessity, even as it is for a painter. But while for the painter it is a matter of uncovering a static reality, or at most a rhythm that can be held in a single image,

for a director the problem is to catch a reality which is never static, which is always moving towards or away from a moment of crystallization, and to present this movement, this arriving or moving on, as a new perception. Film is not sound—words, noises, music. Nor is it a picture—landscape, attitudes, gestures. Rather, it is an indivisible whole that extends over a temporal duration of its own which determines its very being. The people around us, the places we visit, the events we witness—cinema is the spatial and temporal relations these all have with each other, the tension that is formed between them, and the meaning they possess for us today. And our effort as directors must be that of bringing all this data from our personal experience into accord with that of a more general experience, in the same way as individual time accords mysteriously with that of the cosmos. This is, I think, a special way of being in contact with reality. And it is also a special reality: that of film. To lose this contact, in the sense of losing this *way* of being in contact, can mean aesthetic—not to speak of human—sterility.

BC: *Despite what you said earlier, since you write or co-write the scripts of all your films, wouldn't you call yourself a writer as well as a director?*
MA: No, I would not. To repeat myself, I feel that I am a person who has things he wants to show rather than things he wants to say. There are times when the two concepts coincide, and that is when we arrive at a work of art.

Making a film is not like writing a novel. Flaubert said that living was not his profession: his profession was writing. To make a film, however, *is* to live, or it is for me. My personal life is not interrupted during the shooting of a film. If anything, it becomes more intense. This sincerity in art, its being in one sense or another autobiographical, this pouring, as we say, of all our wine into one barrel, is surely nothing more than a way of taking part in life, of adding something that is good—in intent anyway—to our personal patrimony.

BC: *In a world without film, what would you have made?*
MA: Film.

Antonioni in 1980: An Interview

SEYMOUR CHATMAN/1980

SEYMOUR CHATMAN: *In your early, "apprentice" films of the 1950s
(the documentaries, and* Cronaca di un amore, I vinti, La signora senza
camelie, *and* Le amiche) *were you working within the genres or were you
trying to work your way out of them? You wanted to make a film,* Cronaca di
un amore, *so you made a* giallo, *a film noir.*
MICHELANGELO ANTONIONI: Yes, but it happened without my willing
it; I just wanted to tell that story. I didn't want to demonstrate anything
with my movies, you know . . . not to start from an idea and to explain
to the audience that this is my idea, that I want to tell you this and
this. I just wanted to tell a story and depict the emotions it contains.

SC: *Was the story of* Cronaca *more familiar to the public than the kind of
story told by your films of the '60s?*
MA: What you're doing is making a critical analysis and asking my
opinion about it. But I find it very difficult to respond because I scarcely
know how to judge my films from a critical point of view. My films
come from my emotions and correspond to a certain period of my life.
Of course, behind my emotions there are experiences, ideas, thoughts,
observations of reality, and political, social, philosophical, and moral
convictions—everything!

From *Film Quarterly*, vol. 51, no. 1 (Fall 1997), pp. 2–10. © 1997, The Regents of the
University of California. All rights reserved. Reprinted by permission of University of
California Press and Seymour Chatman.

sc: *And aesthetic convictions?*

MA: Of course. But I don't know how to sort these matters out either before or after the film is finished. For me a film is only a record of a period of my life. I find it terribly difficult to say whether I wanted to make this or that kind of film. I have never thought about the public. Only one person is the public. And it's me.

sc: *Were you conscious in 1959, when you made* L'avventura, *that you were entering a radically different phase of your career?*

MA: No. I have to tell you something. I never, never, never think of myself. Never, I'm a "man of action." I have to *do.* And every time I have tried to think about what I was doing it was so difficult that I decided not to do it anymore.

sc: *Does this most recent stage of your work concern general philosophical questions?*

MA: Maybe. Because getting old, you try in a certain way to total things up—ideologically and morally and emotionally. But also because you read new and different things. You change the way you read. I started to read more books about science, for instance. I got very interested in astronomy and things like that, in the world, in the universe. As soon as you talk about the universe, everything is involved.

sc: *Now your new film,* Identificazione di una donna . . .

MA: This is the script [pats it on the table].

sc: *Is the script more like the films of the early '60s, more like* L'eclisse *or* La notte, *than the later films?*

MA: Yes, I think so.

sc: *Set in Italy?*

MA: In Italy, in Rome. But there is something new compared to those earlier movies. That is to say, the milieu—the way they live, these people—is more contemporary. There is a lot of vulgarity. The cars. The people, I mean everything. I am in very close contact with this town. The life of the people in Italy today is very vulgar.

sc: *Am I right in detecting a dramatic change when you stopped collaborating with Suso Cecchi D'Amico and started working with Tonino Guerra?*

MA: Yes.

sc: *Pio Baldelli says that D'Amico's scripts were like high-class* fumetti *[comic strips] for ladies' magazines.*

MA: The movies?

sc: *Not the movies, but the scripts. I think Baldelli was making a distinction between the scripts and your resultant films. He felt that* Le amiche, *for instance, very much weakened Pavese, that D'Amico had sentimentalized it. How do you feel?*

MA: I wouldn't say that D'Amico wrote the script. The script came out of a cooperation between me and two women: Suso Cecchi D'Amico and Alba De Cespedes. D'Amico is not a great writer, but she's a good writer. She knows the feminine mentality very well. But they hated each other, Suso and Alba, so they never talked together. I picked up some material from one and some more material from the other, and then I did the script. Maybe the script was not as good as it might have been. However, I believe that the substance of the film is dramatic enough. The emotional and existential crises of the characters are the same kinds of crises you find in my other films, though the material was structured in a different way.

sc: *You're working with Tonino Guerra again on* Identificazione di una donna.

MA: I had this idea for *Identificazione di una donna* many years ago, and I wrote some scenes. I made some notes, and I kept thinking of it all during those years. And suddenly, two summers ago, I was in Sardinia, and I wrote it. I wrote a hundred pages. Very quickly, in ten days. And then I gave the script to Gerard Brach, Polanski's scriptwriter. Brach is very intelligent and very able. But he did not write much original material; he only developed the hundred pages which I had written. And then, one night he left for Paris and I needed someone to discuss the scenario with, so I turned to Tonino. I work very well with Tonino. He and I wrote the final draft.

SC: *The published English version of* L'avventura *shows that you cut out many things. To me its elliptical quality makes it one of the first great modernist films. Was your method to write the scenario and then to omit parts as you shot and edited the film?*

MA: Yes.

SC: *To let the audience fill in the gaps themselves?*

MA: Yes. It's very instinctive for me, you know. Now I cut my movies by myself, and I like it very much. And it comes very naturally to me to cut something. My two best shots—nobody saw them because I cut them! One in *N.U.* [*Netezza urbana*—on garbage workers in Rome] and one in *Blow-Up.* Oh, it was so beautiful. Do you remember the tunnel under the Thames? There is an elevator. It was in the introduction to the movie.

SC: *What's the shot?*

MA: The protagonist was going toward the elevator, at the end of the tunnel. And he got into the elevator and went up. I moved the light: it was beautiful.

SC: *And what about the shot deleted from* N.U.?

MA: I was on top of Via Sistina, on top of Piazza Espagna, near the obelisk, at dawn. The streets were deserted, and if you look down you see Via Sistina, Piazza Barberini, Via Quatro Fontanne, the whole street—that day you had a gray sky—it was fantastic.

SC: Le Amiche *was still in the narrow screen format, and when you moved to the wide screen—when you made* L'avventura—*it became possible to have several people in the frame without crowding, and to convey a new sense of design. Did you feel liberated by the wide screen?*

MA: Well, I can't say, because, you know, I'm so tied to the reality. I'm like the other Michelangelo when they told him, "Listen, this is the Sistine Chapel; you have to paint it—this size, not larger or narrower." And the same is true of my screen: if it's wide, I have to imagine the composition, you know, according to the wide space; if it's small, to the small one. But I must say that I prefer the larger frame.

sc: *How do you feel about [the made-for-TV] II mistero di Oberwald?*

MA: Well, you know, it's not one of my films. I just directed it. And I tried to do my best. It's a kind of melodrama, a very strong drama between a queen and an anarchist. It also contains some ideological reference to our contemporary scene in Italy: this anarchist could be compared to a terrorist, though the connection is rather slender. But I found it diverting to tell a kind of story which is so different from my own stories. I have never shot very dramatic scenes, but in this film I had to do so. That didn't frighten me because in this strong scene the emotions are very precise. They are not full of nuance or withheld; they are not ambiguous. It is much easier to shoot this kind of film.

sc: *How did it come about?*

MA: Well, Monica Vitti proposed that I shoot Cocteau's *La voix humaine*, but I didn't want to do it because it might seem like a kind of confrontation: Rossellini had already shot a version with Anna Magnani. So we had Cocteau in hand and we selected *L'aigle à deux têtes [The Eagle with Two Heads]*. Maybe it was a mistake: I don't know. But I thought it was easier to do.

sc: *And then you could concentrate on the technical opportunities?*

MA: Yes. It was interesting because of the possibility of writing the film while making it, while inventing it, more than we anticipated. When I am shooting a sequence, normally I try to find the solution, the technical solution, within the set itself. I make a travelling shot here, a close-up there, and so on. When you rehearse on TV you are in touch with the cameramen through a microphone, so you tell them, "Go from here to there," and you see the rehearsal on the monitor. And you find a lot of things in between these two points that you hadn't predicted.

sc: *How about video color-mixing in* The Mystery of Oberwald? *Were you satisfied with your experience?*

MA: Well, you know, the electronic field is something completely new and very exciting. Because you have everything in your hand: you can put in colors, you can make the image more abstract. The possibilities are infinite!

SC: *I hear that you are planning to colorize* L'avventura.

MA: As soon as I have time, I want to try. I mean, of course we have a lot of limits, but I think we can do it. You know why: because there is a picture in *Il mistero di Oberwald*, an old picture, you remember those old discolored photographs, about this big? Suddenly this figure becomes stronger, like a real person. And behind him there is some landscape, and the landscape becomes a little green, and this guy a little blue. So why don't we try to add color to a film? To transfer from film to tape, and then put in the colors, electronic colors.

SC: *For showing emotions?*

MA: Well, to emphasize.

SC: *You've always liked to play off narrative conventions, for instance, the* roman noir.

MA: Yes, but in fact narrative conventions have given me a lot of trouble. Also cinematographic conventions. I always try to avoid them. However, it's not always possible, because you risk failing to communicate. Since the public is used to a certain kind of story, it's necessary to follow conventions a bit—but only a bit. One can't risk being incomprehensible.

SC: *We talked about ellipsis—leaving things out. Now there are other possible developments in narrative, for instance, there is experimentation with point of view or stream of consciousness, interior monologue. You've never been interested in that?*

MA: Yes, I thought of it—interior monologue. But I don't like it for film. I think it's very easy. Too easy. The challenge is to express the same things in a different way.

SC: *By surface appearances?*

MA: Yes.

SC: *Eisenstein wanted to make* An American Tragedy *as an interior monologue film, and have the voice-over of the hero speak his thoughts, though his lips were closed. Would that have been too easy?*

MA: It is too easy. Because as soon as you notice the technique, the film goes down a level, in my opinion.

SC: *Are there any other modern novelistic techniques that you would like to capture on film?*
MA: No, because I never think of technique. I just choose the technique when I start to shoot, not before.

SC: *The subject starts with the visual?*
MA: Yes.

SC: *First you see something, then you make up a story in your head about what you see? Then you write it down. Then you go out and find a location?*
MA: No. I have to see the location while I am writing, not after. I cannot describe a landscape without knowing it. Unless it is a house: a house is very easy to create in my imagination. But if I'm making something in the street, I have to know which street I am talking about. I want to see first, then I place the characters. Actually, the streets give me the idea for the scene.

SC: *But when the original subject is expanded into a full film, then you have to find other locations to match that original one?*
MA: No. If I select a location, I want to shoot in that one, not another one which matches that one. That is my way of being autobiographical.

SC: *You would never write an autobiography?*
MA: No, I don't think so. I could only tell something which happened at a given moment of my life. If I think, for instance, of *Cronaca di un amore* . . . You remember the movie is about money? And what I remember about myself is that I didn't have any money at that time. And that's very important, because I looked at that story from a certain angle.

SC: *From the angle of Guido [the male protagonist]?*
MA: No, it was from the angle of . . . I mean, I acted like I *had* money, because I wanted to have it. I never succeeded.

SC: *I want to ask about the future. You mentioned wanting to do a science-fiction film, an animal film, and a film of violent action.*
MA: Well, I just have some ideas. I cannot tell you about them. But I have different needs now. I'm fed up with psychology, with emotional analysis, psychological introspection. I'd like to try something else.

Life Is Inconclusive: A Conversation with Michelangelo Antonioni

FRANK P. TOMASULO/1982

A S I S P O K E T O A N T O N I O N I O N A D I S M A L, rainy, late September day in 1982 at Cornell University, three analogies came to mind. All involved the cinema.

The first analogy was with the Hitchcock-Truffaut interviews, in which Hitchcock displaced Truffaut's questions about psychology, philosophy, and religion to what was for him the more familiar terrain of camera angles, production details, and star profiles. Antonioni, justifiably displeased with the circumstances under which he happened to be at Cornell, likewise diverted my questions onto other paths. More than once, he replied, "When I was a critic, it was my job to interpret someone else's films. Now it's your job."

The second cinematic analogy related to the horrific tooth-pulling scene in John Schlesinger's *Marathon Man*. To get the information (or the diamonds—I don't remember which), Laurence Olivier is compelled to yank healthy teeth out of a helpless Dustin Hoffman. Just as violence in Antonioni's films generally takes place off-screen, I've left out the gruesome details of the pain involved in this extraction of information.

My final analogy was the most disturbing. In *The Passenger*, an African shaman turns the tables (and the camera) on his interviewer by saying, "Your questions are much more revealing about yourself than my answers would be about me." Since Antonioni's work is the subject of my UCLA

From *On Film* (Los Angeles), no. 13 (Fall 1984), pp. 61–64. Reprinted by permission of Frank P. Tomasulo.

doctoral dissertation ("The Rhetoric of Ambiguity: Michelangelo Antonioni and the Modernist Discourse"), the following questions stemmed from my own research.

Nonetheless, given the circumstances under which this interview was conducted, I will let readers decide for themselves whether the information extracted was worth the effort expended by both parties.

FT: *Your oeuvre, especially after* Il Grido, *fits into that discourse we refer to as Modernism—a term, however, which is all too ubiquitous. In the cinema, Modernism can encompass such diverse filmmakers as Wiene, Eisenstein, Vertov, Cocteau, Deren, Fellini, Resnais, Godard, Duras, Brakhage, and Snow. Some are narrative filmmakers, some are not. Some are representational artists, others are not. How would you position yourself in this form-content dialectic?*
MA: That's really your job. You're the critic.

FT: *To be more concrete, then: as a director concerned with the aesthetics of the image, what is the role of narrative in your work?*
MA: My impulse, even early on in my career, was in terms of story. Even my documentary *Gente Del Po* is a story. The film I consider to be my best short documentary, *N.U.*, is a story. It's the story of a day.

FT: *Do you see any similarities between your work and the films of more avant-garde practitioners like Michael Snow?*
MA: I do like to experiment. Perhaps it's in a different way. As you've described *La Région Centrale* to me, I've probably used the same sort of camera gyroscope to maintain balance and fluidity.

FT: *What is it about narrative that attracts you?*
MA: Film has always been, for me, conflict. A man, a woman: drama. My next film will be different, however. It will be a man versus three other men. It's tentatively titled *The Crew*, and it will be shot here in the United States. I have the locations, the environments, almost all picked out. The story and the characters will follow. I will be meeting my American producer in New York next week to work out the details.

FT: *Why work in the United States again, considering the artistic success of* Identification of a Woman, *your first Italian film in eighteen years?*

MA: First of all, because of the poor state of the Italian film industry. The films they make now are either low-budget or those lightweight comedies with certain actors like Mario Verdoni. I hate them. They're all in dialect.

FT: *Your only previous American film,* Zabriskie Point, *was severely criticized on its initial release, particularly by the Establishment critics, who asked, "What does this Italian know about America?"*
MA: I made ten pictures in Italy and they said that my focus was too narrow. Critics, of course, say the same thing about your Robert Altman—that he doesn't understand America.

FT: *All your films—not just the more overtly political* Zabriskie Point—*strike me as profoundly ideological. What is the role of political ideas in your work?*
MA: I don't start from a thesis, if that's what you're getting at. It's the plot which is most important. As I'm a man who lives in Italy—a very political country—it inevitably enters the picture. We feel everything in regard to politics in Italy! And not just in the cinema, but through the newspapers, art, elections . . . Italy is so corrupted by political scandals now. We're against it, of course, and in favour of social justice.

FT: *Since you mention "social justice," why do your films emphasize the role of the bourgeoisie more than other factions in Italian life?*
MA: Quite simply because I know the bourgeois class better. I grew up with that background, as a tennis champion. That was my milieu. But it was not in Rome or Florence, but in Ferrara, which is not so aristocratic.

FT: *You seem to criticize or satirize the bourgeoisie.*
MA: Yes. I was so against the bourgeoisie and wanted to say something against it. Only in *Il Grido* and *Gente Del Po* do I deal with the working classes. That was in reaction to a government which didn't want films to be about workers.

FT: *Like Renoir, you portray the dialectics of decay of the bourgeoisie. This is an act of negation, in Marcuse's terminology. But is there a solution, something positive?*

MA: The bourgeoisie is sliding into nothingness. They're disappearing slowly. I don't know what the alternative might be.

FT: *Does the reaction of Daria, after "blowing up" the corporate house in* Zabriskie Point, *suggest one answer?*
MA: That was the personal reaction of that girl, of that character. It was not my statement. Let's just say that I'm against certain rules of this society. *Zabriskie Point* really happened, in Phoenix. There was an airplane theft and a police killing. I was visually interested in this fact. The idea of a helicopter going around excited my fantasy.

FT: *Your work is filled with scenes of exquisite visual beauty, moments of pure form. As a modernist, are there other artists who've influenced you: writers, architects, painters, other filmmakers?*
MA: I'm not really conscious of any artistic influences at work on me. I'm now much more intuitive. I ask to be alone on the set or the location for fifteen minutes. Then I shoot the first idea that comes into my head. Pasolini, I know, wants to redo paintings in the cinema. You speak of the beauty of my images, but the best shots are cut from the films.

FT: *If there are no direct influences, are there at least filmmakers who appeal to you?*
MA: Only Steven Spielberg can appeal to all audiences. He's a genius for that, but not on this earth.

FT: *How do you feel about retrospective screenings of your films, when scholars and critics praise your work so extravagantly in public and attribute intentions which you hardly recognize?*
MA: It's very alienating. It's as if they were speaking about someone else. Ned Rivkin gave me his book to read (*Antonioni's Visual Language*). It's very accurate.

FT: *About your artistic intentions?*
MA: You can't ask Jackson Pollock why he made one circle black and another one pink.

FT: *We were privileged to see the American premiere of* Profession: Reporter, *the British version of* The Passenger. *What are the differences between the two versions, and which do you prefer?*

MA: *Profession: Reporter* is my preference. Some scenes were shuffled by the president of MGM, who was a lawyer. The difference is about six minutes.

FT: *Were any changes made in the crucial penultimate tracking shot?*

MA: No. Don't you want to know how that shot was accomplished? (Antonioni proceeded to sketch out a diagram of the camera moves on some scrap paper.) Inside the hotel room, the camera hung from a ceiling until it reached the bars on the window. Then the bars opened. There was a high crane outside the hotel and someone hooked the camera to that crane to continue the movement. This was all on a series of gyroscopes, so that it could even be hand-held later. It was very windy during that scene and it took eleven days to shoot!

FT: *Why was it so important to shoot it in one take?*

MA: *Now* I know why, although I didn't fully understand it at the time. It's a *resume* of the whole film, not just a conclusion. Little by little, I came to understand that.

FT: *This is related to the role of the spectator of any Antonioni film. We must come to some sort of retrospective meaning—"little by little" as you say—especially by the end of your films, which are particularly Modernist in their indeterminacy, their ambiguity.*

MA: Chekhov said, "Give me new endings and I can reinvent literature!" I just got fed up with this traditional way of telling a story, the same pacing. Police stories had to have a certain pace, etc. The pace of life is different. There are dead moments.

FT: *It's interesting to hear a realist justification for your pacing. What about the ambiguities in your narrative closures?*

MA: Life is inconclusive . . . Hitchcock's films are completely false, especially the endings. Altman tries to be real, as in *Quintet*.

FT: *Again, I'm surprised to hear you speak of Altman as a realist. How do you account for the cartoon characters, the play with genre conventions, the style of acting?*

MA: I'm very good friends with Altman and know why he works the way he does. He controls the crew in a sort of collaboration. But his personality has to come out, even if some of his actors are completely crazy, like Elliott Gould.

FT: *How do you work with actors, particularly in English?*
MA: You need good actors, but you can't leave them free. This was entirely different on *Zabriskie Point*. There, I became an acting instructor. The female lead was spontaneous, but Mark Frechette was tough to work with. He had a "guru" named Mel Lyman who influenced him. It was Lyman who sent Frechette out to rob a bank and who made Frechette work in the movie, ultimately to help Lyman himself.

FT: *In* The Passenger, *the Jack Nicholson character is revealed through little gestural codes that seem spontaneous, rather than through dialogue. Were they improvised or your instructions?*
MA: They weren't so spontaneous. I told Nicholson to do that. As for dialogue, it can be completely changed by the lighting scheme of the shot, by the colors, by camera movement . . .

FT: The Mystery of Oberwald *has always remained a mystery to me. I don't see how it fits into the overall thematic and aesthetic unity of your oeuvre. Why did you choose to make this video, based on a melodramatic play by Cocteau, and set in the historical past?*
MA: It is not by me. I made it just to use video technology, but the tape wasn't very good. It had only 625 lines, not the 1025 lines possible today. It will be shown on television. As for the color scheme, it would have been a crime to keep *Oberwald* cool.

FT: *Another disappointing project for you was the Amazon venture. Why wasn't that film ever made, even though the screenplay has been published in French with the title* Techniquement Douce?
MA: Why? Because Carlo Ponti changed his mind one day and decided not to do it. I still insist that it had a beautiful script.

FT: *You indicated that there were no conscious artistic influences on your work. Were there any philosophical sources of inspiration, any modern philosophers who had an impact on you?*

MA: I would have to say that Sartre and Camus played a role. Their philosophy, as a post-war philosophy, was important to me at that time.

FT: *As a postscript, what do you think about your latest honor: being named Professor-at-Large by Cornell?*
MA: Now I'm a professor! It makes me laugh because I'm really more like a pupil. I want to experiment with every film. In Rome, a man once came up to me and said, "Your movies made me grow!" When I told an associate about this incident, he asked me, "Was the man very tall?"

A Love of Today: An Interview with Michelangelo Antonioni

GIDEON BACHMANN / 1983

UNLESS YOU COUNT *The Mystery of Oberwald*, a television experiment based on Cocteau's *The Eagle with Two Heads*, which Antonioni shot for Italian TV three years ago, more of a challenge than a success, it has been exactly 20 years since he has made a film in his native Italy. Now, with *Identification of a Woman*, he has not only returned home, but has also taken up again a subject that was at the center of his best Italian work in the past: the infinite pitfalls of man-woman relationships. Of course, he won't readily admit to this simplification: the film is the story of a man—a film director, in fact—who seeks a woman to play a character in a film, and in the process imposes his own fantasies upon the women he meets. Or does he? The dialectic of the film is precisely this: to what extent does his camera document and to what extent does it invent?

ANTONIONI: I do not believe in autobiography, but every feature film is also, more or less, a documentary. That is, when it's a film on a contemporary subject.

BACHMANN: *Is love the contemporary story documented in this one?*
A: Let's say that there is love in the film, but it is a contemporary love, a love of today. A love for which a man who has two

From *Film Quarterly*, vol. 36, no. 4 (Summer 1983), pp. 1–4. © 1983, The Regents of the University of California. All rights reserved. Reprinted by permission of University of California Press and Gideon Bachmann.

disappointments in a row doesn't tear his hair out, doesn't despair like one used to. He has a mature capacity for suffering, but he controls and in the end dominates it. He has learned to control his feelings and sentiments, especially within the framework of his craft, which has taught him to hold back narrative flights of fancy.

B: *So you think making a fuss about love is old-fashioned?*
A: Let's say it's historical. It's part of other times, of past literature and of past art, past cinema, past theatre. There is something, for example, in an Ibsen play seen today that is untenable, there is a distance emanating from *Ghosts* seen today. I am trying to stay away from making generalizations, and want to concentrate on characters I see; and it is in this sense that I am saying what I am saying, not in a sociological sense. The characters are autonomous; I am only the author, as Pirandello says. Despite what has been said about me, I never identify with my films. It is true that I am emotionally involved with them, but only to the extent that I observe them with the emotion derived of the distance which "narrating" implies. But since your question was addressed to me in a more general way, I admit to believing that nineteenth-century passion today arouses only smiles.

B: *So when you say "control" and "domination" you feel that these are, in a man relating to a woman, achievements?*
A: Certainly. And in a world where we are daily bombarded with catastrophic news and stimuli, the ability to restrain one's emotions becomes essential. In fact, we accept too much: especially in Italy—the Mafia, terrorists, disorder, anarchy—and in the end, without inner control, we might disintegrate. Control becomes a habit. A way of life, maybe the only one.

B: *It could appear that in saying that you imply that your film-making has no participating function; that you only document the descent to restraint.*
A: I don't like to talk in terms of "function." I have difficulty, anyway, to observe myself as a film-maker from the outside. As I am having difficulty, and you can see that, in talking intimately about myself. I actually hate doing it. An artist—in Proust's definition—may be a man ahead of his time, but the man behind the work may not be as far ahead.

B: *Still you are indicating that restraint is being "ahead." While your film, in showing how couples are no longer able to properly relate, seems to say the opposite: that this modern restraint is rather an expression of poverty, a pity.*
A: Of course, the passing of anything is always a pity. It's like pollution: if our organism won't adapt to the new, polluted environment, mortality will increase. And like our organism, so our psyche needs to adjust to new times in order to survive. And in fact, death is only a growing statistical hypothesis. But it is something that I, for one, refuse to accept, and thus life articulates itself in a long series of adjustments which we end up calling "modern."

B: *Is* Identification of a Woman, *then, a film about the modern psyche? I noted, for example, that you devote extreme care to sound, something unusual in Italy, and something habitually considered a psychological medium rather than a rational one like the image.*
A: I do not make this distinction. Hearing and seeing are both "direct" senses; I do not believe either needs mediation. Not like literature that requires a mind. In film, the sound has various dimensions: the effects and noise-recordings are direct, but human voices need interpretation. They are ambiguous and insecure, but voices are the only vehicle we have for comprehension. So they need mediation, orchestration. That's acting. It relates the characters to the world.

B: *Do the two women in your film represent two different worlds?*
A: I had not intended it this way. I know this is a possible interpretation: one from a more aristocratic stratum of society, contesting her origins, trying to make a new life for herself without knowing what this new life may be, and the other a woman who works, who has a sort of place in society and has achieved more of an identity. Thus their problems are not equal. And their behavior, for example in sex, is different.

B: *How is this expressed through the sexual scenes in the film?*
A: It is here, in sex, that the first woman, instinctively, finds herself. That's why the sexual scenes with her are so *osé*, so daring, because they are the most salient parts of the narrative tissue within which this girl

moves. They represent a logical development of her personality. Her sexual activity is a liberating act. It is here she becomes herself.

B: *You mean the other woman doesn't "need" it in the same way?*
A: The other woman is already herself in her work. It is this second woman who is the saner, more human, even if simpler one. And she is simpler because she has a content in her life.

B: *Are you indicating that the seeking of self-realization through sex is a neurotic approach, juxtaposed to the sane approach of doing it through work?*
A: It is sure that the first is more neurotic. That is also a result of her social station and the environment within which she has lived. And thus of her nature. While trying to liberate herself of these ties she remains part of them. Ties which are expressed in gestures, words, acts, encounters. Take the party, where she moves like in a ballet within this world made up of counts, dukes, princes, and the black aristocracy, where there isn't a single object that isn't authentic. She moves at ease within these walls made up of ancient leather wallpaper.

B: *Is the self-liberation through sex within the range of habits of this crowd?*
A: Even hiding it is part of their reality. But remember that I said it was only one way in which the two characters of the women could be interpreted. In creating characters I do not want to plan concepts.

B: *What about the man, then? Does he typify anything?*
A: Well, he typifies the men who exercise that profession and who are of that particular age, which I know, more or less, because while we are all different, we do share that common denominator of being always in search of characters, of themes, of ideas, of stories. It's a common concern. But this business of "typifying" is *a posteriori:* once the film is made you can read those things into it, if you feel the need to do it. I don't. I am not that keen to give my characters a definite ideological position. Imagine all the brakes I would have to apply: instead of utilizing my visual stimuli I'd have to think in terms of translating concepts. I work through inventions and intuitions, which are not necessarily linked to a predetermined dialectic.

B: *Does this put you in the camp of those who now, after so many years of the opposite, defend the view that engagement, in the existential sense, is something of the past?*

A: You could put it like that, if you want. We live in a period of what in Italy is called "riflusso," a reaction against pure social engagement. But of course I didn't make the film just to express this.

B: *Leaving it open like that, and having said what you've said about love, is it maybe you, the thing that is "typified" by the male protagonist?*

A: I do not believe that biography manifests itself through the telling of facts that have more or less occurred to oneself. In fact, to be more precise: the facts that occur in the life of this film director have not occurred in mine. A film is, or becomes, autobiographical in the degree that it is authentic. By that I mean that it is individually yours, tells a story in the way you want to tell it. It becomes part of you because of its being you who are doing it, your way. For example: in the morning, going to the set, I don't usually have clear ideas; I prefer getting there and finding that I have to resolve a certain situation and then doing it in the way it feels, starting from a virginal point. Everything that happens to me that morning—the things I see on the road, the light, the clouds, an item in the paper, a voice I overhear—all these condition me and transform me and eventually become part of that day's shooting, making it individual. What's important is who I am in the moment of shooting. That's where it becomes "autobiographical."

B: *That would mean that your film turns out to be different from the script?*

A: Very much so. If you compare the result with the intent you will find there is hardly a line that hasn't changed. But I do not notice this much during the shooting because I never read the script. I have the feeling of knowing it by heart but actually it is the film I know by heart and not that first version of it, which was written down before the work starts.

B: *Are you happy with the result, then?*

A: I don't know yet, and may not know for years. When I think back to my other films, they keep changing. For example, my "favorite" isn't always the same one. It depends, again, on the experiences I have, the man I am at the moment. How I feel about the things that a film includes and how they concern me now.

B: *You have always been concerned with the couple. In that sense, this film continues a prior engagement.*
A: Probably. But in a developing way. Towards a view of today, a contemporary one.

B: *Couldn't one say, in effect, that the red line of your film-making has been the documenting of this development in an ever more contemporary fashion?*
A: Actually I am quite tired of it. I don't want to be telling the same stories or dealing with the same theme. In fact, my next film will be a very different venture. It will take place mostly at sea, it will be made in America again, and there will be sudden disappearances . . . but it will not deal with a man-woman relationship. There will be interactions between men, but not on a sexual level. It is about the possibility of living together, about possessiveness, about envy, the envy a man can feel for other ways of life.

B: *Do you sometimes have such feelings?*
A: Yes. Also because often, even without admitting it or doing it consciously, a man thinks back upon his own life and makes his reckoning. These are natural examinations that one undertakes, and inevitably certain things in your past don't exactly please you totally. It doesn't necessarily happen often—to me it occurs very infrequently—but when it does, one gets the feeling of there having been other possibilities. On the other hand, the past is a cadaver. Experience is a limited tool only. Also, it can make you sterile or distract you. I really believe that one must annihilate experience. Get free of it. Otherwise it lures you, ties your hands, makes you a victim of false promises. It robs you of that instinctiveness which to me is the most beautiful thing in human behavior.

INDEX

Accident, 102
"action" painting, viii
aigle à deux têtes, L'. See *Two-Headed Eagle, The*
Alice Doesn't Live Here Anymore, 111
Altman, Robert, 111, 164, 166–67
American Tragedy, An, 160
amiche, Le. See *Girlfriends, The*
Among Women Only, 9, 105
amore in città, L'. See *Love in the City*
amorosa menzogna, L'. See *Lies of Love*
anti-novel, viii
Antonioni, Michelangelo: and actors, 16–17, 31, 34–36, 39–40, 48, 49–51, 67, 90–91, 106–8, 140–41; and adaptation, 18–19, 104–5; and architecture, 5; and the audience or public, 8, 53; and autobiography, 136, 169; and camerawork or cinematography, 52, 108–9, 126, 133; as director, 3–8, 61–62, 154; and editing, 52, 110; and female characters, 18, 57–58; and film crews, 49, 109–10; and film eroticism, 53–54, 147–48; and film music, 9, 40–41, 52–53, 111, 141; and improvisation, 7–8, 18, 48–49; and interior or internal realism, 17, 23, 126; and love, 147–48, 169–70; and male characters, 18, 57; and painting, 5; and philosophy, 156, 167–68; and politics, 144–45; and religion, 19–20; as screenwriter, 3–4, 46–48, 66, 104, 142, 154, 161; and sets, locations, or scenography, 16, 28–29, 43–44, 48, 105–6, 137, 143–44, 148; and sound, 9, 51–52, 110–11; and television, 125, 127, 151–53, 159, 169; and theater, 13
Arcalli, Franco, 110
Aristotle, vii
Astruc, Alexandre, xvii
avventura, L', vii–viii, xi–xii, xiv, xvi–xix, 4, 9, 15–16, 18, 29–31, 33–34, 36–38, 41, 44, 73, 80, 82–83, 87, 92, 94–96, 111, 141–46, 156, 158–59

Bacon, Francis, xx
Baldelli, Pio, 157
Bandello, Matteo, 19
Barthes, Roland, xvii
Beckett, Samuel, viii, xii–xiii
Bellocchio, Marco, 101
Ben-Hur, 76
Bergman, Ingmar, viii–ix, xviii–xix, 67
Bianco e Nero (magazine), 81
Bible, The, 95
Bicycle Thief, The, 22, 64
Blow-Up, xix–xx, 53–55, 59, 67–68, 74, 76, 80–81, 83–85, 89–90, 97, 102, 104, 113, 138, 141–42, 145, 147–48, 158
Bosè, Lucia, 31, 39–40
Brach, Gerard, 157
Brakhage, Stan, 163
Brecht, Bertolt, viii, 139
Bresson, Robert, xix, 17
Burri, Alberto, 42

California Split, 111
Calvino, Italo, 125

Camus, Albert, 3, 27, 115, 168
Cannes Film Festival, vii, xv, 31, 82
Carné, Marcel, 14, 62–63, 101
Centro Sperimentale di Cinematografia,
    21, 61–62, 80
Chaikin, Joseph, 149
Chekhov, Anton, 166
China. See *Chung Kuo*
Chung Kuo, 121–24, 127–30
Cinema (magazine), 14
Clair, René, 94
Cochran, Steve, 39–40
Cocteau, Jean, viii, 63, 152, 159, 167, 169
Communism, 144
"confessional" poetry, vii
Conrad, Joseph, 19
Consagra, Pietro, 42
Conversation, The, 111
Copernicus, Nicolaus, 31, 144
Coppola, Francis Ford, 111
Cortásar, Julio, 104
Crew, The, 163
Crime and Punishment, 3
Cronaca di un amore. See *Story of a Love
    Affair*
Cry, The. See *Outcry, The*

D'Amico, Suso Cecchi, 157
da Roma, Eraldo, 52
Daryoush, Hagir, 133
Davidson, Bruce, 75–76
"Death in the Afternoon," 109
De Cespedes, Alba, 157
Deren, Maya, 163
De Santis, Giuseppe, 14
deserto rosso, Il. See *Red Desert*
De Sica, Vittorio, x, 20, 34
Di Palma, Carlo, 91
di Venanzo, Gianni, 91
dolce vita, La, xiv, xix, 146–47
Dostoyevsky, Fyodor, 3, 114
Dreyer, Carl Theodor, xix
due Foscari, I. See *Two Foscari, The*
Duras, Marguerite, 163
Duse, Eleanora, 141

Eagle with Two Heads, The. See *Two-Headed
    Eagle, The*
Easy Rider, 102
Eclipse, The. See *eclisse, L'*
eclisse, L', viii, xiv, xvi, xviii, xix, 88–89,
    94, 142, 148, 156

8½, xix
Einstein, Albert, 59
Eisenstein, Sergei, 160, 163

Faulkner, William, 67
Fellini, Federico, xix, 14, 20, 67, 69, 101,
    146, 163
Feuillère, Edwige, 152
Film: avant-garde, viii; color, 5, 64–65,
    98–99, 106, 159–60; criticism, 61, 90;
    Dynalens, 135; grammar, 79; language,
    60; melodrama, 146, 159; modernism,
    163; neorealist, ix, 6–7, 60, 63–64;
    Panavision, 74; Westcam, 151
Fioravanti, Leonardo, 21
Fitzgerald, F. Scott, 68, 95
Flaubert, Gustave, 154
Fonda, Jane, 137
Fontana, Lucio, 42
Frampton, Hollis, xvii
Frechette, Mark, 77–78, 167
French New Wave, xvii
Freud, Sigmund, 56
Fulchignoni, Enrico, 62
fumetti, 80, 157
Fusco, Giovanni, 141

Garbo, Greta, 76, 141
Gardner, Fred, 70, 72
Gaudí, Antonio, 105
Gente del Po. See *People of the Po Valley*
Ghosts, 170
Gide, André, 19, 63, 67
Girlfriends, The, ix, 4, 9, 18, 42, 44, 88,
    104–5, 155, 157, 158
Godard, Jean-Luc, xviii, xix, 44, 94, 99, 163
Greed, 76
Gremillion, Jean, 63
Grido, Il. See *Outcry, The*
Grierson, John, xi
Guerra, Tonino, 71, 153, 157

Halprin, Ann, 77
Halprin, Daria, 77
Harris, Richard, 91
Hayden, Tom, 137
Hegel, Georg Wilhelm Friedrich, 56
Hemingway, Ernest, 59, 108
Hemmings, David, 80
Hiroshima, mon amour, 41
Hitchcock, Alfred, 162, 166
Hoffman, Dustin, 162

Hofmann, Hans, viii
Hollywood, 41, 75–76, 149
Homer, 32

Ibsen, Henrik, viii, 13, 170
Identification of a Woman, 156–57, 163, 169–74
Identificazione di una donna. See *Identification of a Woman*
Ionesco, Eugène, viii

James, Henry, xiv
Jansenism, 19
Johnson, Lyndon B., 55
Joyce, James, ix

Kierkegaard, Søren, xv

Lady without Camelias, The, 30, 79, 155
Last Year at Marienbad, xviii
Lichtenstein, Roy, xx, 100
Lies of Love, 80
Living Theater, 149
Loren, Sophia, 67, 77
Lorenz, Konrad, 121
Losey, Joseph, 54, 102
Love in the City, 5, 91
Lucretius, 38
Lyman, Mel, 167

Macdonald, Dwight, 97
Maeterlinck, Maurice, 58
Magnani, Anna, 159
Major Barbara, xvii
Malraux, André, 19
Marais, Jean, 152
Marathon Man, 162
Marcuse, Herbert, 164
Marx, Karl, 56, 124
Maselli, Francesco, 102
Mastroianni, Marcello, 11–12, 44, 96
MGM, 70, 75, 149, 166
Michelangelo Buonarroti, 158
mistero di Oberwald, Il. See *Mystery of Oberwald, The*
Modesty Blaise, 54
Monsieur Zéro, 63
Morand, Paul, 63
Morandi, Giorgio, 42
Moravia, Alberto, 92
Moreau, Jeanne, xvi, 11–13, 26, 31, 49–50, 96

Musil, Robert, 19
Mussolini, Benito, 63
Mystery of Oberwald, The, xx, 159–60, 167

Nettezza Urbana, 14, 23–24, 92, 158, 163–64
New York Film Festival, 76
Nicholson, Jack, 106–7, 110–12, 116–17, 122, 125, 150, 167
Night, The. See *notte, La*
notte, La, vii–viii, xii–xiv, xvi–xviii, 4–5, 11, 15, 17, 25–26, 29–30, 34, 36–38, 41–42, 44, 96–97, 148, 156
N.U. See *Netteza Urbana*

Oberwald Mystery, The, 138, 151–53
Olivier, Laurence, 162
Open Theater, 149
Outcry, The, ix, 4, 13, 36–38, 73, 88, 99–101, 163, 164
Ozu, Yasujiro, xix

Padre Padrone, 153
Paolucci, Antonio, 24
Pascal, Blaise, 31
Pasolini, Pier Paolo, 165
Passenger, The, xvii, 104–23, 125–27, 131–35, 138, 145, 150–51, 162, 166, 167
Pavese, Cesare, 3, 9–10, 18–19, 104, 157
Peer Gynt, viii
People of the Po Valley, xi, 14, 63, 163
Peploe, Mark, 122, 125, 150
Pilot Returns, A, 14, 62
pilota retorna, Un. See *Pilot Returns, A*
Pinter, Harold, viii
Pirandello, Luigi, 13, 34, 115, 131–32, 170
Polanski, Roman, 157
Pollock, Jackson, viii, 165
Ponti, Carlo, 167
porte étroite, La, 63
Professione: Reporter. See *Passenger, The*
Proust, Marcel, 146, 170
Ptolemy, 31

Quintet, 166

Rachel, Rachel, 75
Ray, Man, viii
Red Desert, ix–x, xvii–xviii, 52, 57, 73–74, 85, 91, 97–100, 106, 125, 138, 141, 144, 148, 151
Redgrave, Vanessa, 50, 67

Reed, Rex, 81, 91
Région Centrale, La, 163
Remembrance of Things Past, A, 146
Renoir, Jean, 164
Resnais, Alain, xviii, xix, 41, 44, 94, 163
Rise to Power of Louis XIV, The, xix
Rivkin, Ned, 165
Robbe-Grillet, Alain, viii
Rocco and His Brothers, 146–47
Rohmer, Éric, xviii
Romanticism, viii
Room at the Top, xviii
Rossellini, Roberto, xix, 14, 20, 62, 159
Rubin, Bob, 75

Sadoul, Georges, 33
San Francisco Dance Workshop, 77
Sarraute, Nathalie, viii
Sartre, Jean-Paul, xv, 168
Saturday Night and Sunday Morning,
    xviii
Scalera, Michele, 62–63
Scavarda, Aldo, 92
sceicco bianco, Lo. See *White Sheik, The*
Schlesinger, John, 162
Schneider, Maria, 106–7, 117, 121
Scorsese, Martin, 111
Shakespeare, William, 19
Shaw, George Bernard, xvii
Shepard, Sam, 71, 149
signora senza camelie, La. See *Lady without
    Camelias, The*
Snow, Michael, xvii, 163
Spielberg, Steven, 111, 165
Starr, Harrison, 75
Stein, Gertrude, 67
Stendhal, 19
Story of a Love Affair, ix, 4, 13–15, 23–24,
    43, 52, 63–64, 79–80, 88, 96, 155, 161
strada, La, xix
Stranger, The, 115–16
Students for a Democratic Society (SDS), 70
Superstition, 84
Superstitione. See *Superstition*
Svevo, Italo, 19

Taste of Honey, A, xviii
Taviani brothers, 153
Taylor, Elizabeth, 51, 67
Technically Sweet, 125, 167
Techniquement Douce. See *Technically
    Sweet*
Tehran International Film Festival,
    131
Tender Is the Night, 95
Theater of the Absurd, viii
Thomas, Dylan, 88
Titov, Gherman, 148
Truffaut, François, xviii, 94, 162
Two Foscaris, The, 62
Two-Headed Eagle, The, 152, 159, 169

Ulysses, ix
Updike, John, 93
Upton, Jerry, 76

Vanquished, The. See *vinti, I*
Vedova, Emilio, 42
Ventimiglia, Giovanni, 92
Verdone, Mario, 164
Vertov, Dziga, 163
Vietnam War, 137
vinti, I, 30, 88, 97, 101, 155
Visconti, Luchino, 14, 34, 101, 146
visiteurs du soir, Les, 14
vitelloni, I, xix
Vitti, Monica, 12, 31, 39–40, 50, 54, 67,
    151–52, 159
voix humaine, La, 159
von Stroheim, Erich, 76

Walker, Beverly, 76
Warhol, Andy, xvii, 101
Weston, Edward, 116
White Sheik, The, 14
Who's Afraid of Virginia Woolf?, 51
Wiene, Robert, 163

Zabriskie Point, 70–78, 80, 85, 92, 136–38,
    141, 143, 148–50, 164–65, 167
Zavattini, Cesare, 7, 20
Zen Buddhism, 54

CONVERSATIONS WITH FILMMAKERS SERIES
PETER BRUNETTE, GENERAL EDITOR

The collected interviews with notable modern directors, including

Robert Aldrich • Woody Allen • Pedro Almodóvar • Robert Altman • Theo Angelopolous • Ingmar Bergman • Bernardo Bertolucci • Tim Burton • Jane Campion • Frank Capra • Charlie Chaplin • The Coen Brothers • Francis Ford Coppola • George Cukor • Brian De Palma • Clint Eastwood • Federico Fellini • John Ford • Terry Gilliam • Jean-Luc Godard • Peter Greenaway • Howard Hawks • Alfred Hitchcock • John Huston • Jim Jarmusch • Elia Kazan • Buster Keaton • Stanley Kubrick • Akira Kurosawa • Fritz Lang • Spike Lee • Mike Leigh • George Lucas • Sidney Lumet • Joseph L. Mankiewicz • Sam Peckinpah • Roman Polanski • Michael Powell • Satyajit Ray • Jean Renoir • Martin Ritt • Carlos Saura • John Sayles • Martin Scorsese • Ridley Scott • Ousmane Sembène • Steven Soderbergh • Steven Spielberg • George Stevens • Oliver Stone • Quentin Tarantino • Andrei Tarkovsky • Lars von Trier • François Truffaut • Liv Ullmann • Orson Welles • Billy Wilder • John Woo • Zhang Yimou • Fred Zinnemann